MW01094395

African American Midwifery
in the South

African American Midwifery in the South

Dialogues of Birth, Race, and Memory

Gertrude Jacinta Fraser

HARVARD UNIVERSITY PRESS

Cambridge, Massachusetts

London, England

1998

Library of Congress Cataloging-in-Publication Data

Fraser, Gertrude Jacinta.
    African American midwifery in the South : dialogues of birth,
race, and memory / Gertrude Jacinta Fraser.
      p.   cm.
    Includes bibliographical references and index.
    ISBN 0-674-00852-9
    1. Afro-American midwives—Virginia—History—20th century.
    2. Midwifery—Virginia—History—20th century.
    3. Childbirth—Virginia—History—20th century.   I. Title.
RG950.F7 1998
618.2′0233—dc21   97-38661

For Maya Fraser Butler and Gladys Barnes Fraser

Contents

Acknowledgments

Without the support and sustenance of family and friends, the encouragement of mentors and teachers, and the generosity of institutions, I could not have completed this book. Most of all, I am greatly indebted to the residents of Green River County, Virginia. Although I am unable to name them individually, I thank them for allowing me into their homes and lives.

Most recently, I received a sesquicentennial leave for 1995–96 from the University of Virginia to complete revisions for this work. Without teaching obligations, I was able to devote my full attention to the task at hand. I am very grateful. Early in my work, the Carter G. Woodson Institute for African and Afro-American Studies at the University of Virginia provided me with access to excellent library resources, gave me office space, offered the expertise of its capable staff, and valued my work when it was still in its embryonic stages. A two-year predoctoral fellowship allowed me to work in a supportive and intellectually challenging environment. The institute's director, the late Armstead Robinson, gave fully of himself, and I miss his presence. A Ford Foundation postdoctoral fellowship funded me during a year of archival research and writing. I salute them for their support of minority scholars and of my project.

The Department of Anthropology at the Johns Hopkins University provided me with generous financial support during my graduate career. I have had the good fortune to work closely with fellow students and with teachers who pushed me to ask difficult questions and to break down the disciplinary barriers that would restrict inquiry. The Seminar in Atlantic History and Culture provided an always lively forum for the critical discussion of issues related to the African diaspora. It is impossible to unravel the threads of the many conversations and critical insights now woven into the fabric of my work. These provided me with my first exposure to the scholarship that would define my subsequent research interests.

I am grateful to Sidney Mintz, who first introduced me to the field of African American anthropology. He has been a tough and exacting teacher. I thank him for his early attention to this manuscript and to the progress of my development as an anthropologist. Emily Martin has given me the benefit of her considerable expertise on the subjects of science and childbirth and also provided me with a model of a committed feminist scholar and teacher. My colleagues in the Department of Anthropology at the University of Virginia have always provided good cheer and scholarly inspiration. This manuscript has also benefited from a close reading by anonymous reviewers for Harvard University Press.

Sections of Chapter 8 appeared in *Conceiving the New World Order: The Global Politics of Reproduction,* edited by Faye D. Ginsburg and Rayna Rapp, copyright © 1995 the Regents of the University of California, used by permission.

All responsibilities for errors of fact and analysis are mine, but the book is in the end a product of many years' conversation.

As for my family, I cannot conceive of my life without them. My mother, Gladys Barnes Fraser, has offered inspiration and example. She has loved me without reservation, and that has always kept me going. I want also to express my gratitude to my sister Angella, who has walked with me every step of this journey and has given good computer consultation as a bonus. To my brother Mark and family, thanks for the free baby-sitting and for your loud cheerleading. Reginald Butler has been my fellow traveler. He has listened and read, carefully and repeatedly. With hard work, he has made a halfway decent historian out of an anthropologist by giving willingly of his knowledge of African American history and culture in Virginia. To my three-and-a-half-year-old daughter, Maya, who always asked "When is your book going to be finished?": here it is, and thank you for all the good loving and kisses.

*African American Midwifery
in the South*

Prologue

Within the past decade, scholars have begun to reveal the important role African American midwives played in the reproductive experiences of southern women, both black and white. This book is a contribution to the documentation of that African American presence. It is also a requiem to the knowledge, skills, and beliefs that have been lost. If, thanks to the classic movie *Gone with the Wind,* popular imagery has the African American woman faced with the prospect of having to help deliver a baby being completely hysterical, then recent scholarship counters that portrayal. It instead provides one that illuminates the long competence of such women in reproductive medicine. The full impact of this collective scholarship should lead to a rereading of that scene, so that the refusal to reveal knowledge of birthing can be interpreted as an act of deliberate resistance.

Since I began my fieldwork in the mid-1980s and continuing to the present, I have talked to older African Americans in one Virginia community about the material and symbolic shifts in birth that they saw occurring in their lifetimes. Early on it became apparent that the memories of midwifery's presence and absence required me to look beyond Green River County to understand why African American lay midwives, so vital to the reproductive health care in their communities, got pushed aside. Stories of midwifery in Green River County foregrounded the natural disappearance of midwives and home births as if that aspect of people's experience had simply ceased to exist. The naturalizing of this historical phenomena was one way for residents to give explanatory order to the past. I wondered, however, about other ways of telling the same story.

The evocation of "why" in social science methodology implies that patterns of cause and effect are to be discerned. In this work, I prefer to think of the "why" question as a prelude to unraveling a thickly embroidered tapestry. In the near decade of my intellectual and emotional involvement in the story of African American midwives in the South, I found no single set of explanations that satisfactorily answered all my questions. How and under what circumstances did African American women lose their foothold in birthing babies and attending pregnant and laboring mothers in their communities? In always asking why the South gave up on African American midwives, I wanted to remember that the erasure of these women's roles and skills in birthing should not be taken for granted as an inevitable outcome of medical progress and professionalization. The book points out other paths that had been cleared, but then abandoned, in the journey to the dismantling of southern midwifery.

In my discussion of ethnographic fieldwork in Green River County or medical and public health programs from 1900 to 1960, I focus as much on language and the territory of discourse as on what people and institutions did or how they did it. This approach undoubtedly marks me as a product of a particular time and place in the history of anthropology, and specifically of medical anthropology. No apologies are forthcoming; I can only say that much of the data from conversations with residents in Green River pivot around the complex reconstruction of experience and the selective strategies of memory—that is, around talk. Similarly, the writings and programs produced by physicians, nurses, and public health officials contained a universe of ideas about race and gender, the relationship of medicine to society, and the status of the South in the nation's political and social economies. These ideas reflected the world as these authors knew it and established a way of ordering that world in the face of the dramatic transitions that were under way.

Remembering and Forgetting

I am drawn to the nature of remembering and forgetting in the histories and cultures of birthing practitioners and practices. Most current authors allude to the ways in which the African American midwife has been ignored. For example, Rene Reeb describes African American midwives in rural Mississippi as one of the state's "best kept secrets" (1993, 20). The erasure of historical memory about the skills and knowledge of these

African American women existed alongside moments when they have figured on the national and local stage. In this book, I focus on the period from the 1920s to 1950s, when the African American midwife was drafted into service in the social and medical reform initiatives of local state legislatures and the federal government. There were and are other instances suggestive of how the African American midwife has represented a cultural cypher with which others have written their own narratives or blocked alternative readings. This Prologue addresses the rudiments of these interpretive entanglements.

The African American midwife showed up in a most unlikely place when reporter Michael Lewis filed a "postcard" from Montgomery, Alabama, to the pages of *The New Republic* in August 1993. He reported on his meeting with Onnie Lee Logan, a retired African American midwife who is the subject of *Motherwit: An Alabama Midwife's Story,* an "as told to" book by Katherine Clark (1989). A one-woman reading had been adapted from the work (with hopes of a more ambitious play), thus providing the occasion for Lewis's duties as a chauffeur to bring Miss Onnie from Mobile to Montgomery for the reading.

Lewis notes the unlikely reversal of roles in which Miss Onnie was the honored guest celebrity and white men her supplicants. He characterizes Miss Onnie's refusal to dwell on tragedy in her life or to emphasize her experience of racism and professional neglect as a rebuke to those who would use her life to comment on the history and politics of race and racism. The seeming absence of bitterness, in Lewis's view, "posed a problem for modern sensibilities. For a start, a black woman who had suffered the full indignity of pre civil rights Alabama yet does not see herself as a victim threatens those who do" (1993, 11). The dominant note struck in this doubling back on the midwife as public figure—in the text and play and as celebrity—is the veiled insistence on Lewis's part (and not really Miss Onnie's) that her life remain resolutely individualized, sheared from social or historical context. Lewis wants us to take Miss Onnie at face value. That desire has its own conservative motivation. It challenges those of us who would want to give Miss Onnie her due, while insistently speaking to and offering evidence of her victimization, by whom and for what. Lewis's commentary reflects the kinds of issues that emerge in the question of how the African American midwife and her history should be depicted today. Such a challenge is an old one, with perhaps as much at stake in the present, when few traditional midwives remain, as in the past, when they numbered in the thousands.

One remarkable moment in the public depiction of the midwife occurred in December 1951, when in a photo-essay for *Life* magazine, W. Eugene Smith introduced Mrs. Maude Callen, a nurse midwife practicing in rural South Carolina. The photo-essay, sandwiched between advertisements for automobiles by Packard and watches by Longine, showed striking and sympathetic images of the midwife attending a young woman through labor and delivery, nursing the sick and shutin, offering a postnatal check to a poor white mother of twins, helping poor African American residents negotiate business transactions, teaching lay midwives, and assisting the local white physician. While highlighting the competence, caring, and heroism of Mrs. Callen, the *Life* photographs also depicted the substandard living conditions of rural African Americans. Malnourished young children were shown dancing at having received a hand-me-down dress or a few store-bought groceries from the midwife (Smith 1951).[1]

It is not coincidental that these images and text appeared in the Christmas issue. *Life* readers could recognize their own good fortune, while being moved to consider the depressed social conditions of the southern "Negro." As Glenn Willumson documents, barring a few nasty letters to the editor, public response to the photo-essay was overwhelmingly positive: donations to Mrs. Callen allowed her to build and establish a medical clinic for African American patients. The *Life* photo-essay also influenced the state legislature to increase funds to public health, which previously had been steadily cut (Willumson 1992, 167–77). In addition to touching the hearts of readers and legislators, however, Smith intended his story to serve as an ideological counter to the view that African Americans were morally and intellectually deficient (Willumson 1992). By showing the collaboration of an African American midwife and a white doctor, he offered an alternative vision of racial relations in the South and pressed for the importance of increased opportunities for midwifery training.

As a cypher, however, Maude Callen had been carefully selected. She was a college-trained nurse, with a physician uncle and good connections among the public health bureaucracy and local religious philanthropies (Willumson 1992). Willumson is highly critical of Smith's deliberate muting of these facts. With the benefit of foresight, he suggests that the photo-essayist's call for increasing the number of African American midwives could have been detrimental to what would have been the higher goal of medical integration. He is particularly put off by the lop-sided portrayal of Mrs. Callen as a hero-martyr—a rural woman strug-gling to make good by the force of her own will and native intelligence.

Smith's photo-essay worked because it tapped into a cultural icono-graphy of African Americans in which humility and forbearance were paired. Mrs. Callen worked to exhaustion and was smart, but she never expressed anger or stepped outside the appropriate bounds. She looked the part of a midwife, but not in any alien or frightening way. She moved among the African American poor without being too aggressively differ-ent or too much herself a part of that milieu. I see these photographs as reassuring in some ways, at least for white readers of *Life,* because they allowed whites into the homes and communities of the racial and eco-nomic outsider. Furthermore, by ostensibly focusing on the midwife's activities, Smith was able to show scenes of a mother in labor, in tears, in pain, as well as the contorted body of a child near death—moments of such intimacy—that were only available for public consumption in a family magazine because the subjects were African American, southern, and poor.[2] For Smith and others, portrayals of the midwives were linked to a specific set of representations of the African American body and of African American families and communities. These operated in a com-mon fashion, even if the underlying political motivations were wildly divergent.

I show how such public representations appear in the cultural frames of African American residents in Green River County. I indicate, where I can, how residents attempted to shape that public image, particularly through the ethnographic interventions made available to them by virtue of my presence and nagging questions while conducting this research.

On Margins

The margin is a key metaphor in a recent work by Arthur Kleinman, a physician and perhaps one of the best known and most influential contemporary medical anthropologists (1995). Medical anthropology, he writes, operates at the boundaries between different disciplines. It com-ments on the relations among medicine, health, the body, and society but takes a decided and critical stance on the outskirts. Besides the image of the intellectual borderlands as a good place to tackle such issues, I like Kleinman's invocation of margins as a methodological feature of medical anthropology's engagement with ethnography. This, as he puts it, "creates another world and compares it with the taken for granted one" (1995, 195). Ethnography involves writing in from the margins, and in the process it encourages a repositioning of the center. Other definitions may offer more complexity, but Kleinman's perspective on ethnography suits my approach to this study.

Fairly stated, chronologies differ. My ethnographic analysis is based on fieldwork and interviews in African American communities in rural Green River County from the mid-1980s to the present. That dimension of the work primarily focuses on the narratives of older residents. The historical chronology focuses on the period between 1900 and 1960, during which the midwifery question emerged and developed as an issue in the medical, legislative, and public consciousness.

I rely on the tools of the historical trade to track the debates, cultural logics, and personnel involved in the transformation of birthing practices and beliefs.[3] On the margins, no other perspective seemed more useful than to consider how, over time, so much—from the professional status of white southern physicians and nurses to campaigns for racial integrity to national social policy—came to focus on these rural African American women. How the issues waxed and waned also became clear through a reading of medical journals, county records, and legislation from the period. I realize that a reliance on archival material written largely by white professional elites—tantalizing though such material may be— does not afford me a complete picture of what was a complicated process. Neither does such material shed much light on the experience of reproductive transformation and what it meant for midwives and the women they served. Exploring the historical texts gives an extra dividend, however. Within the heart of every public health official, nurse, or local registrar who wrote about the "midwifery problem" lurked a closet ethnographer ready to disparage the personality of the "Negro" midwife or the details of birthing "superstitions."

These naive ethnographies, for want of a better description, proved enormously useful not only in shedding light on the mind-sets of southern professionals involved in midwifery control and public health but also in helping me to understand how the struggles over childbirth involved at some fundamental level a dialogue about southern society and everyone's proper place within it. As the book suggests, the African American midwife proved a pivotal figure in this dialogue. She was used to affirm the status quo and also to question its very foundations. Lest I begin with too passive a picture of these women, the historical materials also suggest that many midwives attempted to insert themselves into contemporary southern discussion about what was good public health and obstetrics. I argue, however, that faced with tremendous constraints, unequal power, and a web of conflicting demands, they found their best efforts short-lived.

As a methodology for cultural comparison, ethnography also figures in this research in another sense. When I began this project in Green River, a county with about 40 percent African American residents, I wanted to understand the local experience of reproductive transformation. How had major shifts in the rituals, the personnel, and the context of birth been experienced by residents? How did residents give meaning to the historical processes that had rendered traditional midwifery invisible to most and a rarely remembered remnant of times gone by to others? The voices of older African Americans in rural Virginia tell their own stories of midwifery's disappearance over the first six decades of the twentieth century. Archival material provides both a context for and counterpoint to these oral testimonies. Older voices speak of the natural dying-out of the midwife. The written documents, by contrast, show that midwifery's demise occurred as the result of public health initiatives.

The central role that African American midwives played in reproductive health care in the South was uppermost in my mind as the issue to explore. Young, well-educated, and having little direct experience of the deprivations and racism that had characterized the community's struggle to gain adequate and accessible obstetric care, I could well take such a position. The African American residents of Green River had a rather more complex relationship to the midwifery tradition. But this would only become clear to me by listening to them speak about the material and symbolic shifts in birth that occurred in their lifetimes.

The tension lie between what might be termed the recuperative impetus and that which privileged silence and restraint as effective tools for containing and holding onto personal and communal narratives. By keeping the history of midwives and the experience of home births on the periphery of public memory, residents protected it from scrutiny while guarding their ambivalence about what had become stigmatized traditions and experiences. These strategies had been forged in the racially charged atmosphere of early-twentieth-century antimidwifery campaigns. Making their own cultural and political sense, they stand in awkward juxtaposition to the growth of a natural home birth movement that has flourished primarily among middle-class, white, nonsouthern women.[4] They also reframed and even destabilized the assumptions that I carried to Green River. The ethnography of memory, of reproduction, and of the body that I had initially expected proved absent, but in its stead remained a much more nuanced perspective on what had been gained and lost in the transformation of birthing in the community and in Virginia.

By working in the field, we are really asked to think about what we hold as the center, what we consider the peripheries of cultural experience, and what to make of it all. For example, at one level, Green River's African American residents mirrored the disdain for midwives sometimes found in medical journals of the early-twentieth-century; at other levels of discourse, however, they spoke with pride and respect for these women's skills and service. In this work, I want to illuminate the world in which such contradictions were created. Yet without losing faith in the strength of these cultural convictions, I also want to recuperate a vision of African American midwifery as a cultural and social resource whose destruction has impoverished us all.

Caribbean Researcher in the South

Begun when I was a graduate student at the Johns Hopkins University, this study has reached an endpoint of sorts with this book, completed while I am a professor at the University of Virginia. In these senses, I am enormously privileged, trained at elite academic institutions and having achieved the dreams of my immigrant parents who came to the United States from Jamaica in 1970. My interest in midwifery and birthing in the South grew out of academic and personal reasons.

At Johns Hopkins, I developed an interest in health and healing traditions in the African diaspora, with a focus on the political and economic dimensions of the interplay of the traditional and modern. But why the South? In the mid-1980s, fieldwork in American culture was still slightly frowned upon, and few studies focused on rural African American communities. Although early research on such communities resulted in what are now considered classics in the field, anthropologists by and large had oriented themselves toward the Caribbean and Latin America when the subject was black culture in the New World (Fraser 1991). Fieldwork in the South attracted me because there seemed still so much to be done. I was also drawn to the opportunity it offered of stepping outside my primary identification as a black person from the Caribbean, raised in Caribbean neighborhoods in Brooklyn, New York, and educated in contexts where the idea of southern African American culture remained an intellectual abstraction. My parents understood the dynamics of race and racism, which joined the interests of African Americans and Caribbean folk. At some level, however, "the black Americans," as they called non-Caribbean blacks, remained elementally unknown and unknowable.

Then again in academic settings, there was always an implicit tension between black students from the Caribbean and those from the United States. I hazard to guess that, small as were the total numbers, Caribbean students outnumbered African Americans in the Johns Hopkins Anthropology Department when I did my graduate work in the early 1980s. And even if numbers did not tell the entire story, there was a perceived difference that mattered in ways large and small. Thinking back, my decision to work in Green River County had to do with such factors: I wanted to make a rapprochement in my own terms with an African American community. I also saw this fieldwork as a rite of nation-building as I became less tied to the immigrant world of my parents and more to the political, social, and cultural context of being black in the United States.

Considerations of my difference in Green River County played a role in residents' interactions with me, even as my similarities offered advantages. For one, older residents in particular often expressed a strong desire to help me in my research because it would uplift the race. At the same time, others commented on my "proper" speech and education with the inference either that I was putting on airs or that it made them feel uncomfortable talking to me for fear that their English would seem "improper." Only rarely was I asked questions about which part of the Caribbean I was from, but as soon as people heard my accent, they would tell me stories of people they knew from "the Islands," or of vacations they or someone they knew had taken, sometimes more than twenty or thirty years before. Because residents of Green River have a long history of family migration to the urban centers of Philadelphia, Baltimore, and New York, they had developed their own views of the nature, mores, and behaviors of these foreigners.

To complicate the issue, I proved unusual on other grounds, as I wore my hair in a natural style, with a part down the middle and braids on either side. All of the women, young and old, whom I encountered in Green River County either relaxed or straightened their hair, or wore it in long extensions. The Jheri curl was still in vogue, offering yet another hair care option. My styling choice drew stares, and then when people got to know me well, direct questioning: "When are you going to fix your hair?" was the preferred form. This bodily symbol generated another line of cultural classification that, although marking me as different, also allowed people to see me as nonthreatening, perhaps even sexually prudish. I am sure my "natural" hair got me into many homes that otherwise would have remained closed to me because I was an unaccompanied single woman, with no kinship among local families. Of course, it might well have kept me out of others.

There is no way to fully measure the overall outcome of my difference(s) on the content and kinds of material I collected, for I had (and still have) no way of stepping outside my identity. Indeed, as I now understand it through years of experience, fieldwork in the United States has to take as its starting point the mutual knowledge of observer and observed. In my own case, sojourn in the South recast the experience of being African American from the Caribbean not through any transformation of the cultural self but through gaining expertise in understanding how others narrated stories about me (anthropologist, West Indian, black, woman, stranger, similar, different), even as I would narrate stories about their worlds. Throughout the book, I have attended to this interplay as both a dimension of the fieldwork experience and, more important, a historical process of defining self and other.

Terminology

Notwithstanding the selective storytelling of her photograper, Maude Callen was a nurse midwife with professional medical credentials. That she practiced in rural areas was an outcome of health outreach programs sponsored by South Carolina's Department of Public Health and the state diocese of the Episcopal church. In a few southern states, African American nurse midwives were hired alongside white public health nurses to supervise and train empirical midwives who are the primary subject of this book. Some recent authors refer to such midwives as "granny midwives." They argue that the name was an honorific used by members of the African American community (see, for example, Reeb 1992; Clark 1989). I avoid this usage for three reasons. Green River residents seemed purposely to sidestep its use, associating it with such terms as "Uncle" or "Aunt," which white southerners used to avoid addressing older African Americans as "Mr." or "Mrs."

Second, the term "granny" suggests that empirical midwives were always elderly, which was not the case in most southern states. Finally, the use of the phrase "granny" implies that these women were harnessed to a static reproductive tradition. As I try to show, they practiced a rather flexible birthing philosophy, incorporating techniques and protocols from their training in health and hygiene by public health departments and through their association with local physicians. They were also required after the 1930s in most states to be licensed and registered. The phrase "traditional birth attendant" (TBA) predominates in the literature on health care in the developing world. For my purposes, however, I simply use the descriptive phrase "African American midwives" and then when necessary specify the level of training or path to expertise.

Memory, Political Speech, and Ethnography

Dialogues of memory in this book title refer to the ways in which older members of the African American community in Green River County speak about the history and experience of childbirth and midwifery. Unlike the approach taken in other works on midwifery, I interviewed not only retired midwives and direct descendants of such women but also anyone who would have lived through the transformations in birth, midwifery, and medical care. How do they narrate the transformations in birth? What is the relationship of these narrations to those discovered in the archives among contemporary medical journals and public health materials from the 1900s to the 1950s? A main thesis of this book is that these forms of speech have a shadow relationship—one mediated by my intervention but present nonetheless.

When they talked about "home remedies" or about the experience of birthing and pregnancy, older men and women in Green River located their discussion in a specific time and place—the community as it had been during the years of their youth through childbearing and child raising. For the most part, they told me that the kinds of bodies that had responded to "home remedies" and to the ministrations and knowledge of the midwives and "old folk" no longer existed. Bodies, along with temperaments and the very nature of the community, had changed, so that scientific medicine now, in their view, provided the only effective and appropriate means of treating and diagnosing illness and birthing children. Given their memories and experiences of the shift to the "professional management of the body" (Duden 1985), I found that one could not reasonably ignore the terms of the dominant discourse.

Yet these memories did not primarily focus on public health initiatives or external pressures not to use the midwife. Talk about changes in childbirth and birthing attendants was framed within a more inclusive narrative of changes in the natural world, in community life, and even in people's bodies and minds. But there were subjects best left unremembered, topics avoided or recast: silence in Green River is as much a part of the ethnography as the spoken word. Some people believed that the past had to be set aside in order to take advantage of the fruits of progress. Others—women who had experienced midwife-attended births or who had kin ties to midwives—emphatically did not want to talk about midwives and their practices. Solicitations for interviews were sometimes met with "no comment" when I explained my interest. Being no Oprah Winfrey, I at first wondered how my curiosity on this subject could be taken as a potential exposé. Because I now know the stigmatization of public health, the pejorative discourses around the use of midwives, and the negative associations between African American bodies and disease, I understand a lot better.

Silence in Green River about these aspects of the past testified to a wish to look forward rather than backwards. But it also marked out an area of distress. Why did informants experience pain in evoking memories of midwives and home births? Silence had many explanations. Individual decisions were made about what to tell the anthropologist. There was the cultural sanction among older people against talking too openly about the experience of childbirth because it was inevitably about women's bodies and secrets. And, finally, silence and remembering were highly politicized acts influenced by the rhetoric of race, shame, and science that for fifty years were so much a part of the public health discourse in Virginia. Social trauma was associated with the decline of the midwife and the cultural world within which she operated. No apologies have ever been made for the mudslinging, for the denial of African Americans' basic humanity, for the stigma of wanting and begging for health care services made available to white citizens, for the vulnerable bodies, and for compromised families and communities.

The past has not been reconciled to the present. Under these conditions, as Peter Lyman says in his discussion of silence and political speech, the historical forces in private lives can remain subdued and repressed, or they can lead to voice: "these voices are texts, fragments of memories from the unresolved past that cannot be mourned and eventually give way to peaceful reconciliation or determined action" (1981, 55–56). When Miss Onnie Logan, the Alabama midwife mentioned earlier, insists on the truth of everything in her book, she is taking action to give voice to the past. When she decries the lack of opportunity for her to "get more learning" when she was a young woman, she is giving voice to her regrets and anger. When she keeps repeating how good white people have been to her, while offering considerable detail of the injustices in her life, she is choosing to speak and to be quiet. She is, in short, exercising mother wit transformed into political speech. It is up to us to hear her. Again Lyman writes that such testifying "raise[s] the question of whether history resists understanding, or whether we ourselves resist understanding the history we have experienced" (1981, 55–56).[5]

Ethnography is about the testimony of others, to use the term in both the courtroom and church sense. My job has been to listen and to connect the fragments, but never to overwhelm the material with my own interpretive desires. Midwives who waited on women in a "family way" are remembered by African Americans in Green River County. But remembering does not necessarily lead to speaking, and speaking carries its own weight and burdens. As an outsider, I am unable to know whether African Americans freely spoke about midwives and midwife-attended births among themselves. In their interactions and conversations when I was present, however, it was clear that they experienced a great deal of ambivalence about bringing this aspect of their personal and collective histories into the public domain.

People did not wish to reveal fully their knowledge about either midwives or the rituals and practices associated with traditional birthing. Discussions of birthing traditions and of midwives invoked a good deal of contradiction and ambivalence. Was the midwife a figure of shame or pride? Did traditional birthing rituals and practices reflect negatively or positively on African Americans? How did one distance oneself from what was now considered "superstitious" or "backward" while at the same time acknowledge the former unquestioned authority of these beliefs and practices? These and related queries informed the ways in which older residents approached the history of midwives and childbirth in their communities.

But these were not the only issues. My initial tendency to see people's reluctance to discuss midwives as directly or solely related to the ideological and bureaucratic power of the state and its "sciences" needs qualification. Beyond the impact of medical and legislative campaigns that discredited midwives, other factors influenced the way in which older African Americans discussed social childbirth and its demise. These are discussed in the work in order to explore the interrelationships between the dominant ideologies of medical and public health authority and the cultural meanings given to birth, the midwife, and treatment of the body by African Americans.

In the work as a whole, I wrestle with ambivalence and contradiction. It is not that I wish to find coherence where there is none. Indeed, in their reconstructions of the past and evaluations of the present, African Americans in Green River County tell many different stories about their lives and their communities: they continually rework the past. But it is important to understand the nature(s) of this reworking and to consider the meaning of silence as well as what is said.

Whenever informants spoke about birthing and midwifery, a subtext inevitably lie just beneath the surface of our conversations—things that individuals did not necessarily want to talk about or things that, I was led to understand, were not normally brought into the open. Even with variations in individual sensibilities, areas of shared reserve or silence could be detected. These were marked in conversations by whispering, by changing the subject, by silence, by forgetting, or by placing events or beliefs further back in time. In some instances, as I have said, people simply avoided speaking to me.

Women sometimes prefaced their remarks by asserting that they had no direct experience of midwives or birth rituals but were simply passing on information that they had heard, or that only "the older folks" in their communities had believed in the rituals involved in traditional home births. Some who would have most likely used a midwife, given the few available physicians in the county during the early part of the century, would often tell me that "this was only how the old folks did it" or "that's how they did it during slavery times" as a means to create distance between the present and the past.

Ambivalence was expressed in other ways. Both men and women often portrayed the midwife as caring, knowledgeable, and a figure of great authority on medical and spiritual matters. Yet few people believed that her approach to birth would be useful or even desirable in the present. None of those women who admitted to having delivered their children at home under the supervision of a traditional midwife expressed any desire to reinstitute home births. Those individuals who were willing to speak extensively about traditional birthing practices, as well as those who distanced themselves from any association with midwives or traditional birthing rituals, shared this point of view. Even as they regretted the disappearance of the "old ways," informants would often concede that "you can't fight progress," and that in the end the insertion of an expert between the body and the self was the best course of action when one was ill. Here I confront these contradictions.

Accounts of childbirth rituals and practices in Green River must be understood as being embedded in a process of closure and disclosure. Older residents were relatively willing to consider the tensions between modern and traditional methods of birth and to offer reasons why the former, while valued in its day, now had to be put aside. By contrast, reticence seemed to be most acute on issues related to the experience of labor and the rituals of postpartum care as mediated by the midwife. It is not coincidental that these aspects of the birthing experience considered by African Americans to be private, domestic behavior were precisely the aspects of home births that public health officials and the state legislature scrutinized and attacked most virulently in the first half of the century.

These arenas of conflict became even more charged when they were brought under the control of the legislature: the element of punishment and illegality substantially shifted the balance of power. In the overlap between culturally normative rules about the privacy of birth, on the one hand, and the official sanctions against traditional midwifery, on the other, one begins to glimpse the dimensions of the struggle over the "said" and the "unsaid" in the recollections of my informants.

The contestation about what is acceptable to talk and remember about the history of birthing and midwifery in Green River County's African American community may appear bewildering to our modern sensibilities. How do we understand the nature of the ambiguities that confronted older African Americans in Green River? Their silence and reserve run counter to contemporary birthing movements that focus on verbalization as empowerment. From this perspective, control is gained and choices optimized by bringing birth into the open, by freely talking about it in the public domain.

By contrast, the degree to which African Americans in Green River maintained some measure of control over birth would have been related to their ability to mask or to hide their belief in and use of the rituals and practices of traditional midwifery. Furthermore, despite their support for medicalized births, older women still hold to the view that it is inappropriate to talk about what should be an intimate, private event. Silence, therefore, is inscribed in the history of midwives and birthing in this African American community. It is part of the dialogue listened to and intiated.

Methods and Setting

The people I spoke with on the preceding topics were African American men and women in their late fifties through their nineties who were bearing and raising children at some time during the fifty years covered by this study. These individuals number upwards of one hundred. Of this group, about two-thirds were women. Two were in their nineties, so they would have given birth in the 1920s and 1930s, and the ages of the other women clustered in the range between fifty-five and seventy. The distribution for men was similar. In addition, I interviewed a public health nurse who practiced in Virginia in this county and elsewhere for almost thirty years. I also interviewed a woman in her twenties who had used one of the last remaining midwives in the county.

Occasionally, I taped formal interviews and later transcribed them. I have a set of thirty completed interviews lasting from thirty minutes to three hours. In addition to the interview format, I relied on conversations overheard in doctors' offices and grocery stores. I lived in Green River County for about fourteen months and paid return visits once I had formally left the field. Conversations took up where we left off or new ones initiated. In the end, I managed to locate four women who had practiced midwifery and five others who delivered babies on occasion but did not consider themselves midwives. The bulk of my analysis, however, is oriented toward the experiences of ordinary men and women whose only criteria for being included in this book is that they lived in Green River County at some time between 1900 and 1960.

Green River County lies in Virginia's Piedmont. To protect the privacy of those who spoke with me as well as those who did not speak, I have used a pseudonym for the county as well as for all persons named in the work. Rather than one African American community, the county is made up of many residential clusters where African Americans have historically lived. These clusters might encompass half a length of a rural state road or an entire section of the county. Another means of reckoning community is by membership in a church. Most residents consider themselves Baptists, even if they were not regular churchgoers. Older residents with whom I spoke—many of them having lived outside the county for some part of their lives—nonetheless considered the church of their childhood baptism as their main church. This claim to primary membership held true even if, for reasons of proximity, for example, the residents attended another church. I often found, therefore, that referrals for interviews from church members were often to people who were kin-related, rather than by virtue of them being neighbors.

Another set of communal connections came through women who had used the same midwife. An interview with a woman whose aunt had been her midwife led to meetings with cousins and friends who had relied on this midwife as well. Midwives, it seemed, especially before cars were routinely available, practiced within a defined birthing territory of no more than ten miles or so, close enough to her clients so that she could reach them by horse and buggy or on foot. But she would also be available to clients living farther away who preferred her services. One got, therefore, a sense of birthing networks among families or groups of women somehow connected to the same midwife.

Census data for the area show that this rural county has fewer than 12,000 residents. Fewer than half this number were African American. I worked primarily in three sections of the county. As is typical of most of Virginia's rural counties, African Americans occupy the lowest-paying jobs in the service industry, have the least years of high school education, and have fewer individuals graduating and going on to college. Indeed, the figures are so low that, for example, almost three times as many whites went on to college as did African Americans in 1980. When compared with whites, fewer than half the number of African Americans had completed four years of high school. I spent 1984–85 in Green River with subsequent visits for shorter periods of time. I participated in local community activities, went to funerals, visited with the sick, attended church, and taught as a substitute teacher. It was in these formal and informal settings that people learned of my presence and found out about my interests. In a pattern that took hold after the first few months in the county, I usually had formal interviews with a tape recorder if it did not disturb the interviewee or intrude in our interaction.

After this first session, however, many informal visits usually occurred when I was not expected to be recording. I found that people usually gave me what they considered to be the "important" facts during our taped interview. Subsequently, we simply talked over a wide range of subjects not necessarily connected to my explicit interests. It should not be surprising that these impromptu conversations were often the occasions on which people let down their guard. In groups, I also noticed that the norms of what was considered acceptable or not acceptable information were not easily maintained. People got involved in the give and take of ordinary conversation and became less self-conscious about giving me the "right" information.

People's concern about giving "wrong" information turned out to be the most problematic part of my role as an outsider with stated interests in a specific topic. Older men and women, who were my primary informants, always wanted to ensure that I got the "correct" information. At times, for example, a dictionary would be taken from the shelf to ensure that I spelled a word accurately. At other times women deferred to men on topics associated with farming because they believed that men were the experts in these domains. Similarly, few men spoke to me about birthing and midwives if women were around. At such times, the issue was not that people were wary of giving me information. Rather, they knew that I was using this project for school and later for public consumption and were quite adamant that I get things right from whomever was considered the expert on a particular topic. Thus I sometimes found myself shunted off to a Sunday school teacher or to the male head of household. Invariably, only after this initial passing up of the system and having been given the specific "facts" was I able to hear less expertly sanctioned testimonies.

The shared themes of the narratives and life histories that were recounted to me, however, make me confident that this work describes how memory, history, and the present come together for the individuals with whom I spoke. Only with attention to the specifics of how individuals narrate their lives and the lives of their community can we come to a clear understanding of both the shared elements and the variations in African American culture and history in the United States.

The Three Bodies

Nancy Scheper-Hughes and Margaret Lock have argued in an enormously influential work that anthropologists should reenvision how they think about and study the body. "We begin," they write, "from an assumption of the body as a physical and symbolic artifact, as both naturally and culturally produced, and as securely anchored in a particular historical moment" (Scheper-Hughes and Lock 1987, 7). They propose three levels to correspond with "the three bodies"—the individual body, the social body, and the body politic.

In my way of thinking, when individual women in Green River remember how they gave birth, the nature and level of pain, how they responded to the umbilical cord, or what it felt like to stay in postpartum seclusion, this constitutes the "lived experience of the body"—something that women shared but that had its individual features. The authors would have us examine the various ways in which individuals experience their minds and bodies and conceptualize the relationships between the "constituent parts."

The social body refers to the "representational uses of the body as a natural symbol with which to think about nature, society, and culture" (Scheper-Hughes and Lock 1987, 7). Drawing on the works of structural and symbolic anthropologists, Scheper-Hughes and Lock suggest that the social body provides a source of metaphor for explanation and justification of the social order: the body is a symbol of society, and society is symbolic of the body. "To a great extent," they write, "talk about the body . . . tends to be talk about the nature of society" (1987, 20). When, for example, a physician blamed African Americans for jacking up the rate of maternal deaths by virtue of their presence in his state, he was expressing the view that the black body was symbolic of decay and disease. His vision of a more perfect polity would not include such bodies, and no amount of health care could change African American women's degraded place in the state. Better to allow them to die out. Other chapters will take up the analysis of lived experience and the social body. Here I focus on the politics of bodily regulation.

With the body politic, the level of analysis shifts in order to focus on "the regulation, surveillance, and control of bodies" (Scheper-Hughes and Lock 1987, 7). Attention is placed on the regulatory mechanisms operating in "complex, industrialized" as well as in preindustrial societies. Regulation in the specific sense meant here highlights the connections between social projects inclined toward organizing and classifying people and processes and assigning power and taking it away. The book's view of regulation acknowledges the constant availability of self-interested evil people who just want to do bad, but also, more important, it underscores the benevolent intentions of those whose work is done according to prevailing ideas of what is good and rational.

Another orientation comes from Lyman's definition of "psychological hegemony" as an effort to teach "subordinates codes of behavior, such as 'reason' or 'politeness,' which subliminates anger into nonpolitical forms of action" (1981, 67). Midwives resisted when they felt imposed upon, but they were also polite, taking a giant step toward transforming themselves into the vision of a sanitized handywomen to birth and public health. Many sets of images from contemporary medical writers and observers capture this emphasis on "before" and "after" midwives, but this formulation is especially exemplary. Dr. James Ferguson almost glows in appreciation of the fruits of midwifery education in Mississippi: "The old Negress in dirty nondescript dress, a pipe stuck in her mouth, and a few odds and ends of equipment thrown into a paper shopping bag or a drawstring cloth sack began to be replaced by a cleaner woman in a white starched dress and a white cap carrying a neat leather black leather bag which contained a carefully scrutinized set of supplies" (1950, 86).

The elimination of African American midwives in Virginia provides a case study of the convergence of the interests of physicians, public health personnel, and the legislature. New concerns in the century's first four decades were mirrored in the calls for an efficient system of vital statistics collection. Birth and death registration certificates filled out by doctors, midwives, or local registrars were avowed to be the basic instruments for data collection. Besides the focus on tracking births and deaths, prenatal care was intended to help preserve the life of mothers and infants. In Virginia but also elsewhere, anxiety about preservation of racial boundaries and fears about the insufficiency of white fertility went hand in hand with the vital statistics and maternal health movement. What was the relationship among these disparate social projects and their connection to African American midwives? All to some extent included the midwife in the regulatory processes, even as she was also to be regulated and supervised. They also created a new set of bureaucratic interactions between the midwife and the women she attended.

The midwife came under scrutiny because she was found everywhere on the social landscape in Virginia and the South, during a time when the administration of American lives came to take on great importance as an essential feature of modernity and progress. The midwife and her clients need not have individually understood how all these pieces fit together, but nonetheless they would have encountered some aspect of the national movement toward rationalization of birthing and dying, seated initially in the mandates surrounding vital statistics and the eugenics of race.

The basic analytic frame of the three bodies shapes the structure of this work. Parts I and II focus on regulation and surveillance—the body and polity. Part III takes up the issues of the social and individual bodies as remembered and experienced by older residents of Green River County.

I

The Body Politic

1

Introduction

Located in the upper South, Virginia has its own history of engagement with African American midwifery. The full weight of the argument developed in Part I is oriented toward the emergence of public health programs and the discourses of race, gender, and society in that setting. Using Virginia as a particular case, I make a broader set of claims about the relevance of the analytic perspective developed here for the South as a whole. The core of that analysis depends on my reading of the rhetoric and structure of race as reflected in the public health and medical literature. I rely on my readers' indulgence as to whether my jump to a regional frame is warranted. (Much of the comparative work that would synthesize what are now localized studies and individually framed life histories is yet to be done.)

A Regional Perspective

In the secondary literature, the trend is toward the documentation of state histories, with an emphasis on the lives of individual midwives. Given the cultural, historical, and political differences among the southern states, the better side of prudence would applaud such an approach. The documentation of otherwise ignored histories and individuals is also an important contribution. Thus, for example, Debra Susie and Molly Dougherty describe midwives in Florida (1988; 1978); Linda Holmes and Katherine Clark document midwifery life histories in Alabama (1986; 1996); Rene Reeb and Susan Smith give accounts of Mississippi midwives (1992; 1994); Beatrice Mongeau and Holly Matthews (1973;

25

1992) focus on North Carolina; and Ruth Schaffer writes of midwifery's functional decline in Texas (1991). These studies bring out the differences but also the shared elements in midwives' practice and belief structures and in their responses to public health campaigns adopted across the South. In this work I use Virginia and the ethnography of memory in Green River County to argue for the regional coherence of midwifery control and public health programs. I also suggest a shared pattern of experiences and responses on the part of ordinary African Americans to reproductive transformation. From this perspective, I am reminded of Harrison White's commentary that in the social sciences, the grammatical definition of case stresses the "relation" of words to "neighboring words" (White 1992, 84).

An African American midwife in Virginia during the first half of the century shared much in common with her counterparts in the South, whether in Florida, Mississippi, South Carolina, Texas, Arkansas, or Alabama. For example, strategies of recruitment included apprenticeship to an older midwife of a younger woman who shared close kinship ties, receiving the spiritual call to practice, or by the 1930s the selection of a woman as a likely candidate by a public health nurse or doctor. At the level of birthing practice and beliefs, there was a shared conviction that formal training, no matter how detailed, could not replace the need for the divine intervention of God to guide the midwife when she was attending a woman. Across the South, African American midwives recognized a shared system of intuitive or charismatic knowledge identified as "mother wit" or common sense and understood as an essential feature of a successful practice. Mother wit functioned as an underlying grammar of midwifery know-how, a requirement of personality that, as Reeb points out in her study of Mississippi, the older midwives she interviewed would not or could not define but "could tell who did or did not have it" (1992, 22).

Allied to the capacity of knowing through intuition was personal temperament. Ideally, midwives were expected to maintain control, to act decisively under pressure, and to handle the diverse demands and expectations of household members who tried to intervene. Specialists in reproductive medicine, midwives gained a higher level of expertise than other women in the use of herbal and patent remedies for other matters of the body. They cared for the sick and in some communities tended to the final washing and dressing of the dead (Bell 1993; Clark 1989;

Dougherty 1978; Fraser 1995; Holmes 1986, 1996; Mongeau 1973; Robert and Reeb 1992; Schaffer 1991; Smith 1951; Susie 1988).

When discourses of race are taken into account, I would highlight the following four factors that linked southern midwifery campaigns. First, the African American midwife shouldered the responsibility for a population of women and children who were by any contemporary measure among the poorest and the least healthy in the South (Beardsley 1990; Farley and Allen 1989; Jones 1981; Ladd-Taylor 1988). No matter how powerful by virtue of her personality and involvement in the most potent stages of the life cycle, the southern midwife ministered to bodies that were extremely vulnerable. They were weakened by the shared structural conditions of ill health, racism, political neglect, and economic distress. Across the South, this social and bodily vulnerability provides the comparative frame for a claim to a regional perspective.

The second factor is that in most southern states there existed an underlying ambivalence about how much, if any, financial resources should be directed at African American communities. At the extreme were those medical pundits who believed that African American ill health was either a consequence of depraved habits or morality or of an inevitable biological-racial disintegration. These views thwarted many of the best efforts of public health personnel and became the point of further heated contention when the federal government made money and resources available specifically for health care reform in the 1930s (Jones 1981; Beardsley 1990; Ladd-Taylor 1988; McBride 1991).

A third factor in the regional experience of midwives and the structure of midwifery campaigns is that federal and northern philanthropic infusions of funds and programs into southern health brought along a common educational and public health approach to midwifery training. For example, Florida, Texas, Alabama, South Carolina, Arkansas, and Mississippi used some of their funds to establish midwifery education programs that had the long-term goal of phasing out midwives and replacing them with clinics, hospitals, and medical doctors and the short-term goal of using midwives to improve African American child and maternal morbidity and mortality rates. Education campaigns shared a similar philosophy, even using practically identical songs adapted from "Negro spirituals" or nursery rhymes to drive home the message of hygiene, limitation of practice, and prenatal care to midwives (Blackburn 1935, 1937; Campbell 1946; Hudson 1987; Lange 1949).[1] Versions of songs taught to midwives in North Carolina, Georgia, and Louisiana have similar, if not identical elements. Here's one from Georgia, meant to be sung to the tune of "That Old Time Religion":

> Give me that good old midwife meeting,
> Give me that good old midwife meeting,
> It is good enough for me.
> We will wear our caps and gowns, *(repeat three times)*
> They are good enough for me.
> We'll use our soap and brushes, *(repeat three times)*
> They are good enough for me.
> We will always clean our nails, *(repeat three times)*
> It is good enough for me.
> Then we'll save our mothers and babies *(repeat three times)*
> And it's good enough for me. (Campbell 1946, 38–39)

From Louisiana, Deola Lange offered a different version, with the same repeat pattern:

> Give me that new time midwife
> She comes to all her meetings
> She uses plenty soap and water
> She is clean, clean, clean
> She knows the danger signals
> She registers all my babies. (Lange 1949, 606)

These songs were likely used by public health nurses to give basic lessons to illiterate women (Bell 1993; Lassiter 1941). As Lynn Hudson rightly suggests in her discussion of midwifery programs in North Carolina, however, the songs' simplicity and repetition indicated a view of the midwife as not only illiterate but stupid. A hint as to the view through the midwife's eyes comes in Marie Campbell's folk ethnography. Campbell documents as having been composed by midwives a song that rivaled the nurse's for complexity and know-how. Here are two sample verses to be sung to the tune of "As We Go Marching On":

> We put on water in a great big pot
> We know of this we must have a lot
> We boil it all, some cool, some hot
> As we go marching on

We report births and deaths and all
When anything is wrong, we the doctor call,
We hope we never from grace may fall
As we go marching on. (Campbell 1946, 39)

The widely distributed training documents, lessons for midwives, retirement and licensing programs, and research reports, for example, created and disseminated supposedly authoritative knowledge about appropriate birthing techniques and comportment. If midwives had culturally specific beliefs and practices in local and regional contexts, they also took part in this totalizing process. "Totalizing" is used here not as a bad word but as a clue to the way in which, by the 1930s and 1940s, the experience and practice of African American midwifery could be characterized as a southern or regional phenomena by virtue of the shared experience of public health training.[2]

To develop this insight, I draw on Bridgette Jordan's observation that the "constitution of authoritative knowledge is an ongoing social process that both builds and reflects power relationships" (Jordan 1991). Public health training and other artifacts were socially produced and marketed to an audience that was simultaneously skeptical and receptive, known and unknown. A close reading of these materials reveals how the southern African American midwife became defined as a category of persons with particular traits and temperaments that justified her location at the bottom of the professional and racial hierarchies. Paired with the ethnography, the textual data expose the interstices where midwives influenced the nature and direction of the flow of authoritative knowledge as well as shaped its content. Cultural negotiation of this authoritative knowledge was a shared characteristic of the history of midwifery and its control in the South.

Besides the educational complex of practices, pedagogies, and ideologies, a fourth regional factor is simply that of race. In his study of southern public health, Edward Beardsley (1990) suggests that the most virulent views against improving African American health care were held by private physicians who, besides their racism, believed that any public health initiative undermined private competition and took money from their pockets. Fair enough; private physicians' distress about improving rural midwifery service had a strong element of professional territorialism. I will widen the net, however, to show that on both sides of the political fence, and in private and public realms, southern medicine depended on a politics of racial and moral difference between blacks and whites as an essential component of its approach to health care issues.

In his discussion of scientific epidemiology and race at the turn of the century, David McBride identifies what he terms a "racialist interpretation" of African American health that prevailed between World Wars I and II (McBride 1991). Great store was placed in the view that physical-genotypic traits predicted African American susceptibility to disease. Nonetheless, proponents of racialism often worked on the same side of the fence as scientists who argued that sociological susceptibility based on degraded lifestyles better explained African American health statistics. Both explanations could be used either to support interventions to ameliorate the health of African Americans or to discourage such efforts (McBride 1991, 31–35). Those who thought it made sense to upgrade midwives' skills so that they could serve an underserved population as well as those who opposed any such efforts used the currency of race. I trace such rhetoric as it developed in Virginia over a roughly sixty-year period but, by example and inference, extend the argument to the rest of the South.

I must admit to a sneaking suspicion that the scholarly propensity to localize the history of southern midwives is connected to the nature of the materials themselves. Perhaps the anthropologist has more latitude than does the historian to give in to feelings about the data. I am going with the flow of that disciplinary liberty in pointing to the ways in which contemporary Virginia nurses and physicians writing at the state level about public health measures rarely acknowledged that the midwifery problem, as they defined it, extended beyond their borders. They also downplayed the involvement of the federal agencies in crafting educational materials or a plan of attack for health care reform. Articles about, for example, teaching midwives how to practice good hygiene or to recognize the symptoms of a high-risk pregnancy were written as if no antecedents existed elsewhere and for which a singular set of interventions had been crafted.

This insular perspective was undoubtedly connected to many southern physicians' and public health departments' mixed feelings about the use of federal funds. They did not want to raise the specter of federal oversight or invite questions about the level of outside supervision that such funds entailed (Beardsley 1990; Ladd-Taylor 1988, 1992). Medical and public health writers of the first half of the century rarely recognized the regional significance of the situation in Virginia. Only by comparing public health training manuals and procedures from different states do we gain a sense of the regional duplication of effort at the level of details—midwife clubs, midwife songs, midwife retirement ceremonies. Common interpretations of the racial bodies of African American midwives and mothers were linked to "ethnographic" mappings of "Negro culture." All of these racial ideas eventually filtered through federally generated materials, scientific-biomedical knowledge, and the local geographies of state programs.

Historian Molly Ladd-Taylor alludes to this teeter-totter between local distinctiveness and regional patterns. Of the 1921 Sheppard-Towner Act, for example, geared to fund health projects to improve maternal and infant health, she writes that

> like other US welfare schemes, Sheppard-Towner was marked by local variation in funding and support. Its decentralized administration allowed communities to devise programmes that suited their needs, but it also made maternity work vulnerable to political opposition, racial discrimination and incompetent administration. Thus, while Sheppard-Towner had a tremendous impact—and popular support—in states where the Children's Bureau worked effectively with local physicians and women's groups, it never got off the ground in others. (1992, 125)

Based on a preliminary classification of states that cooperated and states that did not, it appears that throughout the period, Virginia took advantage of federal public health programs. So did Florida, Arkansas, and North and South Carolina, while Georgia, Alabama, and Louisiana did not. The alternative system of classification that I am proposing, however, foregrounds race and racial hierarchy in defining the South's regional public health issues. These ideological and structural patterns operated regardless of the level of engagement with health and social reform. As we read the historical documents and listen to the voices of the living, it behooves us to uncover the common structures of power and authority, even as we explore local conditions and experiences.

A Primer on Midwifery and Public Health Chronologies

Public health as a concept emerged in the South in the early-twentieth-century. Private philanthropies such as the Rockefeller Foundation initiated large-scale regional sanitation programs in the early 1900s (Brown 1980, 48–50). Doctors, local social reformers, and African American citizen leaders raised the concern about the health status of those vulnerable members of their communities (Beardsley 1990; McBride 1991; Gordon 1994). Although not at the top of the list of public health issues, maternal and infant health had captured the attention of some local health officers and state medical societies.

For example, the first sustained effort to regulate Virginia's midwives began in 1900 in Elizabeth City, a small rural county. This local initiative encapsulated the complex dimensions of what would be the statewide campaign to monitor midwives and to establish a means of measuring the biostatistics of Virginia's African American and white populations. W. A. Plecker, The physician and local health officer who directed the Elizabeth City County midwife program and who was later appointed the state's first registrar, hoped to develop a standardized means of regulating midwives and keeping track of birth and infant mortality rates . A self-described country doctor, Plecker opined on the overall unsuitability of midwives but admitted that "as far as we can see into the immediate future [the midwife problem] is with us to stay" (1925, 809–811).

On the whole, however, southern public health proceeded in fits and starts. Organized at the county level through a system of clinics administrated by a health officer who in turn reported to state-level administrators, public health care depended on the good graces of county and state legislators and finance commissioners (Beardsley 1990; Brown 1980; McBride 1991). Local services, based on an entrenched system of patronage, emphasized the allocation of public goods and services through a personalized distributive system (Greene 1991). Public health's emphasis on some rationalized system of caring for the citizenry must have been anathema, for it potentially circumvented the entrenched set of relationships.

In cash-poor states, legislators shirked from funding health care services for poor whites and African Americans, especially women and children, who were in many respects nonproductive labor. The distaste for public entitlements of this sort only intensified when public heath services were perceived as accruing benefits to African Americans (Beardsley 1990; McBride 1991). As earlier noted, private physicians opposed any part of public health work that they perceived as encroaching on clinical medicine—stealing patients, so to speak. For these reasons, early public health workers were not characterized by any measure of zeal on behalf of African American citizens. In his typical diplomatic fashion, Beardsley concludes that early southern public health "failed [its] black patrons by a wider margin than any other group" (1990, 130).

The philanthropic programs of private foundations and the southern medical establishment's own difficulty in completely burying its head in the sand meant that the social problem of "Negro health" had to be addressed. From one stance, public health seemed a knight in shining armor, duty bound to take on the burden of a species of persons who could not or would not help themselves (Beardsley 1990; Jones 1981; McBride 1991). Midwives came into the picture because they were responsible for the birthing of the majority of rural African American babies.

Evidence suggests that the nation's health care agencies first showed legislative concern for these women and for infant and maternal health with the passage of the Sheppard-Towner Act in 1921. The act was sponsored by the federal Children's Bureau, which handled issues of concern to women and families. Legislative support for Sheppard-Towner funds lasted only through 1928. In its scope and generosity, however, Sheppard-Towner in many respects represented the high point of the progressive social reform spearheaded by northern feminists and their allies in public health and among newly enfranchised women.[3]

Supporters expected Sheppard-Towner funds to reduce infant and maternal mortality rates and improve morbidity statistics. Sheppard-Towner was understood to be a model project whose success would encourage greater state involvement and prove such programs worthy of federal funding. All women of childbearing age, but especially the rural and poor, were targeted for education about pre- and postnatal care, family health and hygiene, and, in some states, family planning. Local physicians did not escape full scrutiny as potential parts of the maternal and infant problem, but midwives were the recipients of the core of instructional programs. Historian Molly Ladd-Taylor, in an overall sympathetic portrayal of the bureau's goals and implementation strategies, concedes that the bureau held a bifurcated racial–class model. In northern, primarily white urban communities, bureau officers linked women and children's health to economic conditions. In the South, however, "the large number of Negro maternal deaths" were attributed not to "economic conditions but to the fact that Negroes were attended by Negro midwives" (Ladd-Taylor 1988, 258).

The Sheppard-Towner model worked through a system of experts. At the top of the organizational pyramid were Children's Bureau bureaucrats in Washington and social science researchers who assessed health conditions and identified and collaborated with local officials. Midwifery education supervisors filled in at the middle level, with their responsibilities for oversight and nurse training determined within the state. Further down the professional base were the public health nurses who directly trained the midwives found to be "worthy" and eliminated those found to be wanting. These Sheppard-Towner–funded nurses also took responsibility for pre- and postnatal maternal care and well-baby checks (Ladd-Taylor 1988; Mulligan 1976). Midwives, of course, spread out at the very bottom of the organizational hierarchy.

Of the many public health nurses hired in the South, a few were African American and worked in African American communities, but local white officials often discouraged such hires because of the status that accrued, the relatively high salaries, and the fear that such women would transgress segregation policies through their association with white co-workers or patients (Beardsley 1990; Hine 1989; Ladd-Taylor 1988; McBride 1991; Weiss 1974).[4]

Even the best intentioned public health nurses faced a daunting task in the South, with rural households widely scattered across counties. Transportation proved an obstacle for those midwives and mothers who wanted to use health clinic services or to attend lessons and training. A later chapter explores how such logistical issues were handled. Here I want simply to identify the main strategies: requirements for mandatory licenses approved by the public health nurse or local registrar; midwifery clubs with regular meetings; a series of lessons held in health clinics over a concentrated period of time; mothers' informational classes; and midwifery institutes such as those organized in Virginia, South Carolina, and Florida, where summer sessions were held typically at "Negro colleges" for midwives selected from across the state. The philosophy stated by the Children's Bureau and endorsed by southern states characterized the midwife as a necessary stopgap until the ratio of physicians to maternity cases increased and women could be educated to cease their reliance on home births and inexpensive female attendants.

Through the Sheppard-Towner legislation, the Children's Bureau undertook an ambitious venture to colonize and civilize African American midwives and mothers. It also offered, however, an infrastructure through which midwives could create networks outside their small communities, gain additional status and expertise on behalf of patients, and secure a professional foothold in reproductive medicine. The desire in that midwife song to never "from grace to fall" takes on interpretive complexity when we consider the hopes offered by the Sheppard-Towner Act.

This federal program affirmed African Americans' basic rights to health care regardless of the biases of local governments. Granted, the recognition of government's duty to secure citizens' health came with many strings attached and with a major bypass around the issues of poverty and political disenfranchisement. As to the program's objective to secure better maternal and infant statistics, scholars are united in their lukewarm assessment of the mixed to poor results during Sheppard-Towner's seven-year run. But the basic groundwork had been established, as had a set of ideological and professional claims and contests about the definition, scope, and utility of public health, especially for women, children, and families.

A primer can establish basic foundations but use quite different pedagogies. Here I want to briefly outline the approach to midwifery control and infant and maternity health for African American women from roughly the 1920s to 1950s in South Carolina, which had one of the highest infant mortality rates in the South. Then I shift strategies by looking at three prevailing historical narratives: the "great" men, the midwife on the rebound, and the suppressed midwifery narratives of southern midwifery history.

South Carolina as a case study provides a sense of the pacing of midwifery regulation and the role and responses of public health personnel and bureaucracies over a thirty-year period. Most noteworthy is the range during these thirty years of midwifery regulation, which spanned from the minimal—permits and birth certificate requirements but little in terms of expenditures for maternal and infant health programs—to the ambitious, which included summer institutes for the professional development of midwives and, by the 1950s, maternity and infant clinics. A nascent midwifery regulation program was born in South Carolina in the 1920s. The state had already established a bureau of child health early in the decade and used this body as a springboard for its efforts in reproductive public health. It required midwives to be issued permits by county registrars and to be responsible for registering all births. Through registrations and permits, public health officers could identify the number of practicing women. Classes in hygiene and in defining the limits of midwifery practice were offered beginning in the mid-1920s through the state public health office. After this basic certification, midwives were expected to report to county or district health officers. This supervision was later extended via the Sheppard-Towner Act to include clinic visits for pregnant women, but until then it largely focused on bag and birth certificate checks and permit renewal.

These early stages of midwifery control in South Carolina reflected the situations and circumstances to be found across the South during the 1920s. Sheppard-Towner and local funds were used to create a local health department in every county in the state, but it is unclear how such departments served its African American and poor patients. A recent history suggests that, owing to lack of funds, the efforts were minimal at best, but a contemporary source from the 1940s gives much attention to the availability of monthly classes for midwives and of prenatal clinics given by visiting public health nurses.

The centerpiece of South Carolina's federal- and state-funded midwifery training program was the midwifery summer institute. These institutes were organized in the mid-1920s, abandoned with the reluctance of the state legislators to fund such enterprises, taken up again in the mid-1930s, and expanded in the 1950s with the increased availability of federal funds and the pressures of African American state and national leaders (Beardsley 1990; Blackburn 1935, 1937; Gordon 1994; Hine 1989; McBride 1991). After the mid-1930s, yearly attendance at such institutes was a prerequisite for permit renewal. Maude Callen's involvement in midwifery training is better understood in this context, although photographs of the period show that most of the instructors at these institutes were white. Besides lessons on hygiene and baby care, basic literacy and leadership skills were taught. Here is the account of one such institute: "The group leader is a source of help and pride to the supervisors and teachers at the institute. This office carries great prestige and is much coveted by the midwives . . . This education of leadership within the group, and thus to educate the whole strata, is an important part of the institute" (Willumson 1992, Appendix B).

Midwives' permit fees helped to fund these seminars. A letter from a midwife to Laura Blackburn, the state's nurse midwife supervisor in the 1940s, suggests that local midwives used church fund-raising to help pay for their housing expenses (fifteen dollars) during the week-long institutes. In her commentary about the impact of such programs, Blackburn voted it a measure of success that midwives were "forcing" patients into prenatal clinics as a condition of offering their birthing services (Blackburn 1935, 1937). With the creation of links between midwives, patients, and public health clinics, the hope was not only to decrease infant and maternal mortality rates but also to secure some approximation of an equal standard of care in a segregated system.[5]

Midwifery control and regulation were predicated on the assumption of a social and political hierarchy in which racial difference was the defining factor. Resistance and often virulent racism on the part of the man in charge of state public health further putrefied the air. His medical wish list included the disappearance of blacks from the state (Beardsley 1990, 142–44). These attitudes did not completely block health care on behalf of the state's African Americans citizens, but they kept services to a minimum, and even those must have been given grudgingly. In 1949, midwives still delivered 60 percent of South Carolina's rural African American babies, while the majority (89.3 percent) of white babies were born in the segregated white hospitals. By its association with African American midwives, mothers, and babies, and by its being subsidized, the public health clinic came indelibly to stand for back-of-the-bus care, reserved for African Americans who couldn't do or didn't know any better. The stigma of blackness and low social status became enjoined, so that all but the poorest whites avoided the public health clinic and the midwife (Beardsley 1990; Gordon 1994).

Three Narratives

What are the features of the narrative accounts identified earlier? As I have said, they divide along these main lines—the "great" men, the midwife on the rebound, and the suppressed midwifery story—but are not mutually exclusive. Rather, they express different valences in the weight given to one or another set of factors, are confounded by the minutiae of state and local programs and personalities over this twenty-year period, and are shaped by the specific points of view and reference taken by the scholar.

Narrative 1, or the "great" men narrative, of which I will have my own version from Virginia, suggests that the variation in public health efforts to intercede in the health care of African American southerners depended in large part on the resolve or character of individuals. Beginning in the 1930s, Louisiana had Albert Dent, an African American physician leader who developed accessible care in a hospital for his people. Dr. Dent worked to decrease infant mortality rates and to offer competitive obstetric rates to entice African American women away from the rural midwife. Mississippi had Dr. Felix Underwood, who brought a system of midwifery education to his state. North Carolina's Watson Rankin and Charles Laughinghouse directed a state health department that spearheaded the employment and training of African American public health nurses in the first half of the century. "Great men" stories work through the chronicling of the acts and beliefs of individuals who fused the public health mission into a highly personalized one. They took on the midwife, as an ally or enemy, in their battle to subdue the forces of death and disease. While most such public health histories tell of good deeds, some—as in the case of Beardsley's evocation of Dr. James Hayne of South Carolina—do not (Beardsley 1990; Hine 1989; Smith 1994).

My protagonist in the "great men" tradition is W. A. Plecker, physician, registrar of vital statistics, midwifery control advocate, and expert on racial eugenics who basically controlled public health in Virginia through most of the first half of the century. Plecker personified the view of public health as a social mission of great purpose. He was also a racist whose driving goal was to clarify and maintain distinctions across the bodies of the state's citizen and to mute others as he saw fit. For example, in one act of public policy he declared that no Virginia resident could identify himself as Indian on his birth certificate, because all Indians were "mixed with negro blood."[6] Zeroing in on a person like Plecker is a good way to understand how the emphasis on vital statistics, birth registration, prenatal care, and the preservation of strict racial boundaries eventually implicated the African American midwife: the relationship among these disparate social projects and their connection to public health start to make cultural and political sense.

The benefits that accrue to the "great men" perspective include the ease with which, depending on the historian's wont, overlapping and contradictory impulses may be built into such a portrait, or simply ignored. There is, however, a danger in wrapping larger processes too tightly either in one person's ennobled or depraved psyche. The "great men's" narrative may best be read as a cultural parable that, in the history of midwifery in the South, should lead back out to the wider dialogues of race, medicine, and society.

Narrative 2, or the midwifery on the rebound narrative, focuses on the consequences of the failed initiative by the Children's Bureau. It argues that the potential benefits of midwifery education and regulation were never realized until well into the 1950s. From this perspective, the retreat of public health nurses and federal funds left the reproductive field up to midwives who continued to deliver the majority of African American babies in a state of relative ignorance of biomedical techniques and philosophies. Any consequences of Children's Bureau education were but unconnected vestiges of specific protocols: eye drops, hygiene practices, or greater willingness to refer patients to doctors and hospitals. The stress in this narrative is on the renegade autonomy of midwives who had slipped from the regulatory bureaucracies of the federal government and out of the reach or interest of local governments and public health officials.

A variant of this emphasis on the persistence of midwifery is the narrative that tells a more romantic tale of the collaborative relationship of midwives and public health nurses in the 1930s and 1940s, a relationship stimulated by early Sheppard-Towner efforts but forged in the mutual respect and professional regard of women working together to battle disease and death. Greatly admired in this account is the supposedly consensual involvement of midwives inp the campaigns of local health clinics and state governments—unpaid workers of public health. In this variation, the post–Sheppard-Towner midwife is a transitional figure, successfully retooled to work in concert with biomedicine. Those who failed to make that transition remain in the shadows, without official permits to practice, bereft of ties to medical personnel to which clients may be referred and stuck in the realm of folk practice (Ladd-Taylor 1988; Smith 1994; Roberts and Reeb 1994; Schaffer 1991; Bell 1993).

The facts of midwifery's persistence and even growth between 1930 and 1950 are uncontestable. The upgrading of midwife skills as a key public health project did not, whether in cooperation or conflict, hit at the underbelly of the health care problems of rural African Americans. Cynicism with regard to these narratives has to do with the muting of any analysis that inserts either the particular grids of power—whether of class, race, or professional status, which framed the interaction of African American midwives and largely white public health nurses—or the larger national context of the administration of bodies and biologies, that kept African Americans grasping for the threads of available care, while unsure if their lives or the lives of their children had been judged of any lasting value.

Suspend for a moment the focus on the midwife's capacities. What the preceding historical accounts underplay are the cultural, social, and political ramifications of child and maternal death. I had a slight discomfort with the midwife-on-the-rebound narratives but couldn't quite say why until I read the eye-opening work of Nancy Scheper-Hughes on infant death in the Brazilian northeast, where rates of 116 deaths per 1,000 births are conservatively estimated. Scheper-Hughes insists that the regularities of infant death in such instances are not caused by the failure of untrained midwives or negligent mothers but by the "social production of official indifference." Baby coffins are everywhere, as are the daily processionals to the cemetery, but municipal officials, factory owners, and state bureaucrats refuse to see the set of social relations that create the escalated rates of child death (Scheper-Hughes 1992, 275–77).

Even with the piecemeal quality of the demographic data, infant mortality rates across the South in the 1930s and 1940s have been documented at levels that met or surpassed these contemporary Brazilian figures. In South Carolina, between 100 and 159 per 1,000 African American infants died compared with 54 to 86 per 1,000 white infants; Virginia had between 99 and 114 per 1,000 African American infant deaths in the 1930s, and in Charleston, South Carolina, there were 213 infant deaths per 1,000 during that decade (Beardsley 1990; McBride 1991). These figures suggest the constant presence of death in the lives of rural African American families in the South—a routinization of mortality that spoke more to the structural conditions of despair than to the roles of any individual.

Narrative 3, or the suppressed midwifery narrative, stresses the gradual destruction of the African American midwifery tradition over the first half of the twentieth century. It is most closely related to the narrative that I develop in this work. It also harbors a particular romance—but this time of loss and tragedy. Here the chronology marks a process through which midwifery education begun at the turn of the century offered but an illusion of a participatory reproductive public health system. This view holds that the integration of traditional midwifery with the modified hygiene-based model taught by local, state, and federal health personnel ultimately did more to limit the midwife's realm of expertise than to widen or enrich it. Holly Mathews takes this view in her discussion of the dismantling of what she calls the "medical self-help tradition" in North Carolina, as does Debra Susie and Linda Holmes (Mathews 1992; Susie 1988; Holmes 1987b).

This historical account exposes the architecture of midwifery education programs: midwives trained within a system that viewed them as a temporary fix until something better (doctors, hospitals) came along. It suggests a scenario of deceit that, with hindsight, must have been difficult to fully camouflage, even in the most ideal circumstances of explicit cooperation between public health nurses and African American midwives. One midwife interviewed by Debra Susie remained puzzled by the abandonment. Speaking of her mother, who had opened a home-based practice in the 1940s, she remembered that "she just got to the place where she just sat there and she looked at her equipment—no deliveries, no one coming. And she got, well, I would say, at first, a little angry about it. This type of thing someone killing your career, is just like killing some member of the family that's real close . . . You ask yourself questions, 'Well, what have I done wrong?' . . . So you just pretty soon feel whipped" (1988:92).

Even with the high rates of midwife-attended births in the 1930s and 1940s, proponents emphasize the decontextualization of the lines of authority and communal relations that gave midwifery its social power. Numbers, then, do not speak for themselves in this weighting of the historical account. As Linda Holmes succinctly puts it, "supervisory structures . . . encouraged dependency and tried shifting authority from the community-empowered midwife to local health departments" (1993, 258). Furthermore, this perspective implicitly suggests that the erasure of key features undermined the entire system of midwifery. Take away the midwife's right to choose her successor, give that decision to the public health nurse, and in many ways, one could argue, the survival of the craft was severely threatened. Ironically, even as this narrative aligns itself strongly with the midwifery tradition, it is least able to envision the possibility that southern medicine could have found a path that allowed midwifery to continue as a birthing alternative. At best, I want to highlight the meaning systems and the contest over knowledge that circulated around the elemental issues of birth, life, and death.

From the safety of my office I can hear the future reader giving me back talk about the certitude of my hindsight. How else could midwifery regulation have been done? What did you expect given the political and social obstacles? Some segregated care was better than none. What other possible model was there given the precedents of white and immigrant midwifery's destruction in the North? The hardest thing for us to do is to think about other possibilities when the past seems to have its own powerful logic. This study is asking for a retreat from surety so that we might rethink the particular unfolding of events and consider the shadow consequences of those events as they did unfold.

2

Midwives and the Body Politic

The midwife delivered babies for African American and white women. She was expected to have some knowledge of the techniques of biomedicine and also to be able to call on God and use the herbal remedies and patent medicines at her disposal. She was a woman, often a mother and wife, but because of her special calling, she transgressed many of the rules and expectations of what a woman should be and do. Few women could leave husband and children at night, or for days on end, unchaperoned and without having to ask permission. She crossed other boundaries—racial, professional, and class-based ones—those that divided life and death, and those that supposedly marked the divide between tradition and modernity in the South.

A Matrix of Conflicts: Niger

Researchers Yannick Jaffre and Alain Prual have recently described the high tensions between hospital-trained midwives, some quite young, and their patients in an urban hospital in Niger. The puzzle was that both these groups of women held very similar views of the social and moral rules governing pregnancy (Jaffre and Prual 1994). Rules included injunctions against pushing during labor, the preference for squatting over the genital exposure of the lithotomy position, the requirement that bodily fluids be safely buried, and avoidance behaviors of young women to older ones (1994, 1,072). Yet the women giving birth consistently complained of the disrespectful treatment they received at the hands of these midwives in the hospital. What was going on?

The authors conclude that midwives found themselves caught between the constraints of their technical knowledge and skills that marked them as professionals and the proscriptions of traditional birthing beliefs and practices. Each set of rules denied the other. The situation created a "matrix of conflicts," which was not "conceptualized by the social actors" (1994, 1,072–73). Midwives responded to this level of discomfort by denying, in essence, the pregnant women's socialness. They ignored and shouted at them. They demanded that women clean up after themselves. Women suffered; midwives turned away. In their complaints, women rarely faulted the measure of technical service, focusing instead on the midwives' moral shortcomings. The intensity of the conflicts experienced in this setting renders one of the most convincing descriptions of the cognitive dissonance that can occur when overlapping systems come into relation in a context of discrepant power and within settings favorable to the dominant knowledge system.

Separated by time, place, and culture, African American midwives in the South, nonetheless, must have experienced a level of conflict similar to that documented for midwives in Niger in the 1990s. We can gain only an approximate sense of how pregnant women and midwives worked out the problem, but we can be sure that knowledge systems with rules that denied one another were well in place. The bureaucratization of childbirth sometimes placed midwives in situations in which a conflict of interest existed between themselves and the birthing woman. The politics of regulation included the paperwork associated with childbirth as it did specific biomedical routines for managing the pregnant body.

The Body Politic: Instrumentation and the Birth Certificate

Let me begin this section with a piece of paper that we take so much for granted—the birth certificate. A pamphlet published in 1948 under the auspices of the National Office of Vital Statistics offers a relatively late example of the government's role in secularizing traditional midwifery. It also provides an unobscured view of the part the midwife was expected to play in the bureaucratic control and regulation of the population. Until she could be effectively eliminated, the midwife, too, was expected to help in the intervention of professional authority into the homes of women. In this way she was to contribute to the nation's growth and progress. Few historians have noted the connections between the birth and death registration movement and the ascendancy of scientific medicine. While not denying that this and other steps toward more efficient governance may have helped individual African Americans to gain access to better health care, I nonetheless think it is crucial to examine the underlying assumptions that fueled the engines of progress.

Titled *A Birth Registration Handbook for Colored Midwives* and written by a registered nurse, the book set out in a series of simple, numbered imperative statements the rules of proper birth registration. Accompanying photographs of African American subjects—mothers, babies, midwives—and of white authority figures—registrars, nurses, social workers, and physicians—mirrored the racial and economic hierarchy (Clayton 1948). They also provided visual affirmation of the text. Thus in one photograph, a midwife, pen and paper in hand, is seated at the side of a well-appointed bed. A young mother lies next to her recently born child. "You are preparing the birth certificate soon after the baby is born," reads the text. Immediately below, the same midwife is shown in the office of the local registrar, a young white woman, whose typewriter is prominently displayed. Again the text describes the procedure: "You have brought the birth certificate to your local registrar. She is checking it for accuracy and completeness. Ask your registrar to look at the spelling on the certificate to see if it is right."

By 1933, most states had passed registration laws. Yet the simultaneously persuasive and threatening tone of the pamphlet suggests that implementation of this legislation had met with some resistance. Cassedy (1965) has suggested that initial resistance to birth and death registration was in great part a result of the populace's general "contempt of law, to some extent, . . . a heritage of America's long frontier era" (1966, 227). Among African Americans, mistrust of secular authority may have had less to do with the frontier and more to do with the day-to-day experiences of institutionalized oppression. Additionally, for midwives, God was the ultimate authority. By comparison, the dictates of vital statistics legislation must have seemed trivial.

In apparent acknowledgment of this point of view, before any instructions are given, the 1948 handbook's author established the religious justification for birth registration, taking as her text a biblical passage from the book of Numbers, Chapter 3, Verse 42: "And Moses Numbered as the Lord commanded all the first born among the children of Israel." This recourse to the Bible linked religious and moral issues to the mandates of the polity. At the same time, it capitalized on the midwife's own sense that she was primarily responsible to God rather than to any secular authority. Birth registration, therefore, according to the pamphlet, was not a divergence from tradition but a continuation of God's will, and a patriotic duty: "In the bible we find a record of a census in the time of the prophets. This book tells you why it is important today to have a record of the birth of all babies. You can help better the health and welfare of our people by following the instruction given here. It will be a service to your country" (Clayton 1948, n.p.).

By the late 1930s, production of the birth certificate had become, for public health officials, as important a crusade as their efforts to teach cleanliness to African Americans. Mongeau's (1973) study of the 1950–60 campaign against midwives in North Carolina suggests that nurses devoted the greater part of instructional time to teaching midwives how to properly fill out birth certificates. Part of the difficulty, from the officials' perspective, was that many older midwives had had little if any schooling. According to Mongeau, medical personnel began to define "literacy" as the ability to fill out birth registration forms. Those midwives who were unable to fill out these forms were usually counted as among the untrainable. Often they were prohibited from practicing or their licenses were revoked (Mongeau 1973). With the birth certificate, the state had the first standardized means of managing and regulating its citizens.

The 1948 handbook reminded midwives of the benefits that accrued to a properly registered individual: "When you are too old to work you may need an old-age pension to help you out. To get this pension you will have to prove that you are 65 years old. Sometimes this is very hard to do. If your birth certificate is on file in the state health department, it will be easy to do" (Clayton 1948).

Older citizens would not be the only beneficiaries; children, too, benefited. When she registered her cases, the "good" midwife allowed these infants to get the care they needed because "the county health doctor will know where to find all new babies." Implicit in the discussion of birth registration both in this handbook and in the discourse of public health officials was that the act of registering would in itself guarantee

African Americans rights that they could not otherwise receive. Thus the midwife was again reminded of the breadth of her responsibilities:

It is your duty to register the births of all babies delivered by you. It is not only your duty; there is a law which requires it. A birth certificate can be used to prove a person's right to: Enter School. Collect insurance. Inherit property. Marry. Get social security benefits for blind and dependent children. (Clayton 1948)

Many places of work require a person to show a person a certified copy of his birth certificate before they will give him a job. During the lst war [sic], defense plants could not hire a person until he had proved he was an American citizen. This was done to protect the security of our country. (Clayton 1948)

Discourse about birth registration mirrored that regarding scientific medicine. If a woman used a physician and a man had his proper birth papers, hardships would fall away. From this perspective, structural limitations and racism simply did not exist. To make the point, another photograph from the 1948 handbook shows a clean-shaven, somewhat downcast African American youth facing a bespectacled and suited white interviewer in an employment agency. The caption reads, "A certified copy of his birth certificate would help this young man get a job."

Because the birth certificate fitted the newborn child to enter properly into American society, its completion superseded other concerns that either the mother, midwife, or family may have had regarding the ritual entry of the child into personhood. For example, the guidelines regarding the naming of children must have conflicted in no uncertain terms with the naming rituals of most African Americans, particularly those in rural, southern communities. The handbook directed the midwife to encourage mothers to choose names for their unborn children. This would facilitate the efficient completion of the standardized forms at the time of birth. "If you do this, the birth certificate can be filled out soon after the baby is born," the author explains.

An accompanying photograph shows a midwife seated across from a woman who apparently has not yet had her baby: "You are in the home of your patient," the caption reads. "You are advising this mother to choose a girl's name and a boy's name before the baby is born. You are also telling

her not to change the baby's name after the birth certificate is made out."
Just as a woman could have a perfect child if she trusted the physicians
and public health nurses, by choosing a name before the birth of her
child she could help her baby to have a "perfect birth certificate."

The birth certificate seemed to offer so much. Based on the culture of
birthing remembered in Green River, it must also have interfered in other
culturally meaningful ways of introducing an infant into the world. First,
as the handbook prompted, a girl's and boy's name should be prechosen
in preparation for birth. But such action could potentially draw unwanted attention: naming the child before its birth implied a certain
assuredness about the outcome of what was essentially outside of human
agency. This then potentially exposed it to the malevolent intentions of
jealous persons or supernatural forces: control of birthing rested not
with man but with God.

Because the future was only clear to God, it would be foolhardy to try
to shape it according to one's own desires by assigning a name to an
unborn child. At the very worst, a normally benevolent God could visit
misfortune on a family, through the death of either the child or mother,
as a means of teaching humility. Given the high infant and maternal
mortality rates in southern African American communities, it is under-
standable that few wished to challenge God's dominion over man in this
manner.

Besides the protective measures taken on behalf of the unborn, the
custom of reserving a name until after the birth corresponded with the
belief that the child itself, by its appearance (who the child resembled,
birthmarks), its behavior at birth (whether crying or calm, its gestures),
as well as the circumstances surrounding the birth (historical events, the
death of a family member, supernatural signs), helped to determine the
name that was to be given. Names were intensely personal, specific enti-
ties. Often a child could be unnamed for a number of days, or even
weeks, if no suitable name showed itself. Because mother and child usually stayed in the birthing room for up to a month after birth, there was
time during this period for a suitable name to be chosen before the child's
emergence into the community. By following the seemingly innocuous
rules for birth registration, however, the midwife could be forced to forgo
the traditional rituals surrounding childbirth. This extended beyond the
actual naming of the child to basic assumptions about man's relationship

to God and nature. In this manner, the guidelines for registration tore at the foundation of what midwives believed to be "the Lord's work."

In other ways, registration laws created a great deal of dissonance for the traditional midwife while giving her a limited role as a functionary in the state's policing of bodies and of individual and family life. These clustered around what the 1948 handbook referred to as "important birth facts," including the mother's marital status and age and the occupation and residence of both parents. For many states, the race of the child and its parents also had to be reported. These facts, for which midwives were reminded in the handbook that they were legally bound to get the "right information," formed part of the public health initiatives of local and national governments. The birth certificate became symbolic of a powerful transformation in science and bureaucracy for which each person was expected to do his or her part, but there was also the implication that such pieces of paper would provide much in return.

Ordering the Life Processes: Monitoring Pregnancy

Regulation of midwifery in the first four decades of the century took place against the backdrop of a national "search for order," to borrow Robert Wiebe's still useful terminology, and a growing emphasis on the efficient functioning of government (Wiebe 1977). With industrialization, it became increasingly important for the state to monitor the life processes of its citizens and to install a regimen in which women expected to have their bodies monitored, in which the intimacies of family life were made accessible to planners and bureaucrats.

By 1928, Virginia's physicians, for example, were encouraged that mothers had "caught on to the merit of the new order of things"; mothers expected to be "questioned carefully and completely examined" (Lowenberg 1928, 263). Such questioning formed the centerpiece of the new prenatal care that, according to one physician, "is that part of maternal care which has as its object the complete supervision of the pregnant woman in order to preserve the happiness, health and life of the mother and child" (Bear 1928, 527). Thus once willing to submit to the gaze of medical men and to the sponsorship of the state, a woman would be rewarded with good health and happiness for herself and child.

Just as government could be made to function efficiently, so, too, could a woman's body, so that even "a half-way skilled" physician (read bureaucrat) would be able to deliver her of a healthy child (Hammer 1931, 376). What kinds of monitoring did physicians consider necessary for the successful delivery of an infant? Their language is, again, bureaucratic. The woman is acted upon on the basis of a set of preestablished procedural rules: "During the first six months of pregnancy, a patient should see her doctor at least once a month, during the next two months, at least once every fourteen days, and during the last month, once every week" (Ware 1931, 246). Dr. Lowenberg concurs: "Six weeks before confinement obstetrical examination of the abdomen is repeated and the duration of pregnancy confirmed; also the positions, presentations, degrees of engagement are determined. The foetal heart is counted, the size of the baby estimated. A vaginal examination should be done, the presentation and position confirmed, abnormalities sought for, and internal pelvimetry repeated" (Lowenberg 1928, 267).

During the visit to the physician, the patient was to be "interrogated" as to symptoms. In addition to having her urine tested, her blood pressure taken, and "the matter of diet, bowels, fluid intake, and general hygiene" emphasized; she was also to be "cautioned to watch for danger signals and urged to report if any of these appear" (Lowenberg 1928, 268).

Thus while fully taking control over the fractionalization of the pregnant body, the physician gave the woman some duties—she was to police the various parts of herself and report to the proper authorities in case of breakdown. Paradoxically, however, the real danger in such an approach, especially for African American women who had limited access to physicians and medical care until the 1960s, was that the woman would lose the capability to judge and interpret accurately the "signs" of her own body and to trust her own judgment. The affluent woman could always depend on the availability of her physician to help "interpret" her pregnant body.

For poor and African American women, however, no such ease of access was available. Potentially, the fragmentation of self inherent in the model used by physicians placed such women at greater, not lesser, risk. In Virginia, African American women were often blamed for the high rates of infant and maternal mortality in the state, precisely because, in physicians' opinion, they had failed to read the "danger signals of pregnancy."

Ordering the Life Processes: Instrumentation

Michel Foucault further illuminates the nature of the relationship be-tween science and government and between science and the body that took shape in the United States. In Foucault's view—one echoed by John O'Neill (1985, 67–90) in his discussion of the metaphor of the "body politic"—the distinction between the individual and the political body was gradually erased during the late eighteenth century (Foucault 1980, 138). Of particular relevance to the history of midwifery's decline in Virginia is the third development. Once the struggle against death no longer dominated the everyday life of the individual then, "in the space for a movement thus conquered, . . . methods of power and knowledge assumed responsibility for the life processes and undertook to control and modify them. Western man was gradually learning what it meant to be a living species in a living world, to have a body, conditions of exist-ence, probabilities of life, an individual and collective welfare, forces that could be modified, and a space that they could be distributed in an optimal manner" (Foucault 1980, 142).

The power of the bureaucratic state came to depend in large measure on its capacity to administer rather than take life. Foucault notes the emergence of population statistics as a legitimate domain of government, of an increasing focus "on the species body, the body imbued with the mechanics of life and serving as the basis of the biological processes: propagation, births and mortality, the level of health, life expectancy and longevity, with all the conditions that can cause these to vary" (Foucault 1980, 139).

In the United States, a similar emphasis on "calculated management" of the life processes becomes apparent. The closer attention by govern-ment to patterns of health and illness, to the social environment of the impoverished, to the birthrate among Anglo-Saxon versus non–Anglo-Saxon populations, for example, expressed a new formulation of the role that the state should play in regulating and intervening in what had been previously understood to be private and domestic. Concerns for the health care and living conditions of the nation's citizens began to emerge in governmental policy (Wiebe 1967; Taylor 1974; Starr 1982; Lemons 1973).

Reformers turned to the twin powers of government and science to mount an attack against the diseases that afflicted the poor and to ameliorate living and working conditions. But the vision of a new order articulated by reformers may have reflected rather than stimulated the interests of the polity to have greater control over the bodies and life processes of the workforce (Wilson 1977; Donzelot 1979).

I have obviously simplified the argument. It is sufficient, however, to note the possibilities within this historical context for an increased supervision of life processes that had previously been contained within the domestic sphere. Birth and mortality patterns, for example, become the focus of intense attention. By the 1930s, not only had many individual and public health issues come under the authority of the national government, but the lines separating the health of the individual and of the nation grew increasingly blurred. In garnering federal support for maternal health programs, for example, feminist social reformers pointed to the links between women's health and the health of the nation: "Each death at childbirth is a serious loss to the country. The women who die from this cause are lost at the time of their greatest usefulness to the State and to their families; and they give their lives in carrying out a function which must be regarded as the most important in the world" (Meigs 1917, 9).

In the same way that physicians called for increased prenatal monitoring of the pregnant female, so did the government take steps to enter what had hitherto been the private domains of birth and death, sickness and health, and so did social reformers open up the homes of the poor to unyielding scrutiny. The upper and middle classes were certainly not immune from this process. Affluent women were, in fact, at the vanguard of the movement to professionalize pregnancy and childbirth (Wertz and Wertz 1977; Ehrenreich and English 1978; Zelizer 1985). When Congress passed acts to educate poor women about pre- and postnatal care, "middle-class women translated its concern into a personal search for the best care they could find, which meant having a specialist and a hospital birth" (Wertz and Wertz 1977, 155).

For African American and poor white women, the ideals of a federally funded health care program were never realized. Nonetheless, they were expected to embrace the gift of science and to abandon the traditional midwife. At the same time, their material impoverishment—the essential factor in the high rates of infant and maternal mortality—was largely ignored.

The new emphasis on professionalizing childbirth—that is, on placing the future (children) of the industrializing nation into the hands of experts (Ehrenreich and English 1973, 187)—complemented the drive to measure the "existing conditions" of the population. Cassedy (1965) notes the "steady growth" of and federal governmental support for the passage of state laws that required not only that all deaths were to be reported but also that the age, color, sex, and residence of the deceased as well as the cause of death had to be duly recorded on a standardized form. Similarly, the birth registration movement may be seen as the first of many steps toward developing a bureaucratic system to count the population as well as to monitor the midwife's activities.

As a means of coordinating and implementing all activities related to measuring the growth and development of the nation, the Census Bureau was officially established in 1902 (Cassedy 1965). Although censuses were taken in the United States since the late eighteenth century, only sporadic and small-scale efforts had been made to isolate natality and mortality statistics (Cassedy 1965, 1969). Beginning in the late 1880s, however, the idea of creating birth and death registration areas with at least 90 percent reporting rates began to gain governmental support. By the early 1900s, states were encouraged to pass legislation requiring medical personnel to report all births and deaths to designated local registrars and to cooperate in national efforts to develop standardized birth and death registration statistics. It was within this context that Virginia enacted vital statistics law. While the legislature offered positive incentives to the local registrars, they meted out varying degrees of punishments to midwives (as well as physicians) who failed to register their cases. Penalties for midwives included revocation of permit, fines, or imprisonment.

The motivations behind crusades for the development of standardized birth and death statistics were complex. Cassedy notes that the "growing registration area became something of a measure of American civilization and, for American registrars and health officers, a symbol of emerging professionalism in their field" (Cassedy 1965, 222). Reminiscent of southern medical profession's concern that the presence of midwives were an index of the South's relative "backwardness," many of the nation's statisticians unfavorably compared the United States with countries in Europe.

For the racists and others who, before World War I, proclaimed the superiority of America's Anglo-Saxon culture, it was bitter indeed to be told that for statistical purposes, at least, the United States had to be classed "with the interior of Africa and other uncivilized regions of the globe from which no vital statistics [were] available" (Cassedy 1965, 225).

Chauvinism may have fueled the efforts of some proponents of registration laws, but others pointed to the usefulness of mortality and natality statistics in developing successful preventive health care programs on a national scale. They argued that these statistics would aid in public health campaigns against tuberculosis, syphilis, and other communicable diseases. Contemporary scientists employed the statistics collected under the registration area legislation to study the etiology of contagious diseases and to isolate the factors that contributed to infant and maternal mortality. In the *Virginia Medical Monthly,* articles, starting in the early 1920s, reported on the state's gross birthrate and on the percentages of maternal and infant deaths. Physicians were not able to use federal registration statistics to compare Virginia with other states.

By the mid-1920s, there seemed to have been a heightened concern with the relative "progress" of obstetrics and on identifying ways in which the discipline could be improved. Once such statistics were consistently used, public health personnel and physicians appeared more willing to examine critically their own methods. Beginning in the 1940s, the Virginia Medical Society instituted a new policy of monthly peer group reviews of maternal mortality cases that occurred in the hospital. Thus the federal emphasis on the collection of birth and registration statistics to some extent benefited women of childbearing age. But registration laws (part of the movement to dissect and rebuild the society through the science of numbers) also narrowed the birthing options of African American and poor white women.

In chiding social historians who view the rise of medical science as simply the triumph of a powerful means of social control, Starr correctly points out that the methods and "values" of medical science "prevented disease and preserved health." It is important to remember, he cautions, that in addition to imposing her bourgeois values, the early-twentieth-century public health nurse "may have taught mothers how to prevent their babies from dying." Public health programs contributed to "the power of individuals to realize their own objectives" (Starr 1982, 192) by providing effective health care and reducing the incidence of debilitating illnesses. Nonetheless, Starr wrongly assumes that developments in medical science took place within a socially neutral context. For the African American, advances in medicine led to very few freedoms and certainly did not allow for the realization of individual potential. The ideology of racism precluded such possibilities.

I agree to some extent with Starr's call for more balanced analyses of the rise in the authority of medical science. But I am also acutely aware that the blind belief in science and efficiency that emerged in the late nineteenth century had a sinister side. In Virginia, for example, birth registration campaigns would become the focal point of efforts to control and eliminate midwives and, in the end, to leave poor and African American women with greatly reduced access to reliable and familiar assistance during childbirth. The new faith in science meant that alternative philosophies were suspect. This itself was a powerful form of social control even if we refer only to Starr's definition of the term as "actions of mechanisms that tend to suppress deviations from the dominant rules in society" (1982, 192) and prevent the attainment of individual objectives.

Unquestioning belief in the utility of science led to another set of circumstances—the practice of science for science's sake and efficiency for the sake of being efficient. Many of the actions taken against Virginia's midwives, for example, were not based on any "objective" assessment of their ability to safely attend childbirth but rather on their divergence from supposedly scientific methods. The campaign against midwives in Virginia may be seen as part of wider societal changes of which Wiebe has written: "bureaucratic thought, . . . made 'science' practically synonymous with 'scientific method.' Science had become a procedure, or an orientation, rather than a body of results" (Wiebe 1967, 147).

Physicians writing in the *Virginia Medical Monthly* used their colleagues' relative willingness to comply with registration laws as an index of their efficiency and modernity (McCleod 1927, 524). By definition, then, midwives, many of them illiterate, were inherently inefficient and had to be trained in the methods of proper registration. Midwives' inability, or refusal, to register the births they attended became for public health officials a primary indication of these women's inability to do the work of obstetrics.

One is inevitably drawn to the affinities between such a point of view and the theories of scientific management developed by Frederick Taylor in the late 1890s and early twentieth century: "Taylor's system started with a close study of every step in manufacturing. By applying the resulting data, by breaking the process of manufacturing into separate parts, and by specializing the function of the worker and machine involved in each part, he could substantially increase the rate of production. For Taylor efficiency was a fetish" (Blum, Stampp, et al. 1985, 633).

The Body Polity: Instrumentation and the Birth Certificate

What medical practitioners and the polity demanded of midwives was the ability to treat their craft as a process with clearly defined functions, to which particular procedural methods could be routinely applied. Yet this was antithetical to the way in which midwives had traditionally attended births. Thus the campaign against midwifery in late nineteenth and early-twentieth-century America, although most frequently described as an instance of professional rivalry (Kobrin 1966; Wertz and Wertz 1977), is better understood as an instance of a severely imbalanced competition between opposed philosophies of method.

In the scientific discourse about birth and death registration, the very act of collecting and publishing statistical data was imbued with a certain curative efficacy. Officials of the Children's Bureau, established as an advocate for the welfare of the nation's children, exemplified such a point of view. They "quickly set about to promote birth registration as a means of attacking infant mortality" (Wertz and Wertz 1977, 203). Wiebe notes a similar emphasis on the collection of statistics and scientific management among early-twentieth-century social workers in the immigrant settlements of the urban North: "The original settlement workers had entered the slums and served the poor as moral acts. By the [First World] [W]ar many settlements had grown into centers of efficient procedure and expert management. Casework in the nineties had meant a personal concern for an individual's spiritual and material elevation; two decades later it meant the scientific analysis of a life in process" (Wiebe 1967, 149).

In a parallel vein, African American midwives had perceived their craft as a gift from God. They were "called" to practice just as ministers were "called" to preach the word of God. But by the 1920s, public health officials took on the task of secularizing traditional midwifery. Much of their work focused on teaching midwives to obey a list of carefully laid out commandments (including rules on the proper way to fill out birth registration forms). In what turned out to be futile attempts to survive, many midwives responded by appropriating the outward symbols, if not the philosophy, of scientific childbirth: white uniforms, physician-type satchels, rubber gloves. By their overwhelming emphasis on the power of science and the importance of efficient management of childbirth, public health officials would eventually foster among midwives what Wiebe describes (in his discussion of the revolution in bureaucratic thought during the Progressive era) as a shift in focus from "essences to actions" (1967, 148).

In the next chapter I turn our discussion to the work of William A. Plecker, a "great man" who was at various times a general practitioner, a local and state registrar, a midwifery bureau supervisor, a race theorist, and a passionate advocate of rationalizing the fields of maternal/infant health and epidemiology in Virginia.

3

Race and Regulation

In Virginia, two major approaches to the midwife "problem" emerged. Public health personnel supported what might be termed the education and supervisory approach. They argued that in rural "districts which cannot support a physician of any type," midwives could not be immediately eliminated (Plecker 1925, 809). Because few physicians wanted to practice in rural areas among a population unwilling and unable to pay for medical services, then, according to proponents of this point of view, midwives were a "necessary evil."

Some physicians took an opposing position. They expressed ambivalence, if not outright hostility, toward federally supported initiatives to educate midwives. At the annual meetings of the Southern Medical Association in 1924, the argument against training midwives as paraprofessional birth attendants was clearly articulated. Commenting on the official training and licensure of midwives in Germany and England, one physician admitted that for the most part "the well trained midwife under strict government control had no doubt greatly reduced the maternal and infant mortality in many of the European countries"; however, he doubted that such a system could be effective or welcome in the United States, as it gave "the midwife a professional status and establish[ed] two standards of service, when there should be but one. This being true it would seem to be poor judgment to attempt to make competent obstetricians out of the great army of ignorant women now practicing midwifery in this country" (Hardin 1925, 347). For many physicians, therefore, the midwife problem would be solved only with the rapid abolition of these practitioners and the ascendancy of obstetrical science. Yet despite these apparently opposed approaches to the problem, both public health personnel and private physicians in the South eventually envisioned that midwifery would be eliminated. Their disagreement revolved around the timing of the process—whether midwives were to be immediately outlawed or their numbers gradually reduced.

Some scholars, writing about a similar dynamic in earlier midwifery debates in northern states during the nineteenth century, have characterized these differences as essentially contradictory (Litoff 1986; Donegan 1978; Kobrin 1966). The evidence from Virginia suggests otherwise. These seemingly opposed strategies were part of the same process. As Armstrong writes of medicine in postwar Britain, "perhaps, when the history of the medical profession comes to be written . . . the apparent diversity of analytical perspectives—from liberal to repressive—will be seen to be simply different components of an overall system of disciplinary power" (Armstrong 1983, 54).

Elizabeth City: A Case Study

In Virginia, neither side believed that the midwife could ever be a positive good. Given the limited availability of physicians and hospitals to most African American and rural poor white women, however, it was impossible to completely eliminate the midwife over the short run. Virginia took a series of actions to define the boundaries of midwifery practice and, just as important, to institutionalize a system for regulating and training midwives. From 1900 to 1912, a pilot midwifery supervision and vital statistics program was established in Elizabeth City County. Drawing on this experience, the state legislature in 1912 enacted a model vital statistics law followed closely by legislation in 1918 that placed midwives under the jurisdiction of the Bureau of Vital Statistics and required that they be licensed and registered. Not coincidentally, the increasing attention to the midwife problem, from 1900 to 1950, paralleled the state's developing interest in monitoring the life processes of its citizens through vital statistics legislation, health and social welfare initiatives, and stringent attention to the issue of "race suicide;" that is, to the perceived threat of white racial extinction.

In his early campaign in Elizabeth City, W. A. Plecker, a physician and county registrar of vital statistics, wanted to create an efficient and scientific bureaucracy for managing reproduction. This concern was reflected in his complaint that midwives' "efficiency seldom increase[d] with experience"(Plecker 1925, 809). Thus in a fallacy that guided his (and later public health personnel's) training of midwives, it was argued that the empirical means by which these women gained knowledge about childbirth was flawed. From this point of view, midwives either stubbornly perpetuated outmoded customs or simply obeyed instructions. They were unable to innovate, or to use their accumulated experiences, when faced with new or unusual birthing situations.

Midwives' supposed inability to improve—to learn from their mistakes and to develop methods to handle complicated births—provided the dark antithesis to science. Plecker wrote that midwives, regardless of their experience, inevitably panicked in emergencies: "helpless, blundering along and delaying, until, frequently too late, the family would send for a physician." They "knew nothing of rendering assistance and of speeding up the delivery of the after-coming head" (Plecker 1925, 809). The secondary literature as well as my fieldwork suggest that midwives not only expected complications during the many births they attended but also often successfully employed a combination of strategies—ritual, manual, and otherwise—to deal with such emergencies (Holmes 1987; Logan 1989; Robinson 1984; Susie 1988).

It is at once remarkable and expected that such a discrepancy should have existed between midwives' abilities and medical personnel's denial of these women's expertise. In order to fully justify the involvement of medical science in childbirth, it had to be argued that midwives were completely unable to handle complicated births by recourse to their experiential knowledge. Thus they had to be fully supervised or taught by medical practitioners, masters of an always expanding body of scientific knowledge.

Given the insistence on their intellectual inferiority, it is with considerable exasperation that Plecker complained about midwives' confidence in their own powers. These women's "arrogance and self complacency," he wrote, "knows no bounds" (Plecker 1925, 809). As early as 1900, therefore, the agenda was clear. The objective was to curb the "self-complacent" midwife while making her more efficient and "less dangerous." In this manner, Plecker justified to his reluctant colleagues the benefit of teaching midwives a fixed number of simple rules about childbirth. At the same time, she would be closely supervised to ensure strict compliance.

Plecker devised such a supervisory program in Elizabeth City County. He hoped that standardized birth and death registration records would allow him to compare the "work of physicians and midwives" and to "study [the] health conditions" of the populace by race. Clearly, Plecker was aware of the possibilities for combining supervision of midwives with a study of epidemiology. In this respect, the Elizabeth City trial program took the basic form of those that had been instituted earlier in northern states such as New York and Massachusetts (Litoff 1986; Wertz and Wertz 1977). Discipline of the midwife came in the wake of a growing interest in monitoring the population. Ironically, with the institutionalization of methods to measure and regulate the life processes, physicians, too, found themselves open to greater scrutiny. But they were both collectors and interpreters of the amassed information. Midwives had no such access or control.

With the support of local county government, Plecker created a standard birth registration form that required the attending midwife or physician to list the child's sex, date of birth, and name and the parents' names, ages, occupation(s), skin color, and marital status. The form also called for information on the "presentation of the child." (Later state forms would drop this question, asking instead if the infant was born full term.) These standardized birth certificate forms were distributed to physicians and all known midwives practicing in the county.

Plecker's methods suggest his interest in making the collection of the county's vital statistics more efficient while keeping track of midwives and providing a means for comparing their work with that of doctors. Some twenty-five years after his initial experience in Elizabeth City County, he recalled that "in order to make a correct study of the comparative birth and death rates of the two races in the county, extraordinary efforts were made to secure complete registration of births as well as deaths" (Plecker 1925, 810). Writing to an audience still interested in how best to develop midwifery regulation and vital statistics collection, Plecker offered precise instructions:

A complete list of the midwives was secured fifty in all. The number is now *less than half of that* [my italics]. They were listed on a sheet ruled with columns for their names and residences, and thirteen other narrow columns, one for each month, and one for the total. On this sheet at the end of each month, was checked off the number of births reported by each midwife, as well as by each doctor. A glance at this sheet showed the number reported by each of them for any given time. (Plecker 1925, 810)

On the surface, the Elizabeth City program's intent was to monitor the activities of both midwives and physicians. In his article, Plecker neglects to give the full results of his "comparative work" in the county. The drastic decline in the number of practicing midwives, however, seems to have been directly related to the strategies used to supervise them: discouraged by the surveillance, the need for literacy, and the emerging bureaucracy of birthing, many women stopped practicing.

Plecker's description of his sheets of paper with their carefully drawn lines and columns reflected his interest in applying a scientific method to all dimensions of the life processes. His policy of strict enforcement of local health department rules preceded and did much to influence the enactment of statewide vital statistics in 1912. Indeed, the emerging power of bureaucratic management is aptly encapsulated in the image of Plecker's list, with the names, production levels, and success rates of doctors and midwives neatly entered in the appropriate spaces. Midwives in Elizabeth City were open to scrutiny when, according to Plecker's tallies, they appeared to be ignoring health department rules on birth registration. Besides the monthly list of midwives, he informed his colleagues that, "a pocket memorandum was kept of any who were not reporting, and as I passed their homes in my regular rounds, I would call to inquire why no births had been recently reported. Almost invariably I was assured that none had occurred" (Plecker 1925, 810).

Given Plecker's confidence in his system, he took at face value these women's assurance that they had not delivered children within the reporting period. Yet percolating up from his account is a subtext. One wonders whether midwives who neglected or refused to report their birthing activities would have admitted having done so when asked by the health officer. Plecker's system may not have been as efficient as he claimed, for these women would have simply not complied with his rules. Yet it is difficult to assess the nature of midwives' response to this intervention.

The fifty women on Plecker's midwife list probably exercised a range of options in making decisions about whether to report a birth or withhold that information. At the time of the initial program, there appeared to be no penalties for failure to report births. Indeed, a semi-official connection to the health department could have enhanced rather than diminished these women's already considerable authority in the African American community. From 1900 to 1912, therefore, the Elizabeth City County pilot program had not yet taken on the coercive dimension that later midwifery education projects would. It is likely that most midwives did not yet regard this program as a threat to their activities as birth attendants.

Only in 1918 were health departments and registrars of vital statistics given the authority to determine midwives' fitness to practice and to license women who attended births "for pay" (Bennett 1925, 523). With the use of legislative sanctions to encourage midwives' compliance, the nature of the relationship between these women and medical personnel changed. Commenting on the effects of midwife regulatory efforts in his state, for example, a North Carolina physician informed his colleagues at a meeting of the Southern Medical Association that midwives had developed a "wholesome fear of the law and of the 'State Doctor'" (Hardin 1925, 348). By 1918, to ignore the regulatory and supervisory efforts of public health officials was to break the law.

Although my analysis focuses on the negative aspects of the increased monitoring of midwives and the birthing process, it is not meant to diminish the ingenuity of the program in Elizabeth City County. Not only did Plecker initiate a means of linking vital statistics collection, standardized forms, and close supervision of midwives, but he also saw these techniques as applicable to improving health care, developing an epidemiological profile of the county, and evaluating physicians' competence over time. Regarding physicians' performance, for example, Plecker noted that with his system it was "an easy matter to check off the work of any physician for a series of years when he is suspected of irregularity. This record is also frequently made use of in deciding a physician's fitness for holding positions of trust" (Plecker 1925, 810). The beauty of Plecker's plan was that it allowed for the insertion of the scientific and bureaucratic gaze at different points in the system.

The development of a well-articulated relationship between the medical profession and the legislature in the late nineteenth and early twentieth centuries has been described by Smith-Rosenberg (1985), Petchesky (1984), Haller (1963), and Starr (1982), among others. Smith-Rosenberg writes, for example, that as a means of increasing the status of the medical profession, physicians increasingly "turned to politics, bolstering their self-esteem through frequent contacts with state and national political figures." For gynecologists in particular, "it became of critical importance . . . to establish the right . . . to set public opinion, sway votes in state legislatures, determine legislative policies" (Smith-Rosenberg 1985, 234).

The evolution of the Elizabeth City regulation of midwives is a revealing case study of this process. Plecker considered himself the model of the physician as statesman. In discussing his efforts to institute a program of birth registration and midwifery control, he noted with pride that "the vital statistics and midwife supervision in . . . [Elizabeth City County] were organized upon plans which were found successful, and well adapted for the whole state later" (Plecker 1925, 809). Indeed, he believed that his close monitoring of the Elizabeth City midwives and of the life processes of the population in that county, although imitated statewide and by his colleagues in other southern states, had never been surpassed. "I am satisfied," he assured them, "that now, under a far more efficient law, birth registration in no county in the state approaches . . . [Elizabeth City's] at that time [1900–12] as to completeness (Plecker 1925, 809).

Backing away somewhat form the focus on one person, it is valuable to realize that even though Dr. Plecker formulated and wrote about his early birth registration and midwifery regulation program as his "one-man crusade," he wielded considerable institutional power. He was a white male physician, a member of an increasingly authoritative profession, and a person who implicitly relied on the legislature and the state hierarchy to support and implement his attempt to supervise the life processes of Elizabeth City's populace.

To return to the use of the birth certificate, the Elizabeth City health department, under Plecker's guidance, recognized the power of birth and death registration. With the birth certificate, in particular, it would be possible to insert an instrument of measurement and management into previously uncharted and unmanageable territory. The standard birth registration form, with its links to the county bureaucracy, marked a significant departure from the ways in which rural families had previously recorded the births of children. Not only was the child's birth or death brought into the public sphere, but intimacies about the parents' marital and occupational status, about the timing and numbers of births, and about the parents' racial identity became part of official county records. Once made official, this information could not be easily manipulated or reshaped according to the needs or preferences of those most closely involved in the birth. For example, with birth certificates, public health clinics could easily keep account of those poor women who were having children out of wedlock.

Mongeau (1973) reports that as late as the 1960s in North Carolina, public health nurses refused to treat African American women who were pregnant with a second "illegitimate" child, which often forced these women to marry in order to participate in prenatal care programs (Mongeau, 1973, 180). Similarly in Virginia, with the advent of birth certificates, which required information on marital status, the stigma attached to illegitimacy by medical personnel could be easily institutionalized. Indeed, much of the power of mandatory birth registration rested in the opportunity it offered the state to become a primary participant in reproduction and in defining the realm of what constituted normal family life and structure.

The development of the Elizabeth City program reflected an early consolidation of legislative, medical, and bureaucratic power. Based on this experience and the nationwide movement to develop model vital statistics programs (Cassedy 1965), Virginia's state legislature in 1912 created the Bureau of Vital Statistics under the auspices of the State Board of Health. Plecker, who had argued for the linkages between health care policy and vital statistics, was appointed state registrar by the Board of Health—an appointment that officially acknowledged the emerging importance of the state's ability to administrate the life processes and of the medical profession's role in that enterprise. Vital statistics registration now required that birth attendants file standardized birth certificates within ten days of the birth of the child. In the case of stillbirths, both a birth and death certificate were to be filed: "It shall be the duty of the attending physician or midwife to file a certificate of birth, properly and completely filled out, giving all the particulars of birth . . . including a statement of year, month, day and hour of birth, and whether the child was alive or dead, with the local registrar of the district in which the birth occurs, within ten days" (Virginia State Board of Health 1924, 514).

Any birth attendant who failed to file these standardized forms could be charged with having committed a misdemeanor and fined up to ten dollars. Local registrars were encouraged to be vigilant. They received twenty-five cents for "each registration certificate properly made and returned to the State Registrar" (Virginia State Board of Health 1924, 511). Because these registrars were either the "principal executive officer of the local board of health," the justice of the peace, or an individual appointed by the state registrar, midwives were immediately drawn into the bureaucratic order once they registered the infants they delivered. Perhaps more than the fines levied against midwives and physicians who did not register births, the registrars' intrinsic ties to the legislative and policing controls signaled a new dimension in the politics of reproduction. Birth was no longer either strictly a family or even a medical event.

Some physicians resisted this intrusion of the legislature into what they argued was the private relationship between the doctor and his patient. Articles in the *Virginia Medical Monthly* often rebuked these individuals, especially those identified as country doctors—a breed of practitioner viewed with a mixture of tolerance and disdain by younger, more progressive physicians. Despite the resistance from within the ranks, however, for most health personnel there was a certain inevitability to the process. The issue was not simply one of improved health care but of an increased efficiency and professionalization of the society.

The birth certificate was one marker of this new efficiency. It also helped to bring the state's midwives under some degree of bureaucratic control (previously there had been no such supervision except for Elizabeth City). Still, with its focus on the midwife's role as birth registrar, the birth certificate offered no means of monitoring her activities as birth attendant. Consequently, in 1918, the legislature, following close on the passage of the vital statistics law, expanded the responsibilities of the Bureau of Vital Statistics to include midwifery "control." Plecker remarked on the historical aptness of this legislation in recalling that "as no branch of the State Board of Health was exercising any supervision over the midwives, and as the Bureau of Vital statistics, had them already listed, the legislature . . . placed them under the supervision of the state registrar" (Plecker 1925, 810).

While the African American midwife had emphasized her practice as a spiritual calling, the new rules set up under the bureau focused on the secular and ultimately medical nature of a midwife's duties. According to the law, any woman who attended births for pay was to file her name and address with the registrar in her district of residence. In turn she received a "permit to practice" bearing her signature and those of the state and local registrars (Virginia State Board of Health 1924). With the appearance of the permit, midwives lost a good measure of their autonomy and received in turn official recognition of their presence in the state. The exchange was not an equitable one, as it allowed for sanctions to be brought against those women who committed infractions against the new laws but did not provide an official mechanism by which midwives could participate in determining the rules governing licensure.

Public health officials, physicians, or local registrars had the authority to request the denial or revocation of a midwife's permit if in their view she was "unfit" to practice. The 1918 statute declared that permits could "be revoked by the State Registrar upon evidence that the midwife has failed to comply with the law in the reporting of births, or to obey the sanitary rules of the State Board of Health governing midwives." In addition, "any person who practic[ed] the profession of midwife for pay without a permit [was] subject to a fine of from one to ten dollars" (Virginia State Board of Health 1924).

Printed on the reverse side of each permit issued by the state registrar's office were eleven "elementary safety rules" that the midwife was legally bound to follow. On receiving her permit, she was required to sign a pledge card acknowledging her responsibility to uphold the law governing birth registration and to follow the procedures set down by the health department: what had been an informal social contract between midwife and patient was now superseded by the formal one between midwife and state.

The "elementary safety rules" had been developed in response to medical personnel's concern with the "risks" that midwives presented to their patients. Indeed, to the extent that they helped to reduce the infant and maternal mortality rates, there was nothing implicitly sinister about these standards of practice. According to Plecker, in announcing what he described as the "first move toward midwife control,"

> the chief aim of the "Rules" [was] to make the midwife less a source of danger to the mother and child. She is forbidden to make vaginal examinations or administer drugs, and is required to practice cleanliness, so far as it is possible to accomplish such a thing with the type of women who generally pose as midwives. She is enjoined to call upon a physician for help, if there are any complications, or if the delivery is not accomplished after twenty-four hours of labor. (Plecker 1918, 13)

These and other public health rules were seen as essentially preventive. Although they responded to the infant and maternal mortality crisis, they did not address the unequal access to health care that African American women and their children were experiencing. Rather, under these rules the midwife was to provide primary care for those patients who could not afford to pay a physician, but at the same time she had to be brought under bureaucratic and professional control. Depite its focus on prevention, the Virginia legislature and its medical supporters did not consider the underlying economic and social causes of infant and maternal mortality. Attention was fixed on the birth event itself, and as a consequence the midwife was viewed as the main cause of the mortality crisis. The hope was that control of midwives would precede their eventual elimination.

It is important to note that during this period (approximately 1900 to 1920), legislation as an instrument in the fight against disease and high mortality rates in Virginia shared more in common with criminal law than it did with later legislation such as the Sheppard-Towner Act (1922), which focused to a greater extent on broad social programs. Given this early orientation, it became essential to identify a culprit, to pin blame on easily observable individuals or groups of individuals. In Green River County, to take a situation that I discuss more fully later, I often found that residents' memories of midwives were characterized by an undercurrent of secrecy, and in some instances by a sense that these women engaged in "illegal" behavior. And indeed they did. Only after having examined the historical background and legislative dimensions of the story did I begin to understand fully that medical personnel classified much of midwives' routine activities and certainly their interventions in emergencies as outside the law and subject to a range of sanctions.

While the punitive approach must have greatly affected midwives' sense of autonomy, from the perspective of those in power, it provided an efficient, visible means of attacking health care problems. The safety rules printed on the back of the midwife's permit or the lists of midwives maintained by the Bureau of Vital Statistics fell into the category of "real things," whereas references to social problems, poverty, or the lack of prenatal care as causes of ill health belonged to a more abstract world of ideas. These were the ideas, in fact, that many Virginia health care providers and legislators perceived as coming from an imperious federal government and its cadre of female physicians and social workers in the

Children's Bureau. From the perspective of enforcement, therefore, a set of rules—rules that when broken incurred specific penalties—must have seemed to local officials as an eminently more sensible way of dealing with infant and maternal mortality and the midwife problem.

What was eventually tragic about midwifery supervision programs (and the laws that created them) was that the lines of authority and power were unidirectional: midwives and pregnant women received information and were expected to alter their behavior, but given the acceptance of their assumed inferiority, neither medical personnel nor the legislature expected that these women possessed any useful knowledge that could be passed up the system.

The point holds for most officially recognized interaction between African Americans and white public health authorities. As I have shown, with his experience in Elizabeth City County and as state registrar, W. A. Plecker had enthusiastically applied his medical and bureaucratic expertise to creating a hierarchically structured midwife control and vital statistics program that would provide some measure of preventive health care, insert a system for measuring the life processes, and ensure that the medical profession maintained its privileged position.

Following the rules, however, did not guarantee that midwives would be accorded a measure of professional recognition. Plecker, for example, reported that as a result of "strict enforcement" of the rule forbidding midwives to enter the birth canal, deaths among the "colored" population as a result of childbed fever (puerperal infections) had declined from seventy-six in 1922 to fifty-five in 1924. By contrast, he explained, white physicians continued to make repeated vaginal examinations of their patients and thus the mortality rates owing to infections among white patients had shown no improvement during the same period.

The implications of the findings for these two years are astounding. At the least they overturned medical personnel's argument that African American midwives were untrainable disease bearers. These findings also provided a potential avenue for opening the debate so that the issue would not have been merely confined to discussions of the "midwife problem" and of dirty women but focused on the need for more careful antiseptic procedures on the part of all birth attendants.

From a public health perspective, this approach would have proved the more effective. Yet ironically, despite his glorification of science and efficiency, Plecker was incapacitated by his professional and racial biases.

In what now appears as disregard of his own findings, he ignored the scientific conclusions and immediately turned instead to a cant against the midwife: "Those not familiar with the habits of these untrained and dirty midwives may not appreciate the importance of this requirement [forbidding vaginal examinations] and of the difficulty if not impossibility, of teaching them the practice of aseptic methods" (Plecker 1925, 811). Even when his results showed that midwives followed the "safety rules" mandated by law, Plecker found reason to damn them.

Plecker's inability to "see" that physicians had higher incidences of maternal deaths reflected an attitude common among American physicians since the mid-nineteenth century. For years they resisted—indeed, ridiculed—the findings of Ignaz Semmelweiss, a Vienna physician, that doctors who did not practice asepsis were responsible for the spread of puerperal fever among their patients (Wertz and Wertz 1977, 210–11).

Although he ignored the culpability of his colleagues, Plecker nonetheless implied in a sort of backhanded praise that although African American women had inferior creative intellects, they nonetheless were willing to obey carefully set out instructions. By way of comparison, he noted that the smaller number of white midwives, "of a distinctly Nordic type," and "proud of their present supposed attainments" were more resistant and less inclined to "carry out our rules" (Plecker 1925, 811). Here again the racial dichotomization comes to the fore. For Virginia's medical personnel, the white, "mountain" midwives disobeyed because of their proud ancestry and independence, whereas black women obeyed because of their intellectual inferiority. They were in fact accustomed to obeying. When they didn't follow instructions, it was either because of their inability to understand or their proclivity for filth, not as a result of any heritage of resistance. Thus the self-complacency, of which Plecker and his colleagues complained, took different forms in the conduct of the few white midwives and the many African American ones.

Midwifery and Surveillance:
Racial Integrity as Public Health Crisis

Elizabeth City had set a firm example of the need for surveillance and regulation. Another social policy issue further made the point when it tied birth registration to racial accounting. I may be accused of expecting early-twentieth-century physicians to have the sensibilities and worldview of their more enlightened counterparts today. Far from it. I simply want to point to the ways in which medical discourse about scientific rationality did not replace deeply embedded racist beliefs but was simply layered over them. Still, the concept of racism, one could argue, is itself a modern construction. Medical personnel in Virginia rarely made distinctions between their ideas about, for example, the germs that could cause puerperal infections and the commonly held notion that African Americans were biologically and culturally subordinate to whites. In their view, these were all legitimate scientific concerns. Within this context, campaigns to supervise midwives inevitably mixed arguments about the need to reduce maternal and infant mortality and to improve health care with those confirming the importance of maintaining the racial and social order. Indeed, for Plecker, public health personnel, and the Virginia legislature, these were convergent rather than opposed objectives.

Use of the midwife as a functionary of the state took on added dimensions in 1924, when the legislature passed a set of laws for the "preservation of racial integrity." Now twelve years after the first vital statistics legislation, Virginians must have grown increasingly accustomed to state regulation of formerly intimate life events. The role of the state in bringing private acts into public view has been discussed by Rosalind Petchesky in her study of the history of abortion. Laws to prohibit abortion, she writes, "did not suppress" as much as they "revealed," "regulated," and "certified it as a legitimate domain of public intervention and control" (1984, 73). Similarly, Virginia's racial integrity laws, which appeared at the height of a national eugenics movement, brought out into the open the issue of miscegenation. To medical and legislative personnel, the need to maintain white racial "purity" and prevent "race suicide" was as pressing a public health problem as birth registration or midwifery control—and as potentially damaging to the population as infant blindness or high infant and maternal mortality rates.

With perhaps even more passion than in his discussion of vital statistics and midwifery control, Plecker informed his colleagues outside of Virginia of his work on this "problem":

> In closing . . . I beg to be allowed the privilege of calling attention to a still greater and far more difficult work [than midwifery control] imposed upon the Bureau of Vital Statistics—that of enforcing the racial integrity laws . . . We have published a booklet on eugenics and racial

integrity which will be mailed upon request. We are contemplating enlarging the scope of the work by an educational propaganda amongst college, normal, and high schools, aimed at staying the progress of race suicide amongst our best native American stock. (Plecker 1925, 811)

Significantly, the racial policy behind this law did not focus on discouraging African Americans or other racial minorities from having large families, as was the case in other eugenics movements (Petchesky 1984; Haller 1963; Kevles 1985), but rather directed attention to the importance of maintaining strict racial boundaries so that the white genetic pool would not be tainted. This variation on the eugenics theme was rooted in the historical configuration of race and slavery in Virginia. With the support of its medical experts, the state's interest in the end was on providing instruments to monitor and control miscegenation.

We need to look more closely at the racial integrity statute. A "white person" was defined as having "no trace whatsoever of any blood other than caucasian," although individuals who had "one-sixteenth or less of the blood of the American Indian and [had] no other non-caucasic blood" (Michie 1924, 1,259) were also classified as white. Three interrelated strategies were developed to maintain the integrity of this racial group. For those individuals born before the mandatory birth registration laws, the Bureau of Vital Statistics made available standardized forms for voluntary registration of one's racial "composition." On these "registration certificates," the local registrar, indicated whether the person was "Caucasian, Negro, Mongolian, American Indian, Asiatic Indian, Malay, or any other mixture thereof" (Michie 1924).

Well aware of the range of possible permutations, the legislature also required that for those individuals of mixed parentage, "the racial composition of the parents and other ancestors . . . so as to show in what generation such mixture occurred" was also to be certified. The law assumed a scientific basis for judging "admixture" of blood and further expected local registrars to be capable of making these assessments (Michie 1924).

While the racial registration part of the law had been ostensibly voluntary, that section relating to marriage allowed no such leeway. Unions between whites and any other racial groups were strictly forbidden. Of course, while explicitly invoking the threat of racial dilution caused by "Mongolians," "Malays," and other racial groups, uppermost in the con-

sciousness of Virginia's white elite was the specter of the black population. At all costs, its members were to be classified as a separate category
of persons. Indeed, the law did not prohibit the intermarriage of any
other racial group. Safeguards were established to ensure that individuals
did not succeed in subverting the process. County clerks were enjoined
to certify the "color of both man and woman" before issuing marriage
licenses: "If there is reasonable cause to disbelieve that applicants are of
pure white race, when that fact is stated, the clerk or deputy clerk shall
withhold the granting of the license until satisfactory proof is produced
that both applicants are "white persons" as provided for in this act. The
clerk or deputy clerk shall use the same care to assure himself that both
applicants are colored, when that fact is claimed" (Michie 1924, 1, 259).

Thus in the war against "race suicide," no crossovers would be permitted, either for "those of colored mixture . . . striving to pass over into the
white race" (Plecker 1925, 811) or for whites wishing to reclassify themselves as "Negro." The "willful falsification" of racial information was a
felony. Correspondingly heavy punishments followed such a conviction.
Individuals so charged were imprisoned for a year in the state penitentiary. Even if punishment was rarely implemented, the threat of sanctions
was no doubt extremely effective in preventing even surreptitious inter-
racial marriages.

The third section of the racial integrity law used the birth certificate as
an instrument to shield against white "race suicide." In the privacy of the
birthing room, the possibilities for slippage across the color line must
have seemed to multiply. Thus midwives were enjoined to report the race
of each child they delivered. Misrepresentation of the race of a newborn
was a felony that was also punishable by a year in the state penitentiary.
More than any breach of the new laws relating to health care, failure to
accurately report a newborn's race brought down the full wrath of the
state, and similar punishments applied. In essence, midwives and physicians were given the legal mandate to notify state officials of the sexual
behavior of the women they delivered. While the marital license ensured
that legitimate unions maintained the boundaries between the races, the
birth certificate policed informal sexual interactions between blacks and
whites.

For African American midwives, the responsibility of reporting on this
highly charged, taboo behavior was an onerous one. Limited discussion of this subject in Green River County suggests that this was espe-

cially the case when midwives waited on white women who delivered mixed-race children. After all, for southern eugenicists, white women represented the salvation of the Anglo-Saxon race. A mulatto child born to a white woman exposed the fallacy of racist claims that sexual unions between white women and black men were always the outcome of a rape.

With these violent overtones, midwives who attended white women who gave birth to mulatto children must have faced excruciating decisions once the racial integrity laws had been passed. On the one hand, they risked imprisonment; on the other, reporting the birth of such a child could have recriminations for the black community as a whole and its male residents in particular.

It is extremely difficult to uncover midwives' varied response to the racial integrity laws. In Green River County, relatives of midwives who practiced in the 1930s and 1940s informed me that sometimes mulatto children were indistinguishable from their white siblings or cousins, who, of course, did not publicly recognize the kinship ties. Mr. Brewer's grandmother, for example, was a midwife who practiced in the county until her death in 1930. She had borne a son by a white man before marrying Mr. Brewer's grandfather. In remembering this "outside" child and others like him, Mr. Brewer recalled that "you couldn't call them white back in them days. The old folks used to call them . . . [he attempts to recall the term] the 'latta child.' They used to call them the 'latta child.'"

Here mulatto is contracted to "latta." It is significant that Mr. Brewer, sixty-three at the time of our conversation, at first had difficulty remembering the appellation. He seemed not to connect the word "latta" to mulatto. Rather, he conceptualized the phrase "latta child" as a categorization imposed from without to refer to these particular kinds of people, as "you couldn't call them white." While white women may have at times been able to register a mixed-race child as white, African American women could not, even if they so wished. The stories from Green River County drive home the historical rather than scientific basis for racial distinctions. Yet for the medical and legal community, the racial preservation law had its foundation in a science that was not open to question. This community felt completely justified in drafting African American midwives to aid them in preserving white "racial purity."

The systematic integration of midwifery control programs with other dimensions of social and reproductive control of the population provides the clearest evidence that health care policy cannot be understood as simply an instance of the polity performing a public good. For example, Virginia's physicians seemed completely unaware of any contradictory motivations behind the two legislations—prevention of infant mortality on the one hand and preservation of racial integrity on the other. Their confidence both in their methods and in the scientific accuracy of their observations—whether about health care, racial composition, or the behavior of the "Negro"—was predicated on the acceptance of the system as a whole. And if these physicians were willing to accept their professional role as guardians of this system, then midwives were expected to follow their lead. It is as a man of science as well as a political appointee that Plecker preached against the dangers of "race suicide." Midwives had been warned, he wrote, "that they must not report as white, children born to the mixed breeds of white-red-black, or white and black. Our colored midwives, being usually true negroes are faithful in obeying our injunction. They seem pleased to place these would-be-white mulattoes in the class to which they properly belong" (Plecker 1925, 811).

The midwife, from this perspective, was to be a sort of gatekeeper. Out of jealousy, according to Plecker, she would police the women she attended so that no mixed-race children got the opportunity to "pass" into the white world. For Plecker, African American culture is transparent. So, too, are the motives of midwives. As the scientist-bureaucrat, he purports to predict that midwives will comply with the racial integrity law because they are darker complected and unable themselves to "pass as whites." When he enforced the law, therefore, he assumed a scientific (ethnological) familiarity with the "workings" of the "Negro" mind while depending on his coercive power as the state registrar to ensure that the law was obeyed.

David Armstrong (1983) alerts us to the analytical danger of personifying the power of individuals who are themselves functionaries in an institutionalized and ongoing system of surveillance and control. Indeed, although he was instrumental in developing the new permit system and obligatory birth certificates in Virginia, Plecker the physician was part of a broader process that, as I have shown, was linked to the new emphasis on administrative efficiency, scientific observation, and professionalism in the nation as a whole. Ironically, although they had no control over the administrative bureaucracy of the state, midwives, too, were involved in this system of surveillance. The functional analogies between midwives and physicians had no connection to their relative power in the system. In fact, the effective control of life processes required no such equality of access. As Armstrong reminds us: "[the] observer . . . [is] neither unique nor important. Discipline depend[s] not so much on a person as on an observing gaze. It matter[s] little who the observer [is], more that he function[s] as a component in a unified observation" (Armstrong 1983, 4).

From 1900 to 1924, therefore, Virginia took its initial steps to institutionalize a "unified" field of observation in which not only midwives but also physicians, pregnant women, births, deaths, "health conditions of the races," marital patterns, and sexuality could be systematically monitored and studied and the racial and economic hierarchy of the society reproduced and maintained. Once in place, this system, as Plecker himself referred to the program, would allow data to be collected by any functionary. Even the midwife herself could be used to monitor the women she attended during birth. Therefore, as Armstrong points out, the efficacy of state monitoring of life processes is directly related to this ability to decentralize power—indeed, to engage the individual (in this discussion the midwife or the pregnant woman) in disciplining her body/self. It is important to realize, however, that this decentralization is not of the kind that empowers the individual. Rather, it concentrates state power by making it part of the routine, by making it ordinary and expected.

Seen in these terms, the seemingly contradictory motives that guided Virginia's health care policies and its midwifery control program are easier to interpret and reconcile. On the one hand, some health care policies, when taken in isolation, seemed to have worked for the benefit of the public. Collectively, however, the goals of administrative and medical professionals were not to create equity in the system but to maintain the status quo. The professionalization of reproduction was to completely push the midwife to the margins. In the interim, however, she occupied an ambiguous position as a functionary in the medical and legislative bureaucracy—as both observer and observed in the administration of life processes.

4

Race and Mortality

The basis for intervention into maternal and infant health, as public health officials had repeatedly pointed out, was high mortality rates among African American women. In this chapter, I explore the mortality issue and its rhetoric. There is no effort here to challenge the desperate situations of poor rural African American women. Figures (some cited in Chapter 1) indicate that these women and their infants died disproportionately during the first half of the century. But what, in the minds of Virginia's public health and medical personnel, caused these discrepancies? A frequent response was to point the finger at midwives. It makes sense, therefore, to consider mortality through the eyes of biomedicine. (For this analysis, I used articles in the *Virginia Medical Monthly* from 1900 to the 1950s, supplemented with reports from the *Virginia Public Health Bulletin,* oriented to public health workers in the field.)

Leading from the rhetoric of mortality, I confront more directly the underlying conflation of mortality with the midwife's body—out of place in reproductive medicine because of her race and gender.

Mortality Compared

In 1914, W. A. Plecker identified what he considered the crucial issue facing his profession. Great strides had been taken in "preserving human life, and in banishing disease and suffering" (Plecker 1914, 456), but "physicians, surgeons and public health men" now needed to direct their efforts "to the prevention of the unnecessary deaths and injury of mothers and infants in the practice of midwives during childbirth, from infection, ignorance and neglect" (1914, 456). Although he expressed general concern about the high rates of maternal deaths in the state, he focused his attention on urban deaths, and on the proportionately higher numbers of urban "colored" women (more than three to one) who had died from puerperal fever.

It was important that the main thrust of Plecker's argument be directed to urban African American maternal mortality figures. Although the majority of African American midwives were located in the state's rural areas, a greater proportion of urban African American women than urban white women relied on the services of these traditional birth attendants. Plecker used the higher rates of maternal mortality among urban African American women to argue that midwives were the essential problem. The comparison of urban deaths suited his argument. Although reasonably certain about the accuracy of the sixty-five rural white maternal deaths reported by physicians, Plecker expressed grave misgivings about the thirty-three reported cases of maternal deaths of rural black women. These, he felt, were grossly underreported "on account of the death of many being allowed, without even being seen once by a physician" (Plecker 1914, 456). Because his figures for maternal mortality among rural African American women failed to substantiate his thesis, Plecker based his interpretive conclusions on urban materials. The questionable givens in this scientific exercise were the assumptions that "the city rate represent[ed] the true State rate" and that figures for maternal deaths among rural black women, if they could be unearthed, would undoubtedly exceed those for rural white women delivered by physicians.

Calculated from birth and death certificates, his urban data for 1913 showed that 1 out of every 331 white women died from childbirth-related infections, as compared with 1 in every 102 "colored" mothers (Plecker 1914, 456). "I believe," he concluded, "that this great difference . . . is due to the fact that the colored women are attended chiefly by midwives. Some of the white women also, who died, were delivered by midwives, which makes the case still stronger" (1914, 456). In explaining the deaths of white women under the care of physicians, Plecker suggested that many of these had been actually delivered and already infected by the midwife before the doctor had been consulted. His thesis that the high numbers of maternal deaths among black women was the direct result of midwife care remained essentially unchallenged.

Similar studies appeared in Virginia medical journals through the

1940s, but especially between 1900 and 1930. A 1925 study of maternal mortality rates in Richmond, for example, concluded that "coincident with the decrease in the percentage of [white] births attended by midwives, there has been a decline in the maternal death rate from puerperal causes among the whites and an increase in the maternal death rates among the negroes" (Hudson and Rucker 1923, 302). Thus for many of the state's physicians, the maternal mortality problem was the "midwife problem." Furthermore, their urban data led them to conclude that the situation in rural areas would be heightened. Few researchers acknowledged that midwives attended the majority of high-risk cases in rural areas.

An article co-authored by two doctors, a health officer and the chairman of the midwife examining board, suggests the manner in which even results favorable to the practice of midwifery and detrimental to physicians could be twisted to support the push for greater physician and hospital involvement in the birthing process (Hudson and Rucker 1923, 300–304). In a statistical survey of maternal mortality for Richmond, the state capital, Hudson and Rucker wrote that "any consideration of maternal deaths from puerperal causes brings up the midwife question" (1923, 302). They then cited a New Jersey study that found that maternal mortality rates in midwife-delivered births were lower than those for mothers attended by physicians—a pattern that emerged from the Richmond data as well.

How was the 67 per 1,000 maternal mortality rate for midwives as opposed to the 78 per 1,000 for physician-attended births to be explained? The authors cited four possibilities, all of which directed attention to the manner in which the statistical results had been inordinately weighted against the physician and never entertained the possibility that midwives actually had greater success: "First in one case at least, a midwife was called and, upon seeing the patient's condition, refused to assume the responsibility of attending her; secondly, in all cases of convulsions physicians were called or the patient was sent to hospitals; thirdly, pregnant mothers who either have chronic impairments or have acute diseases always call physicians; fourthly, cases of pregnancy in very young girls are usually treated by physicians" (Hudson and Rucker 1923, 302). The figures may in fact have been slightly skewed by the greater numbers of high-risk women attended by physicians. Yet the authors had, by their own account, taken this into consideration when they included deaths in the hospital or under the care of physicians as "midwife-attended deaths" if the midwife had been the initial birth attendant.

It is also important to realize that in the state's urban areas, the debate about the "midwife problem" had already led, by the 1920s, to a decreasing pool of licensed midwives. Rucker's midwife examining board had, for example, reduced the number of practicing midwives in Richmond from 105 to 47 in a 3-year period. Furthermore, the overall percentage of women delivered by midwives in this urban area fell from 41 percent in 1907 to 18 percent in 1922, while physician-attended births rose from 59 to 82 percent (Hudson and Rucker 1923). City physicians were therefore attending the majority of pregnant women, not merely high-risk cases.

In another article, a graph showing the steady rise of births attended by physicians is plotted above the line showing the precipitous decline in white births attended by midwives from 1928 to 1949. A second graph for the same twenty-one-year period plots the downward slope of the maternal mortality rate so as to suggest an inverse relationship between mortality rate and percentage of midwife-attended births, as opposed to a direct one for physician-attended births. Yet the downward slope of the maternal mortality graph was far from perfect: even as the percentage of midwife-attended births continued to decline, mortality rates rose in 1931, fell for the following three years, and then rose again through 1937. Such evidence clearly shows that physicians greatly overstated the threat that midwives posed to the scientific profession while exaggerating or misrepresenting the relationships between midwifery and high maternal mortality rates.

Furthermore, although the overall maternal mortality rate among African American women was higher throughout the period from 1900 to 1940, it appears that fewer African American women died as a result of puerperal infections when compared with white women in rural and urban areas. For example, when the newly formed Children's Bureau of the U.S. Department of Labor conducted an independent inquiry into maternal morality in Virginia during 1927–28, its researchers found that in a sample of 767 maternal final trimester deaths (276 urban, 491 rural), "puerperal septicemia caused 50 percent of the urban white deaths, 48 percent of the urban colored deaths, 35 percent of the rural white deaths, and 33 percent of the rural colored deaths" (Rothert 1933, 238). This exception to the general pattern contradicted physicians' assumptions that women attended by midwives were more likely to contract puerperal infections.

The study also revealed that maternal mortality rates were higher in the state's urban areas in every category of death except for "puerperal hemorrhage which was the same for both urban and rural areas" (Rothert 1933, 238). Again, such a finding suggests that, at least for the 1920s and 1930s, increased access to hospitals and physicians' care did not always result in reduced risk of death for women in childbirth. The figures for hemorrhaging are especially revealing, because doctors commonly believed that they were eminently more capable than midwives of handling such emergencies: puerperal hemorrhaging was in fact one of the conditions for which doctors insisted that midwives consult them.

As with local studies by Virginian physicians, however, the Children's Bureau failed to explore the implications of their report's findings, as they related to the comparative similarity of outcome between physician- and midwife-attended births. Perhaps as federal government employees and members of a bureau that state physicians had regarded with hostility, the researchers were careful not to make recommendations but only to report the results of their statistical analyses to the Medical Society of Virginia and the Virginia State Department of Health. Yet Frances Rothert and her team, all physicians, seemed blinded to their own statistics when they were favorable to midwifery. In explaining the results for the maternal mortality data, they concluded that "the large proportion of deaths . . . among women who died after physicians' care, particularly among the colored women, suggests that the physicians had an unfavorable selection of cases" (Rothert 1933, 243).

Obstetric Uncertainty

As long as African American midwives delivered children and delivered them safely, they challenged the dominance of the medical profession. Fear of the midwife's real power—her ability to do the work of obstetrics—translated into a public portrayal of such women as primarily responsible for long labors and puerperal deaths. Physicians, by contrast, associated themselves with painless labor and safe childbirth. As one physician suggested in his support of a new program to preach the value of preventive maternal health, "prenatal care will do more than reduce the obstetrical mortality; it will do away with the midwives by teaching the people that the doctor can relieve them from death and discomfort" (Baughman 1929, 750).

The equation of the maternal mortality problem with the midwife problem provided a clear, comfortable, closed logic. If midwives were the problem, then the cure could be easily seen. They were less able to create such closure when they had to draw on their own expertise. In the *Virginia Medical Monthly,* one of the state's most influential medical journals, doctors offered their diverse, sometimes contradictory, opinions about effective care for puerperal infections, toxemia, hemorrhaging after childbirth, and a host of other complications normally referred to as "accidents of pregnancy" (Hudson and Rucker 1923; Plecker 1918; Williams 1936; Riggins 1942). They also struggled over the problem of creating antiseptic conditions during childbirth. Furthermore, general practitioners and obstetricians alike faced a great deal of uncertainty about the actual prevention or treatment of "complicated" or high-risk pregnancies.

Issues that now seem elementary were also subject to a variety of "scientific" interpretations in Virginia's medical journals. In the 1920s and 1930s, and to a diminished extent in the 1940s, articles in the *Virginia Medical Monthly,* for example, discussed the normal progress of labor, the proper method of delivering the placenta, the diagnosis of pregnancy, and the proper use of anesthetics such as ether and chloroform and of uterine stimulants and depressants, the most frequently mentioned being pituitrin. Physicians disagreed on major issues, such as the value of home versus hospital birth, and took opposite views on minor ones such as whether it was necessary for expectant women to toughen their breasts (by rubbing with a rough cloth) in preparation for breast-feeding.

Journal articles served a didactic purpose. Physicians reported to their colleagues on their empirical experiences and their personal successes and failures. Much as Mary Poovey has shown for nineteenth-century papers in the British medical journal *Lancet,* these articles reflected an underlying attempt to formulate a set of principles that would take obstetrics out of the realm of practice and into that of science (Poevey 1986, 149). Not infrequently, however, these "scientific" reports provided conflicting information or, at the least, revealed an underlying tension.

For example, his colleagues may have had some difficulty in identifying the intended message in A. M. Showalter's articles. To start, he advised that "when you know it is safe to sit down and wait, do so, for proper intervention in abnormal cases is just as important as no intervention in normal cases" (Showalter 1922, 137). He ended, however, by confessing that "earlier in the practice of medicine I followed a very conservative policy and chose to let nature take its course in all normal and questionable cases, but my own experience has taught me that was a great mistake" (1922, 139). Although physicians wanted to assert scientific dominance over the physiology of pregnancy and birth, their own experiences suggested that such control was never guaranteed.

Virginia doctors' increasing concern with the "management" of parturition suggests a trend toward the view of pregnancy as a scientific rather than natural event—a pattern that is widely discussed in the literature on the professionalization of birth (Wertz and Wertz 1977; Oakley 1984; Litoff 1978; Arney 1982). Although scholars usually depict this pattern as having been completed early in the century, in Virginia and I suspect elsewhere as well, a great deal of ideological indeterminacy and interpretive dissonance continued well into the 1940s. It is within the context of this uncertainty that doctors, with relatively little dissent, viewed the midwife as the primary cause of the state's high maternal and infant mortality rates. It was easy to equate mortality with midwifery and reassuring to think that the solution simply rested in its elimination.

Diana Scully finds it ironic that nineteenth-century physicians "who were, at the time, incapable of reducing the mortality rate claimed that the elimination of women-midwives and the expansion of obstetrics constituted the solution to high infant mortality rates" (Scully 1986, 57). I see no irony here. Rather, it was precisely the inability of obstetrical science to find a cure for, or assert complete control over, maternal and infant mortality—indeed, over pregnancy itself—that led its practitioners to attack the midwife with such vehemence and so loyally to defend their own imperfect craft.

A few doctors did call their colleagues' attention to the need for better trained physicians and for an avoidance of "operative intervention in obstetrical cases that are progressing normally" (Ware 1931, 24). In general, however, most doctors treated such suggestions with considerable skepticism, if not outright hostility. As one rural physician put the matter:

I do not believe the imputation of the high mortality rate to the doctor is absolutely just. For instance, an obstetrician gets a high mortality rate because he gets the most complicated cases. Then the high mortality rate of the general practitioner is due to the incompetency of the midwife . . . In the majority of cases of death of the mother, the doctor signs the death certificate, thus getting an increased mortality rate which he is not justly entitled to: because, as I say, the obstetrician will sign the death certificate in the most complicated cases referred to him by the general practitioner, and the doctor will sign the death certificate in the cases sent to him by the midwife. (Harris 1924, 852)

Similar arguments appeared in journal articles through the 1940s. At the bottom of the birthing hierarchy, midwives were said to create falsely elevated maternal mortality rates for all physicians by referring up their "botched" high-risk patients to the general practitioner who referred his most difficult cases in turn to the obstetrician (Hudson and Rucker 1923, 302; Laneford 1924; Baughman 1929, 383). In this manner, doctors shifted the greater burden of responsibility for the state's high maternal mortality rates onto the shoulders of the African American midwife.

Few physicians drew any direct connections between significantly higher rates of African American infant and maternal mortality (almost three times that of whites in some regions) and the economic impoverishment of the state's African Americans. A search of articles in the *Virginia Medical Monthly* over a sixty-year period yielded four references to the probability that maternal mortality was linked to poverty: the most explicit appeared in 1941. In a map of Virginia pinpointing the places of residence of maternal fatalities for December 1939, the author suggested in passing that "the black belt and mountainous districts are well represented, which fits with the growing belief that maternal mortality is as much an economic problem as it is a medical one" (Rucker 1941, 141). Despite this evidence, the perceived association between puerperal infections, maternal mortality, and African American midwives remained constant in the medical discourse through the late 1930s. Only in the 1940s did physicians begin to examine methodically their own procedures with any measure of serious criticism.

In his critical history of American obstetrics, William Arney correctly argues that the eventual success of male obstetrics came as a result of "well-orchestrated actions" and effective political strategizing on the part of practitioners (Arney 1982, 42). Yet he endows obstetricians, individuals as well as the profession, with a degree of self-consciousness that is unsupported by the discourse of Virginia's doctors. In the articles they wrote for the *Virginia Medical Monthly*, doctors seem to lash out at the midwife with little regard for the internal contradictions in some of their arguments. Oral narratives from Green River County suggest that mid-wives and expectant women were often terrorized, rather than logically wooed, to the side of science.

Midwives were allowed no firm ground on which to stand. On the one hand, they were maligned for being unable to deal with high-risk cases or complications; on the other, they were equally chastised for attempt-ing to handle such situations themselves—and, indeed, at times, for being able to handle any births at all. Doctors complained that the "in-competency" of midwives forced medical men to accept the greater per-centage of high-risk cases. Yet as a part of their continuing campaign to gain authority, they encouraged practicing midwives to refer high-risk patients to local physicians, insisting that they request help whenever complications arose during delivery and denouncing those women who, in their estimation, waited too long before calling the physician.

The discourse on mortality contained other paradoxes. As the scien-tific representation of birth in the state's medical journals underwent changes that would culminate in a model of birth as a pathological and potentially dangerous condition, the state medical society mounted pub-lic education efforts that contained a similar message. Birth was too complex an event to be left to the untrained midwife. As a part of that message, however, physicians warned women that the "puerperal state" itself was "a cause of death" (Williams 1936, 67).

In pushing birth to the extreme edges of potential abnormality, physi-cians risked suggesting that childbirth was indeed beyond the control of any expert. From this perspective, neither the midwife nor the physician could be fully blamed for all the things that could go wrong during pregnancy and childbirth. This was not, however, the conclusion that doctors wished the public to draw. Whenever possible, the physician was to remain blameless, having done all that science could do, while the midwife took all the blame for not being able to do enough.

Women's Choice: Dirty Midwives, Clean Doctors

When doctors linked midwifery to high rates of maternal mortality, they wished their message to reach beyond a purely professional audience. Although I focus on medical texts, I want to invoke the presence of a lay audience composed primarily of women of the childbearing age. Inevitably doctors wanted these women to reject midwives and to choose physician care, whether at home or in the hospital. The first wave of women consistently to choose physicians over midwives included urban whites from all social classes and rural affluent and middle-class white women. Next, it appears that in Virginia, middle-class urban African American women increasingly turned to doctors when possible. Finally, rural poor white and African American women were the last to depend almost exclusively on midwives to deliver their children.

Unlike some authors who write of this pattern in the northern United States and in nineteenth-century Europe, I use the words "choose" and "choice" with some reservation. Women chose doctors as a result of the diminishing availability of traditional midwives and the increasing power of the medical establishment's discourse and of its monopoly of life-saving pharmaceuticals and techniques. Even if we accept the view that affluent women in Virginia freely chose the service of physicians, and later birth in a hospital, any considered sense of the word would restrain us from suggesting that poor African American women freely chose, without coercion, to use physicians and to deliver their children in the hospital. Contemporary physicians seemed well aware of the task they faced in "weaning" women away from the midwife:

> The doctor has not the time to sit on a normal primipara for twenty-four hours to the neglect of his other patients without adequate remuneration. The midwife who frequently is a neighbor, is willing to spend her time for the prominence that it gives her in the community, for the friendliness that she has for the neighbor, as well as for the chance to recount or hear the latest gossip, and will consider herself well paid if she receives only her meals. (Baughman 1928, 750)

Physicians also saw the "problem" as one that involved changing women's basic evaluation of the relative "worth" of birthing services. Another wrote that

> so far as the individual is concerned, pregnancy and labor are often regarded as of minor importance. As one evidence of this may be cited the low comparative value placed upon the services of the doctor who delivers them. It is a matter of common knowledge that the average patient will willingly pay more for a simple appendix operation than for the most difficult labor. This often results in the labor being planned on

the cheapest plan possible, and, to some extent, is responsible for the midwife problem. (Andrews 1924, 148)

Virginia's doctors realized that the midwife was frequently the logical choice for the majority of African American women. The doctors' task, therefore, was to restructure perceived circumstances so that what had previously been a logical choice would appear ill-conceived, unsophisticated, risky, and perhaps even immoral. Thus the shift to medicalized birth was not an inevitable one. Women did not make choices in a free market of birth services in which midwife and doctor competed fairly. Doctors actively worked to convince women that their primary choice lie elsewhere than with midwifery care and inexpensive births.

Additionally, in Virginia—and I suspect in the South in general—the campaign against African American midwives reflected physicians' wider concern that medicine in the South was not far enough advanced. Southerners, particularly white southerners, were sensitive to the portrayal of the South as economically and medically underdeveloped when compared with other regions of the United States (Andrews 1944; Cooper 1953; Rucker 1941; Laneford 1924). Evidence of such concerns appeared in many forms. The following captures one physician's assessment of the problem:

> This [program to establish maternal centers and reduce the number of midwives in rural areas] brings up the problem that McCord so graphically described in his presidential address before the American Association of Obstetrics . . . namely the poverty of the South. At the end of his address some of my Northern friends asked me if it were as bad as that and I had to reply that every word of it was so, but that we did not like to brag about it. The people of the South have gotten so used to being poor and of not being able to afford anything that they think that they cannot afford good maternal care. (Rucker 1942, 443)

The overall concern about the South's perceived backwardness extended to any public depiction of the African American midwife. Mississippi's Felix Underwood, director of the board of health, refused inquiries from *Life* magazine to photograph midwives in his state, for fear that the magazine would make the state look "backward" (Willumson 1992, 276). It was also Underwood who, even though he instituted midwifery training programs, referred to midwives as "filthy and ignorant and not far removed from the jungles of Africa" (Mathews 1992, 65). Mortality and midwifery both conveyed symbolic associations of the South as Africa in America.

Except as a temporary measure, physicians saw no role for the African American midwife in the delivery of "good" maternal care. Even in light of evidence to the contrary, she was irrevocably associated with maternal mortality. In 1933, for example, Plecker again made his case that the essential problem was puerperal infections caused by midwives. As registrar of vital statistics, he informed his colleagues that "we have forbidden these midwives to make vaginal examinations under any circumstances." By the strict enforcement of such regulations, he hoped to "save, each year, fifty to seventy-five deaths of mothers from septicaemia" (1933, 84).

To reach their primary audience—women of childbearing age—physicians built their arguments about the unsuitability of midwives upon a substrate of racial and cultural stereotypes intertwined with an ongoing discourse about high rates of maternal mortality in the state and against the backdrop of a radical redefinition of pregnancy and childbirth. Certainly doctors were genuinely concerned that midwives maintain as antiseptic a birthing environment as possible. Beyond this medical fact, however, they were obsessed with the view of these women as unclean—a state of being that was immoral as well as unhygienic.

Arguments most damning to the moral character of the African American midwife revolved around her supposed inclination to abort pregnant women. For example, one rural physician, in arguing against the efforts of public health officials to offer classes in hygiene to midwives, warned against the dire consequences. In a double-layered attack, he also suggested, as did other physicians, that African American women were more likely to abort their pregnancies than were white women. In giving lectures to midwives, county nurses, he believed, were unintentionally "teaching negro women how to produce abortion" (Kerns 1927, 369). Once midwives were given scientific knowledge about childbirth, they would naturally use it to destroy rather than to save life. Thus notwithstanding the well-meaning efforts of public health officials, this physician advised against exposing any midwife to such information. "No negro midwife should be taught the anatomy of the genital organs," he argued. As evidence, he raised the specter of the back-alley abortion: "I have had twenty-seven abortions within the past seven months. The majority of these cases had consulted some negro granny, who told them how to do the work" (Kerns 1927, 370).

What is revealed in this discourse is the close association between midwife and the immoral, dirty "work" of abortion. Only in the hands of white men did science become ennobling. Physicians viewed themselves as the ultimate defenders of individual and family health. They had a duty, therefore, to warn families about the enemies within their own homes, whether that enemy was the anthropomorphized household germ, the African American maid or the "granny" midwife. Even those who recognized the midwife's important function in providing care in areas poorly served by physicians spoke of the "risk" of employing "these dirty untrained women" (Plecker 1914, 457), called for their "eventual elimination" (Hardin 1925, 350), and lauded the activities of health departments that had "done a splendid piece of work by reducing the number of midwives in the state from nine thousand very ignorant and dirty creatures, to four thousand eight hundred and forty, only one thousand two hundred and thirty-three of whom are really active" (Baughman 1928, 749).

As the primary source of domestic labor, African American women sanitized the homes of southern white families. They were the ones who performed the work associated with achieving a properly clean, hypersanitized domestic sphere. As part of their duties, those same women were also expected to nurture and attend to children and the infirm elderly. In one sense, then, it would be ironic if southern white women completely accepted the representation of the African American midwife as immoral or dirty. Information from narratives in Green River County suggest that white women did not all share this view.

Older African American residents Green River County remember that midwives delivered for "both colored and white," and that even the most affluent white women in the county used their services. In these circumstances, the distinction between midwifery and housekeeping became blurred as the midwife stayed on to care for the women and child. Informants also remember that whites would sometimes place the "honorific" title "Aunt" or "Nanny" before the first names of older, respected midwives.

From another perspective, however, the intimate association, in the minds of whites, between the African American woman and housecleaning, laundering, caring for the sick—all activities that involved some form of pollution—could be easily turned on its head so as to support the view of doctors that midwives were inherently filthy and thus dangerous to women in childbirth. Such women were unfit to enter either the homes or bodies of southern white women.

After the 1930s, the movement of higher status southern women into the hospital or under a physician's care began to replicate the pattern in the North, where such women were at the vanguard of the campaign to create safer, cleaner, more scientific, and painless births. By a reasoning that can be traced to the history of slavery in the South, the once-benevolent "aunt" (Aunt Jemima) could be effortlessly transformed into a slovenly harbinger of destruction and death. Both portrayals—the selfless caretaker or malevolent menial—fit within accepted cultural stereotypes of the African American woman who served—whether as maid or midwife.

As a corollary to the sanitation of the individual midwife, public health personnel also hoped that they would reach the unclean masses of "negroes." A public health nurse noted, for example, that "in addition to better, cleaner deliveries by the midwives as a result of the educational program, it has been noted that the families and friends of midwives tend to practice better general health habits as well as better maternal care and to seek medical supervision more often" (*Virginia Health Bulletin* 1951, 11).

Not only does this passage illustrate the public health department's focus on preaching the "gospel" of cleanliness to African Americans in Virginia, but with equal force it points out the way in which health professionals hoped to gradually bring this population into the "church" of scientific medicine. Ideally the midwife provided the bridge between African Americans and medicine. But eventually she would no longer be needed as an intermediary. Ironically, once made "fit," the midwife was to be replaced because, as public health personnel argued, "delivery by a physician, preferably in a hospital is . . . [ultimately] more desirable than midwife service" (*Virginia Health Bulletin* 1949).

In speaking to the white public health nurse who practiced in Green River County between 1950 and the mid-1970s, I first became convinced that midwives were often judged as unsuitable on the basis of cultural rather than strictly "scientific" criteria. According to Mrs. Stewart, only fifteen practicing midwives remained in the county during the 1950s.

She remembered that "these were the last of the group. We wanted people to go to the hospital. We were trying to phase them [midwives] out." Descriptions of her interaction with midwives suggest an ongoing battle to bring the remaining women into line with the health department's guidelines (equivalent here to the dominant culture's model of correct behavior).

Much of the behavior described by Mrs. Stewart reveals that midwives actively responded to claims that they were unclean or caused puerperal infections by adopting some of the tools (symbols) of scientific medicine—rubber gloves, for example. For Mrs. Stewart, however, an alternate interpretation carried more validity. She interpreted such behavior as either "stubborness" or the inability of these elderly African American women to "take instruction." One midwife in particular broke all the public health department's rules about proper and hygienic comportment. Mrs. Stewart remembered that "one old lady would work in the fields almost like a man. And then someone would call her . . . She would go to deliver babies, straight from the fields, dirt and all. Not even to change her clothes. We had a hard time with her."

In Mrs. Stewart's typology, one that was mirrored in doctors' discourse in the medical journals, midwives could be roughly divided into two types. All leaned toward being habitually unclean, but there were some midwives who could be taught the "rules" of hygiene, while most (like the midwife who farmed) were simply unable to learn, or as Mrs. Stewart put it, were mentally unable to "take instruction." From this perspective, the "teachable" women were unhygienic because they didn't know better, while the "unteachable" ones were irrevocably unclean, animallike, or primitive in their personal hygiene. In assessing efforts to teach midwives, Plecker wrote with exasperation that "we have tried to give them some instruction as far as it is possible to teach these ignorant creatures" (1933, 84). Again the contradictions in the representations of these women emerge when texts are compared. On the one hand, some doctors and public health personnel spoke of African American midwives as incapable of understanding basic instructions about cleanliness, but on the other, many argued that midwives developed effective techniques for abortion when they were taught even the simplest lessons in the physiology of birth.

Richard and Dorothy Wertz report that in the urban North, Italian and Irish women who practiced midwifery were also portrayed as dirty. They

.e negative stereotypes provided a contrast with descrip-
:erile environment" of the hospital in early-twentieth-
ical literature. The starkly posed disjunction between the
t midwife and the antiseptic hospital appealed to the sensibilities of the affluent and middle-class women who used hospitals or
doctors with increasing frequency after the 1920s (Wertz and Wertz
1977, 161):

> A number of social and cultural changes encouraged women to think
> that the hospital was safer, apart from mortality statistics. The popular
> culture in the form of advertising, for example, had alerted women to
> the danger of the "household germ" and of their obligation to rid their
> homes of it with new cleaning products. Germs at the home were
> thought to be unsafe for birth, for most people knew by 1920 that
> germs somehow caused infection and sickness. At the same time, the
> hospital began to picture itself as superclean, germ-free, safer than the
> home. (1977, 155)

Pejorative characterizations of African American midwives in Virginia
may be partially understood as a part of this movement to counterpoise
the sterility of the hospital against the "polluted" state of the home. Such
a view is incomplete, however. In Virginia, many physicians, especially
those in rural areas, contended that home deliveries could be clean and
safe: "While we do not undervalue the numerous advantages the hospital
offers in the management of a normal labor, we are convinced that the
majority of cases can be handled safely and satisfactorily in the homes"
(Hammer 1931, 378).

Satisfactory deliveries would only be possible, however, if "strict asepsis" was maintained, anesthesia was properly administered, and careful
attention was paid to "abnormalities" (Hammer 1931, 378). Following
the logic of this argument, such prerequisites could only be met by a
trained physician. Any other kind of home birth would be "unsatis-
factory."

Representations of the midwife as filthy and eventually as immoral
were so virulent, I believe, because physicians had not reached a consensus about the necessity of births in the hospital. When the disputed
terrain involved the home, doctors found that even greater distinctions
needed to be made between themselves and the midwife. Up to the
1940s, much of the task of southern medicine (particularly in rural areas

with few hospitals) was to convince women (especially middle-class white women) that even home births should be attended exclusively by the physician; only he could direct the transformation of the birthing room into the likeness of the hospital. As the intermediary, the physician supervised the preparation of the patient as well as the home.

While the portrayal of traditional midwives as incompetent, immoral, and unclean was directed to all women in Virginia, the undertones of the physicians' and the public health personnel's discourse were markedly different. The middle-class white woman responded to arguments about the greater capacity of the physician to reduce pain, to maintain a clean birthing area, and to fight the germs that caused childbed fever. For white women (particularly the urban and rural middle class), the doctor would assist them in maintaining a sanitary domestic sphere. For African American women, by contrast, doctors and public health personnel alike preached a different message: that these women's own inclinations to slovenliness and immorality (aborting fetuses, for example) could only be surmounted by accepting the gifts of science and hygiene and rejecting midwifery.

In addition to social class and race, the debate about midwifery versus physician care and home versus hospital birth varied over time and between the state's rural and urban areas. From the turn of the century to about the 1930s, doctors largely directed their arguments against the midwife to an audience of white women who could afford their fees. In the city, these women were encouraged to use the hospital; in rural areas, they were urged to rely on the physician, who could give them the experience of hospital birth. In either situation, doctors argued that "to allow a mother to go through the so-called natural birth experience without such relief as we may give from suffering [was] the most inhuman and unkind thing" (Langston 1929, 381). In essence, to allow midwives to deliver these women was to commit a moral breach, but then for a poor woman (whether African American or white), physicians found that they were unprepared to give "any considerable help," "except it be an operative case, which must be admitted to the hospital" (Andrews 1924, 148).

Although they continued to denounce the midwife, physicians were unwilling to offer their services to women who were unable to pay, and most often such women were African American. For these women in particular, doctors were willing to dim their sense of outrage about the supposed cruelty of natural childbirth. These doctors argued that is was "folly to advocate the extermination of the midwives," because "in the country . . . with few doctors, great distances to travel, and a tremendous obstetrical service, much of which would be absolute charity, the doctors would work themselves to death and die broke" (Baughman 1928, 750). Physicians and public health departments wanted to reduce the autonomy of traditional midwifery by bringing practitioners under the full authority of physicians. But until the late 1940s, when the state and federal government increased investments in clinics and community hospitals, few physicians wanted to have total responsibility for the care of large numbers of indigent parturients.

Bodies Compared

Scholars of the history of midwifery often assume that the discourse and praxis associated with the elimination of the midwife was duplicated in England, the northern United States, and in the South. Most focus on the latter two contexts and suggest that the situation in the South with African American midwives was different only in chronology. Yet the situation in Virginia varied in essential ways even though physicians had the same goals as their counterparts in nineteenth-century England and in the northern United States during the nineteenth and early twentieth centuries: to eliminate alternate birthing philosophies and practitioners.

I want to consider the portrayal of midwives that appeared in the discourse of Virginia's doctors and public health personnel. As I have shown, these were drawn from racial stereotypes about African American women and African Americans in general: that they were dirty, slow to learn, animallike, potentially unsafe, and needed to be continuously watched. None of these pejorative labels is remarkable by itself. In other contexts and historical periods, doctors used similar characterizations to assert control over the birthing process and to deny midwives access to the birthing chamber (Wertz and Wertz 1977; Donegan 1978; Eakins 1987; Laqueur 1986; Arney 1982), but never in this exact configuration. Also revealing is the absence of some of the central arguments waged against midwifery in England, France, and the northern United States during the nineteenth and early twentieth centuries.

Of these arguments, the most conspicuously absent in the discourse of Virginia's doctors were cultural representations of African American women as either too "delicate, modest, docile, submissive [or] gentle" (Donegan 1978, 151) to attend deliveries. In nineteenth-century England and France, such views dominated arguments about the unsuitability of women to participate in midwifery and the developing science of obstetrics. Grounded in the "Victorian separate-sex culture" (Wertz and Wertz 1977, 58) these arguments also appeared in the discourse of nineteenth-century American physicians—in Massachusetts, New York, and Pennsylvania, for example (Donegan 1978; Wertz and Wertz 1977; Eakins 1987). This "social theory of sexual incommensurability" rested on arguments about the biological differences between men and women (Laqueur 1986, 31). Such differences were thought to be replicated in the social sphere: the delicacy of woman's biology (largely equated with her reproductive organs and brain) prevented her from professional participation in childbirth.

Women, it was believed, "lacked the power to act that was essential to being a birth attendant" (Wertz and Wertz 1977, 56). Connected to this idea that women were emotionally too delicate to attend childbirth was the view that their inherent sexual instability made it impossible for them to be taught about the female anatomy. Physicians argued that women would be unduly and inappropriately stimulated by such knowledge. Not only would they jeopardize their purity, but they would also risk exciting male colleagues to acts of sexual abandon (Donegan 1978, 24). For similar reasons, women would be unable to handle the new technologies associated with scientific birth. If they were not to overturn the scientifically determined boundaries of male and female, their proper place was in the home, as "primarily wives and mothers, and dependent upon husbands and other males" (Wertz and Wertz 1977, 58).

In Virginia, the campaign against African American midwives drew on representations of black womanhood that departed significantly from those of white womanhood. For nineteenth-century British and North American doctors, the danger in teaching the white woman about the female anatomy lie in inadvertently damaging her purity or overtaxing her emotional resources. Just the opposite characterization held for the African American woman. Rather than having an overabundance of emotional sensitivity, the black woman had too little or none at all: exposure to scientific knowledge about female physiology would stimulate her propensity to mischief and evil. Thus, as I have shown, physicians cited statistics that showed that African American women had higher rates of self- or midwife-aided abortions. They argued that midwives caused painful labors, disproportionately contributed to maternal and infant mortality, and unnecessarily injured women during childbirth. Ultimately, Virginia's physicians held the view that they had to protect defenseless white women, in particular those of "sufficient means," against the pernicious midwife.

In a parallel vein, representations of African American midwives suggest that physicians and nurses saw them as being intellectually dense (reflected in the colloquial use of the word "ignorant"). But the African American woman's inability to comprehend scientific childbirth was a result of her mental (racial) dullness, not because her brain was structured for more genteel duties or because menstruation sapped her of "the mental and physical energy" (Laqueur 1986, 32) necessary for practicing scientific midwifery.

That the former public health nurse in Green River County was unable to see resistance in the midwives' refusal to follow carefully laid public health rules is certainly connected to this notion that African Americans were inherently slow. From the medical texts and my interview with Mrs. Stewart, it appears that midwives were thought incapable of consciously acting against the medical establishment. Rather, evidence of infractions of rules were taken as a measure of their failure or inability to comprehend. In her study of traditional midwifery in a North Carolina community during the 1960s, Beatrice Mongeau (1973) suggests similar interpretations of midwives' reluctance to follow public health procedures.

Besides the centrality of racism in structuring the debates about traditional midwifery in Virginia, the historical involvement of African American women in work—whether as slaves, as sharecroppers, as domestic servants, or as factory hands—must necessarily have led to a separate set of representations about the relationship between the black female body and the social order. Unlike upper-class white women, African American women were never able to withdraw into idealized domesticity.

Indeed, African American women were perceived as sharing certain characteristics with men. (Mrs. Stewart, for example, hinted at this possibility in her discussion of the recalcitrant midwife who was "almost like a man.") In addition, descriptions of the ease with which African American women gave birth suggest that some whites believed that these women were less susceptible to the dictates of (white) female biology because they were closer, in these whites' view, to some primitive, animallike state.

Ironically, the supposed masculinity of the African American woman did not raise her value in the eyes of nineteenth- and early-twentieth-century physicians and social theorists. Instead she came to represent a repugnant anomaly, a kind of woman who shared the basic biology of white women but who, by virtue of her lower position on the evolutionary scale, was coarse, immoral, lacking in intellect, sexually promiscuous, and well-suited for hard and intensive physical labor (Ehrenreich and English 1978; Barker-Benfield 1976; Jones 1981; Haller and Haller 1974; Haller 1972).

These convoluted representations meant that the same woman who nurtured white children (sometimes serving as wet nurses) and attended to white women during childbirth could also be portrayed as potentially destructive. It also meant that an ideology of biological differences between the races coexisted alongside experimentation and research on black bodies for the purpose of refining and advancing the medical treatment of whites. Writing of nineteenth-century southern medicine, Todd Savitt notes that "despite the political rhetoric then current in the Old South about a separate medicine for blacks and for whites, the research and teaching reflected, in fact, the opposite. Negroes did not seem to differ enough from Caucasians to exclude them from extensive use in southern medical schools and in research activities" (Savitt 1978, 332).

When they conducted anatomy lessons with or performed surgery on African American bodies, physicians, deliberately or unconsciously, ignored the contradictions. In other instances, however, ideas about biological difference, on the one hand, and similarity, on the other, were conflated. For example, scientific notions about African Americans' supposed higher threshold for pain, or about their greater insensitivity to physical discomfort, when compared with whites, could be used to endorse using them for medical experimentation. Here the ideology that biological differences existed between the races provided rather than subverted the logic of biomedical practice. Physicians oftentimes used African Americans as the subjects of clinical trials and experimentation precisely because they were seen as more suitable subjects: they shared enough biology with whites to allow the direct implementation of

re different enough so that ethical issues need not be
en 1985; Jones 1981; Ehrenreich and English 1978;

.ise when J. Marion Sims performed his surgeries in the
_.∪5 in Alabama (Barker-Benfield 1976; Sims 1884; McGregor 1985;
Axelsen 1985; Harris 1950). He operated on slave women in search for
an effective treatment of vesico-vaginal fistulas. These were tears or rips
between the vagina and bladder that sometimes accompanied childbirth
and often left woman completely incapacitated. Working without anesthesia, which was not yet generally available, Sims conducted numerous
operations on slave women over a period of four years. By his count, one
of these women had been subjected to thirty different surgical procedures during this period.

Lucy, the first of his slave patients, underwent more than an hour of
surgery in which she was "crouched on her knees and elbows, fortified
only by opium and hope against the searing, racking, operative pain. The
entire base of her bladder had been destroyed, leaving a gaping hole two
inches wide. The surgeon was confronted with the problem not only of
closing this fistula but also of first scarifying its callused edges so that
when the membranes were sutured they would have sufficient vitality to
grow together" (Harris 1950, 88).

Yet except in passing references to Lucy's "great heroism and bravery"
(Sims 1884, 237), Sims seemed remarkably nonchalant about the excruciating tortures she and his other slave patients endured as he sutured,
pared away flesh, inserted catheters, and examined their inflamed vagi-
nas. This scientific detachment did not extend to his white patients,
whether male or female. In his memoirs, he recalled his hesitancy in
treating the wife of a white planter: "I could not make up my mind to
introduce my finger into the rectum, because only a few days before that
I had had the occasion to examine the rectum of a nervous gentleman
who had a fissure, and he made so much complaint of the examination
that I thought that this poor woman was suffering enough without my
doing so disagreeable a thing" (Sims 1884, 232).

When he had perfected his surgical techniques on slave women, Sims
could safely turn to whites. Again he found it of sufficient interest to note
these women's sensitivity to pain—a sensitivity that, to his dismay, im-
peded his work. With white patients, his empathetic nature came to the
fore: "The pain was so terrific that Mrs. H. could not stand it and I was

foiled completely." In another instance, he recalled that "the patient insisted that it was impossible for her to bear the operation," and after one episode, he commented that "patient, assistant, and surgeon were all worn out" (Harris 1950, 109).

The crucial difference between these white women and their slave counterparts was obviously not biology but power (Axelsen 1985; Barker-Benfield 1976). Where Mrs. H. could express her refusal to submit to the violence of unanesthetized surgery, neither Lucy nor her slave sisters had any such voice. Under these circumstances, they had no choice but to endure the pain. Was it that these women didn't complain about the pain, even if they believed that Sims was making efforts to alleviate their miserable condition? More likely, the physician did not think their complaints important enough to document in his surgical notes.

Throughout the nineteenth and twentieth centuries, physicians continued to read biology into the social domination of African Americans (Beardsley 1990; McBride 1991). More than one hundred years after Marion Sims's first excursion into gynecological surgery, his physician biographer, for example, writing in the fourth decade of the twentieth century, could still comfortably promote a view of the African American as innately submissive. Offering an interpretation of the ability of Sims's slave patients to withstand surgery without anesthesia, this medical scientist dismissed the coercive nature of the relationship between the slave women and the white physician on whom they depended for food and shelter in addition to medical care. Instead he theorized that

> only in a small degree was their complaisance due to the fact that, as slaves, they were conditioned to yield implicit, unthinking obedience to the white man's orders, even if as in this case, the white man was not their legal master . . . Sims's experiments brought them physical pain, it is true, but they bore it with amazing patience and fortitude—a grim stoicism which may have been part of their racial endowment or which possibly had been bred into them through several generations of enforced submission. (Harris 1950, 99)

These constructions of the African American woman, it is important to point out, were not exclusively products of the South. Neither were they held only by men, nor restricted to the descriptions of black women. Working-class and immigrant white women were discussed in similar terms (Wertz and Wertz 1977; Ehrenreich and English 1978; Petchesky 1984). When he moved his practice to New York, Sims, for example, continued surgical experimentation on Irish working-class women. Illustrative of the equations that were sometimes made between black and working class white women are the opinions of northern physicians such as one Dr. Lucien Warner, who believed that "the African Negress who toils beside her husband in the fields of the South, and Bridget, who washes, and scrubs and toils in our homes of the North, enjoy for the most part good health, with comparative immunity from uterine diseases" (Ehrenreich and English 1978, 114).

Regardless of the convergences of representations of white and African American women, the essential racial differences were always paramount. Many nineteenth- and early-twentieth-century scientists believed that African American women occupied the basest position, on the lowest branch of the evolutionary tree. Despite the similarities in function, "Bridget," the named servant, did not exactly fit in the same biological and social category as the unnamed "African Negress." Thus in an investigation of the health conditions of working girls in Massachusetts factories during the 1890s, Carroll Wright, the white investigator, could empathize with the harsh lives of the white women who worked in the state's mills. "However strong they may be at the beginning," she declared, these women eventually succumbed, for in the words of one of her interviewees, "they cannot stand white slavery for ever" (Ehrenreich and English 1978, 114). In its unmodified manifestation, slavery was bearable only by African Americans. It was precisely the potency of the term "white slavery" that drew the ire of Wright and other of her reformist colleagues.

In sum, the scientific ideology of an essential biological difference between the races meant that the southern discourse about the midwife question diverged in many respects from that which had surrounded debates about the appropriateness of white female midwifery in the northern states during the nineteenth century. This discourse did not reflect concern with issues of modesty, delicacy, and appropriate female activity, because in the eyes of physicians and public health personnel, the African American woman did not fit within the normal male-female typology. In their arguments against the midwife, physicians drew on sometimes contradictory ideas about the pathological psychology and biological inferiority of African American women. They used the language of presumably objective statistics to argue for an association between midwifery and mortality and then implied that such links were to be expected from women who had a natural affinity for uncleanliness. Furthermore, even in their limited efforts to train midwives, medical personnel evaluated their successes and failures on the basis of the racial and intellectual inferiority of these African American women.

Such depictions of traditional practitioners mirrored racist assumptions about African Americans in general. Negative characterizations of the midwife could be extended to include all those who used her services. The stigmatization of the African American female body blocked the possibility for a professionally recognized role for traditional midwives in the South's medical hierarchy. It also influenced white southerners to retreat from the public health clinic where black bodies received and gave treatment. Negative representations of the capabilities and limitations of the African American body and mind still have power.

I am convinced that the almost total success of the dominant ideology among African American women, especially among the middle class, came in large part because these women wanted to distance themselves from the pejorative racial stereotypes used to characterize the traditional midwife and those who depended on her skills. Going to the hospital or using a doctor at home became a marker of status among African American women. Ironically, the relatively inexpensive service of the midwife became less desirable because it was seen as an indication of poverty and "backwardness," and perhaps even as a measure of a woman's "insensibility" to the welfare of her unborn child.

A case could be made that the process by which hospitals and doctors took center stage in the events of birthing was an inevitable and perhaps not totally undesirable one. Others have noted that African American women turned to physician care and hospitals to take advantage of anesthesia, forceps deliveries, and biomedical technologies and services (Clark 1989; Schaffer 1991; Susie 1988). But the degree of alienation from the history of midwifery expressed by many women in Green River County need not have accompanied their eventual acceptance of scientific obstetrics. Entirely bound up in the South's regulation of midwives and delivery of public health services was a language of shame, stigma, and pollution keyed to racial difference. How much should this have mattered given the eventual offer of maternal and infant care? Certainly the rhetoric did not keep African American women from claiming public health services when they needed them. Those pragmatic acts should not, however, turn us away from the damaging cultural narratives that were served alongside the menu of improved reproductive health.

II

Authoritative Knowledge

5

Nurses and Midwives in the Classroom

The core metaphor for public health personnel was the classroom. Midwives and mothers were students; nurses and doctors were teachers. The metaphor of the classroom extended from the public health clinic to the homes of pregnant women and midwives. Churches were drawn into service as the likeliest of classrooms for midwife clubs; demonstration projects focused on bringing new lessons in health care and the body to the untutored citizenry. Even women's bodies could be drawn into service. These various public health classrooms proposed an idealized model of midwifery as submissive to the authority of obstetrics—a classroom based on consensus—but there was also the threat of punishment should there be resistance. Like other classrooms, the teachers were primarily women—public health nurses who, in a manner of speaking, had taken their medical training to the streets. In this chapter, I examine the relations between teaching and punishing, coercion and consent. By so doing, I take another step in uncovering the struggles over authoritative knowledge (Jordan 1989, 1991).

In her work, Bridgette Jordan has described the operation of authoritative knowledge from birthing rooms in rural Latin America to hospitals in the United States and in the control towers of airports. As she defines it, authoritative knowledge may be horizontally or vertically distributed, but it is that knowledge which is understood by participants to be officially sanctioned and "accepted as grounds for legitimate inference and action" (Jordan 1991, 1). Participants might move between coexisting systems of legitimate knowledge. They may become good at drawing on separate knowledges to suit the situation and to avoid failure as it is defined within that sphere. In many instances, however, "one kind of knowledge gains ascendance," the "legitimation of one kind of knowing as authoritative is the devaluation, often the dismissal of all other kinds of knowing" as backward or irrational (Jordan 1991, 2). Through this negation, Jordan believes that the learning of authoritative knowledge invents and mirrors power.

Public health lessons, in the analytic lens proposed here, worked to erode midwives' base of knowledge gained through experience and mother wit. Unpacking the midwives' claim to special powers included offering replacement knowledge in health and hygiene, but it also meant that those women who failed to take to the new lessons could be replaced by younger women who were deemed more intelligent and less likely to be burdened with the weight of old beliefs and practices. The need to display the social power of authoritative knowledge weighted the preference toward the bodies of younger women: "health workers . . . should definitely plan to train a younger woman in the neighborhood of each older one . . . and thus gradually eliminate the unfit midwife," and the "older ones might be encouraged to return their permits and discontinue practice"(Daniel and Gafafer 1935, 1,813). It also explains the tremendous emphasis placed, in the South's midwifery education programs, on rituals of performance, inspection, and demonstration.

Jordan is emphatic in her claim that the teaching and acquisition of authoritative knowledge need not carry any explicit signs of conflict or antagonism. Most often sanctions are in place, but just barely under the surface of participants' recognition. I would stress a greater consciousness of sanctions and punitive measures than Jordan's analysis allows. The point is, however, that the hierarchy of bureaucratic, professional, and racial power made its presence known alongside the expressions of mutual affection and admiration.

Midwives and Nurses: A Model Partnership?

Of the recent scholarly perspectives on the interaction between midwives and public health nurses, one is most antithetical to the position I have set out. The midwife and the public health nurse in this model worked together in a joint project to improve maternal and infant health care. Consensus developed in the interaction of the committed nurse and the eager midwives. This joined professional relationship prospered despite racism and the challenges of working with pregnant women who had little if any prenatal care and who lived in conditions of dire poverty. Where African American nurses directed midwifery education, the analysis further accentuates the collaborative bent of education and regulation programs (Bell 1993; Roberts and Reeb 1994; Smith 1994).

These authors tend to cast any conflict as cultural barriers posed by the midwives' insufficiencies. For example, one author commends the accomplishments of a public health nurse who "found ways to instruct midwives despite their advanced ages, superstitious beliefs, and widespread illiteracy" (Bell 1993, 166). Another describes a typical midwife meeting: "The nurse prepared her set-up and the midwives began to arrive. It was a bit tense as bags were inspected; then as people began to greet one another and bags were determined to be 'C.C.S.' (clean, complete, sterile), a real bond of mutual respect and appreciation sprung up" (Roberts and Reeb 1994, 62). This description gives an almost a fairy-tale quality to the encounter. The setting is Mississippi, where in another instance we are told that "plantation storekeepers' wives, who often helped with birth certificates, frequently came to these meetings to support the nurses" (Roberts and Reeb 1994, 60).

It may well be that I am recounting a horror story where others see happy endings, but my project seeks to observe what's going on behind the curtains of the stage set. Why, for example, is the plantation storekeeper's wife present? What are the contexts of power that create tension with bag inspections? By what means did public health nurses evaluate the criteria for good, efficient midwives—"eager learners, strongly motivated" and trained to take over from the "inefficient ones" (Roberts and Reeb 1994, 60)? How, if at all, did midwives contribute to the exchange beyond offering their open bags and submissive natures?

Virginia's midwifery programs intended to clean up the midwife, strip away her superfluous rituals and beliefs, and make her, so far as was possible, a creature of science. When William Plecker wrote about the midwife problem, his concern extended beyond these women's uncleanness. He was equally, if not more intensely, disturbed by midwives' lack of "efficiency" and their seeming inattention to any fixed rules either in their acquisition of knowledge or in their birthing methods. "None of Virginia's midwives [either black or white]," he wrote, "can be rated high from the standpoint of culture and efficiency" (1925: 809). The absence of order, of a scientific approach to the birthing process, contradicted his and other physicians' sense that efficient and scientific methods of child-birth would automatically lead to decreased maternal and infant mortality. In an article written in 1925, seven years after his initial efforts in Elizabeth City and just at the beginning of the state's federally sponsored child and maternal health programs, Plecker described for his public health colleagues the informal means by which women became midwives:

> They are usually women who have had a number of children themselves, and who have witnessed other women passing through the pangs and perils of childbirth . . . They usually begin by acting in their own families or are called in emergencies when a "midwife" or woman of greater experience is not available . . . After supervising a few successful deliveries, and receiving, perhaps, small fees for their services, they enter upon the calling as regular midwives, and respond to calls throughout the neighborhood. (Plecker 1925, 809)

Plecker was not alone in paying such close attention to the apparently unstructured manner in which women learned to be midwives. Their comparative success belied the assumption that birth could only be managed by appropriately trained experts. Throughout the period, physicians and nurses devalued the knowledge of midwives yet seemed fascinated by that knowledge's empirical or experiential base, by midwives' recourse to the supernatural, and by the personal rather than professional nature of the relationship between midwives and the women they attended during childbirth.

Emily Bennett was hired in 1922 as a "field education nurse" and was later given the title "midwifery education supervisor." Based in the Virginia Bureau of Child Welfare, she held jurisdiction over county public health nurses. This white professional nurse encountered the "untrained" African American midwife across the chasm of contradictory agenda. She provided a bridge between midwives and the medical bureaucracy, carrying out the educational campaign while working toward eliminating "unfit" and eventually all practitioners. Scholars have examined the roles and impact of a new breed of women professionals in the early twentieth century—rationalizing housework (Ehrenreich and English 1978; Lemons 1973), providing scientific health care (Morantz-Markell 1982, 1985), and disbursing social welfare (Petchesky 1984; Kennedy 1970; Johnson 1975). The meeting between white women professionals (nurses, physicians, social workers), who were themselves at-tempting to redefine their social roles, and African American women (midwives, healers), who had considerable communal authority by vir-tue of their skills but no bureaucratic power, is a story yet to be told. It is not surprising, however, that Virginia's health department hired a woman to direct the educational component of the midwifery project. While men headed the board of health and disbursed the federal funds, women like Bennett transformed an accepted area of expertise for women into a professional calling. As part of their new professional responsibilities, however, these women were expected to play a role in controlling and restricting the authority of the African American midwife.

Nurse Bennett, with the support of local nurses, devised and encour-aged midwives to attend a series of eight instructional lessons that she offered in counties having the largest numbers of home births. Much like a circuit preacher, Bennett moved from county to county, spreading the message of hygiene, prenatal care, and scientific childbirth. Eventually, local public health clinics took over these duties on a more sustained basis. But whether formulated along the lines of Bennett's eight-lesson plan or in a community-based clinic with ongoing programs, Virginia's midwifery education project remained essentially the same.

A characteristic of public health programs throughout the South was in fact the unchanging nature of their midwife education materials for decades on end. Programs retained the same songs, the same lessons on hygiene, and the same restrictions on practice as if midwives existed in a virtually static realm of knowledge acquisition. In Mississippi, "policies have remained virtually the same . . . [T]he [midwife] manual was dis-tributed to other states and abroad . . . [E]xcept for minor revisions and updated pictures and deletion of some of the early sing-and-do songs, it remained the guide for midwives until 1985 when the last was retired" (Roberts and Reeb 1994, 60). A similar pattern held for North Carolina, where the *Book for Instructions and Illustrations for North Carolina Mid-wives,* first printed in the mid-1930s and disseminated until the 1950s, underwent few changes (Hudson 1987).

Public health personnel intended to closely define the boundaries of midwifery practice, offer hygiene basics, and transform these women into auxiliary health practitioners. The passage through which midwives could make a way into the practice of medicine, however, had to be tightly guarded. The exchange of authoritative knowledge threw nurses and midwives into conflict about which kinds of information and techniques belonged to which domains. It was in this context that public health personnel wanted to keep it simple, while midwives likely expected that increased knowledge should be matched by widened spectrums of practice and abilities.

In the case of Virginia, Nurse Bennett tackled her job with the conviction and passion of a missionary. African American midwives initially welcomed her endeavors. They embraced the opportunity to increase their knowledge and offer improved care to their pregnant clients. Just as important, midwives and their clients may well have perceived Bennett's involvement as the first signs that the state and county governments had finally decided to place some resources at the disposal of the African American populace.

Working on the front lines, midwives were well aware of the economic impoverishment of families and the need for better and more accessible health services. Bennett, whose career (1922–39) spanned the two decades of federal support for maternal and infant health care in the state, reported that after an initial period of distrust, most African American midwives greeted her efforts with considerable enthusiasm. Three years after the start of midwifery training in the state, she recalled that "there is no difficulty in getting the midwives to attend [instructional lessons]; some of them walk many miles to get to the appointed place. One woman, who is over ninety years old, did not miss a single class and came through a thunder storm to one, and through a snow storm to another" (Bennett 1925, 524).

Besides the emphasis on hygiene and sanitation, the instructional courses initiated by Bennett closely defined the midwife's realm of jurisdiction in childbirth. Under no circumstances were vaginal examinations permitted, whether as a part of routine checks or as an emergency measure. Furthermore, Bennett directed her efforts toward discouraging midwives in their resort to "superstitions" during childbirth or in their follow-up care of mother and child. As defined in these early lessons, as well as in the more regimented clinic classes that eventually replaced them, "superstitions" included all activities that fell outside the immediate domain of physiological childbirth. Bennett and subsequent public health nurses discouraged the use of ritual incantations to ease a difficult birth. They preached against the use of any home medicinals and ridiculed traditional beliefs related to food restrictions and the use of smoke to protect mother and child. The public health nurse's objective was to delineate a narrow band of activity deemed appropriate for midwifery. Besides teaching basic lessons in hygiene, the goal, according to these professionals, was limitation of midwifery practice.

As part of their policing activity, nurses conducted periodic checks of midwives' bags. Mrs. Stewart, the public health nurse who practiced in Green River County for twenty years, recalled her efforts to convince midwives to carry only those items specifically allowed by the board of health. She considered all other items to be contraband—at the least unnecessary for birthing and at the most "dangerous" and "unhygienic." These were the items "allowed": soap, clean towels or cloth, a white apron and hat, scissors to cut the umbilical cord, silver nitrate ampules to prevent blindness, and birth certificate forms. These were the rules passed down from the board of health, and Mrs. Stewart and all other public health nurses in the state were expected to be rigorous in applying them.

Both scheduled and impromptu inspections of midwives' bags formed part of the routine of the relationship between public health nurses and African American women. Strictly forbidden were any items that could be construed as related to superstition or as reflective of a midwife's attempt to use birthing techniques not recommended by the public health clinic. For example, gloves were strictly forbidden. A midwife caught breaking this rule could have her permit revoked (Plecker 1918; Bennett 1925). The appearance of gloves in the midwife's bag suggests that some women continued to use their knowledge about checking the progress of labor by vaginal exam. But this was precisely the activity that public health personnel and physicians defined as outside the midwife's jurisdiction.

Other forbidden items included the various salves and herbal teas that midwives used to treat mother and newborn. According to Mrs. Stewart, "we [her public health colleagues and herself] would have inspections . . . They were not supposed to have any instruments, no rubber gloves or anything else. You would always find those gloves . . . They were taught never to go into the birth canal, [but] they probably did all kinds of things. They tried to deliver breach, though they shouldn't have. But they probably did all kinds of things [without her knowledge]."

Bag inspections were a common feature of midwifery control programs throughout the South (Ferguson 1950; Holmes 1986; Mongeau

1973; Susie 1988). Mongeau argues that in the North Carolina county where she conducted her research, inspection of the midwife's bag "was to become the official agency's first mechanism of control and the means through which changes in the midwife's practice was to be brought about" (Mongeau 1973, 83). As was certainly the case in Green River County, midwives and their patients followed their own culturally sanctioned rituals during childbirth and after the birth of the child. These activities could not be closely scrutinized by public health nurses. Nurses did make "surprise" visits to midwives' homes to check on domestic cleanliness and observed midwives during deliveries. This was to ensure that the rules were being obeyed (*Virginia Health Bulletin* 1949, 11; Bennett 1925).

Because there were not enough nurses to monitor the private relationships between midwife and client, the bag inspection and the immediate threat of sanctions provided the public health nurse with a visible symbol of her authority. The bag inspection became, therefore, the site of the struggle between the nurse professional and the African American midwife. Mongeau writes that "instruction in behavior at the bedside could be given, but the extent to which these instructions were carried out at the bedside could not be controlled. The items which the midwife carried in her bag to the bedside which reinforced old practices could be more stringently supervised" (Mongeau 1973, 83).

Contemporary literature is replete with descriptions of these rituals of inspection and display (Campbell 1946; Ferguson 1950), and these descriptions teetered on the edge of cultural lampooning, with the dialect of midwives coming up for attention. In a footnote, Susan Smith mentions that nurses kept running lists of midwife sayings and malapropisms—what she terms "midwife illiteracies" (Smith 1994, 43). In Virginia, public health nurses attempted to write in dialect to convey the flavor of midwife personality. They did so, in particular, as a means of describing midwife responses to lessons and inspections. Given the way that the nurses dramatized the fervor of midwives caught up in the pomp and ceremony of being retired, descriptions of retirement ceremonies are almost a genre in and of themselves. Not only was the midwife to be transformed into a good-enough-for-now birth attendant, but she was also good for a laugh now and again.

The entire complex of midwife clubs, white uniforms, bag inspections, and midwife songs (what one author called "sing-and-do songs") encoded an array of conflicting associations. Midwives are like nurses. Midwives are not like nurses. Midwives are professionals. Midwives are childlike. Midwives are like us. Midwives are strange creatures. The forms of midwifery supervision also led, as Mongeau implies, to ever evolving patterns of front- and back-stage behavior. Part of the interactional dynamics involved nurses' quest to catch midwives who ignored the expected protocols and for midwives to avoid being caught. Susan Smith documents the "bag to go and bag to show" strategy by which Mississippi midwives kept an officially sanctioned bag solely for the purpose of inspection and used another for actual deliveries. Nurses and doctors knew of such deceptions, punishing midwives when discovered (Smith 1994, 34).

Another area of control was the clothing that midwives wore. As early as the 1920s, Virginia began to enforce a uniform code. Midwives were told to wear white caps and dresses or aprons when they attended women in childbirth. This concern was partly related to hygiene, but the use of this clothing symbolized the transformation of the midwife from the outside to the inside. In a sense, the African American practitioner was to be made into a "nurse's helper"—a semiprofessional. Just as important was the symbolism of the color white. The alien, somewhat frightening African American woman was to be made less primitive and more aesthetically pleasing. White clothing also befit the new categorization of birthing as a medical, scientific event, occurring under pristine conditions. In her discussion of this policy, Emily Bennett expressed the complex motivations that guided the public health department:

> Their [African American midwives'] clothes were not always clean, and in winter they wore woolen clothes. They said they must have "something warm" as they have to go out at night in all kinds of weather. A regulation cap and apron has been adopted in order to minimize the danger of infection from soiled clothing. The apron covers the entire dress, back and front, and the cap is large enough to cover all the hair. They are made of white material and make quite a difference in the appearance of the midwives. (Bennett 1925, 523)

Photographs from the 1940s and 1950s that appear in the *Virginia Health Bulletin* show midwives in clinic classrooms all dressed in regulation white dresses and hats. In one photograph, they sit in rapt attention as a white public health nurse demonstrates how to fill out a proper birth certificate. In another, a group of midwives cluster around a table while yet another nurse demonstrates how to wash and diaper an infant (a white doll). In a laudatory report on Bennett's efforts in Virginia, Carolyn Conant Van Blarcom, a national leader in obstetrical nursing during the first three decades of the century, commented on the transformation of the African American midwives who had undergone training. She described a midwifery education class held in a county clinic:

> The rows of pupils with tidy heads and hands, immaculate in their wash uniforms, might have been the staff of any visiting nurse association. There were no leathery, rheumy-eyed old crones. Only alert young women. Their bags with washable linings and appropriate contents, conformed to State Department of Health requirements. They were evidently put to practical use and were not merely for exhibition. The quizzing and responses were intelligent and showed that the midwives in that group had a good working idea of what could and should constitute their service; and more important, still, under what conditions they should summon a doctor and what they could not do for their patients. (Van Blarcom 1930, 331)

Here, then, was the vision of the properly socialized African American midwife. In many senses, these women with their "tidy heads and hands" represented for Van Blarcom and her white colleagues the perfect embodiment of the proper "Negro"—satisfied and happy with her place in the social and economic hierarchy. The coercive element in the uniform requirement tied it directly to appearance, to hygiene, and to birthing practice. Midwives could and did have their permits withdrawn because of their failure to wear the proper uniform, just as they could lose the right to practice if they were found doing internal examinations.

The use of the white uniform may have contributed to the midwives' sense that they were to be part of the permanent structure of the public health system. At the same time, however, older midwives were being "persuaded" to retire, according to the *Virginia Health Bulletin's* editor. These were the "unfit" midwives. Again, the methods used suggest that public health nurses acted on a set of presumptions about the simplicity of the African American mind. Thus, for example, women were actively pressured to "give up the work." In compensation, the board of health printed large "certificates of retirement" (appropriate for framing) that were given to older midwives, often with much offical puffery. Supposedly, these women would be satisfied with these certificates, unmindful of the fact that their craft and incomes had been appropriated. According to the *Virginia Health Bulletin*, "Many midwives who have served their communities well for many years are becoming too old to do such hard work and are being retired. An appropriate certificate of retirement is presented by the State Department of Health. In some instances suitable programs are held in their honor" (1951, 10).

In her study of the Florida midwifery control program, Susie writes that many women resented these retirement ceremonies. They felt coerced to retire, but there was little that they could do to challenge the officials (Susie 1988). In Virginia as well as in Florida (Dougherty 1978; Susie 1988), Mississippi (Roberts and Reeb 1994; Smith 1994), and North Carolina (Mongeau 1973), public health personnel often held these retirement programs in the midwife's church. Thus, they drew on the ritually powerful sanction of the midwife's God to approve the retirement. Having the ceremony in church also served to announce the retirement to the community at large. Given their coercive nature, these retirement ceremonies were not perceived by the midwife as the final recognition of her worth to both the community and public health (Bell 1993; Smith 1994). Indeed, the retirement ceremony almost perfectly inscripted the administrative power of midwifery regulation: the midwife faced sanctions should she seek to unretire herself.

The midwifery education and control program formed an integral part of Virginia's implementation of federal maternal and infant health care legislation. At the local level, we can examine the ways in which efforts to upgrade health care services were tied to existing racial attitudes toward African Americans and supported the professional dominance of medical practitioners. Education was offered to midwives with one hand, while the other attempted to take away their autonomy and eventually their craft.

What Does the Midwife Know?

Health initiatives gave midwives access to information about asepsis, nutrition, and contagious diseases, as well as the ability to recognize women who were likely to be at greater risk during pregnancy and childbirth as a result of preexisting illnesses (hypertension being the most dangerous). Over the course of Virginia's involvement in reproductive

As info/tech grew,

health care, more and more women were classified as "at risk" and judged unsuitable for home deliveries under the care of a midwife. The range of normality became increasingly narrowed until, by the 1950s, midwives found themselves without clients: all pregnant women were to be attended by a physician, preferably in a hospital setting. This, however, was the end point of a process. Until then, midwifery programs in Virginia combined education with restriction, support with antagonism.

Written sources and fieldwork offer every indication that midwives believed that they should and would be central participants in finding solutions to the health problems of women and children. Public health officials hoped that only a few "properly" trained women would remain during the transition phase and that eventually all midwives would be replaced by physicians. Reflective of the focus on gradual elimination, the *Virginia Health Bulletin,* looking back over three decades, lauded the Department of Health's successful efforts to reduce the numbers of active midwives: "At present there are 1,671 midwives in the State. In 1920 there were 5,916. In 1947, thirteen per cent of all deliveries in Virginia were by midwives; in 1920, the rate was 37 per cent. It may be significant that in 1947, 68 per cent of the deliveries in the State were in hospitals as compared with 15.4 per cent in hospitals in 1935, the first year the record was kept" (1949, n.p.).

What lie behind the numbers? These reflect an elemental and specific location of power in the hands and minds of medical professionals as the appointed representatives of local, state, and federal governments. They also reflect a certain bravado because public health personnel were always anxious about the efficacy of their information programs. The tension that emerges in the primary sources suggests a confidence in the numbers that showed that the fight against home births (equated with high infant and maternal mortality) was being won but uncertainty as to whether the numbers really reflected processes on the ground. As they attempted to assess midwifery knowledge, public health workers were well aware that midwives were not empty vessels waiting to be filled with new forms of knowledge and birthing skills. The gap between what midwives said they knew (utterances) and practices (what they did when attending women) continuously occupied the attention of public health personnel.

Researchers from the U.S. Public Health Services (USPHS) occasionally came to Virginia to conduct research on just these matters (Daniel and Gafafer 1935; Dewberry and Daniel 1936). Based on a study of midwives in rural Brunswick County, USPHS researchers concurred that the midwife was an impediment to the "progress of the practice of obstetrics" and that her "incompetence [was] a contributory cause of high infant and maternal mortality" (Dewberry and Daniel 1936, 1,507). They directly observed rural midwives after having administered a battery of knowledge inventory interviews. For example, midwives were asked, "What food other than breastmilk do you give the baby?" Boiled water received the highest score of 1. "Sugar bubby or a pinch of soda and water" received a score of "0," while answers such as "burnt feathers under the nose" or "raw red onion" or "snuff in the face" received a score of "-1." Having collected data to provide an index of discrepancy between what midwives knew and what they practiced, the authors concluded that "what the midwives said they taught their patients did not agree with what they taught on observation visits. Apparently much of the knowledge that the group obtained from 12 years of instruction and supervision was not of sufficient importance in their eyes to merit application" (Dewberry and Daniel 1936, 1,814). The path to authoritative knowledge was not as straight as public health personnel would have it: midwives took detours and moved between systems.

Pamphlets, manuals, and health bulletins alerted practitioner readers to the potential for breakdown in the transmission of knowledge. Mothers and midwives, nurses and midwives, and nurses and mothers were simultaneously drawn into alliances and conflict around the need for and uses of any specific part of the health information offered them. What the midwife knew would be a central occupation of the southern public health personnel.

Like it or not, by framing the issue of maternal and infant mortality as the midwifery problem and then by taking on the job of providing midwives with correct birthing and health knowledge, southern public health officials had to confront the African American midwife as a privileged knower and knowing subject. Here is a plea in a 1924 midwifery manual from Virginia's Department of Public Health authored by W. A. Plecker: "What are the most important things you should learn from these lessons? (a)WHEN YOU SHOULD CALL A DOCTOR. THAT YOU MUST BE CLEAN. (b) THE TERRIBLE RESPONSIBILITY THAT LIES IN YOUR HANDS. (c) A graduate nurse who spends three whole years studying these things would never undertake to deliver a baby if a doctor could be found. Her training has made her realize that the mother should have the very best possible care at this time" (Plecker 1924, 50).

The fear was that the midwife would assume too much authority. The goal was to inculcate her with a healthy respect for the professional know-how of the physician and the high level of technical expertise needed to attend childbirth. Contemporary portrayals reflect the struggle on the part of public health professionals to pin down the mind of the midwife, to classify her according to some general index of intelligibility and suitability.

For example, on a research visit to Virginia in the late 1920s, Carolyn Conant Van Blarcom, a white obstetrical nurse active on the Midwife Committee of the National Organization for Public Health Nursing, reported on the activities of African American midwives, or as she termed them, "these strange old people" (Van Blarcom 1930, 325). She subsequently published an article in *Harper's Monthly* titled "Rat pie: Among the Black Midwives of the South," a reference to a remedy used by these women in treating sick infants. Readers were introduced, for example, to Aunt Georgina, who carried a vial of "murky looking fluid" in a "small shining vanity case" that "she explained was April Snow Water for the new babies' eyes. 'Ain't nuttin' better . . . fo' babies eyes dan Ap'il snow wattah. Mah'ch snow is good, but Ap'il is de bes'" (Van Blarcom 1930, 326–27).

Van Blarcom sought to convince her audience that obstetrical care in the United States needed to be improved by "raising the status of the midwifery profession" (Van Blarcom 1914, 204). Training should be provided through accredited schools as in England, and midwives licensed as visiting nurses. (It is not clear from her writings whether she expected that African American women such as Aunt Georgina would receive the kind of training she advocated or would be simply replaced.) What better means of driving these points home than lampooning the rural southern Negro midwife? Such characterizations as a simple, perhaps even childlike mentality; an attraction to "shiny" objects; and an unerring faith in bogus remedies legitimized Van Blarcom's call to action and no doubt helped to mobilize her middle- and upper-class white readers.

In a prologue to the first in a series of articles on rural midwives appearing in the journal *Public Health Nurse*, Helen Moore, M.D., staff member of the American Child Health Association, evoked images of a primal battle between science and progress, good and evil: "Quietly, persistently, here and there forces are breaking through a wall of superstition and ignorance and throwing light upon what once seemed only darkness" (in Bennett 1925, 523). As if to reinforce this imagery, Emily Bennett, in sections of her article titled "Midwife Sketches" and "Some Midwife Superstitions," described the beliefs and attempts to reproduce the dialect of the southern "colored" midwife:

> One midwife remarked, "I tol my daughter-in-law, dat Lizzie, befo her fust baby come not to drink so much water case she might drown dat chile."

> During a meeting held in Essex County, the question was asked, "Are there any members here who would like to give up the work?" Aunt Judy Marshall, tall and black, arose and said, "Yes Ma'am, I is done come to the pint whar I specs to give up. I is done bin down here wid dese here folks all my life, and when dey gets in distress and calls for me I is been obleeged to git up and go, but I'm come to de pint now whar if dey calls dey will jes hafter keep on a callin', case I can't come." When asked why she had come to this decision she replied, "case on my last birthday I was seventy-nine years old, and den agin my second reason is dis: I am gwine to git married agin and my second husband he don' care to have me work." (Bennett 1925, 526)

Both Bennett and Van Blarcom portrayed the Negro midwife as somewhat charming in her misuse of the English language and ignorance of human anatomy but potentially dangerous to the welfare of the pregnant woman unless "constantly supervised" by professionals. Thus they constructed a characteristic type of African American midwife and used this model to argue for the medicalization of childbirth. In the passage from Bennett's article, the measured, tolerant questions of the white narrator are counterposed against Aunt Judy's impassioned and supposedly comical responses.

My intent here is to point to the emphases placed on the "exotica" of African American culture and to the contrast posed between midwifery and science. Often it appears that, more than the possible negative effects of traditional midwifery on infant and maternal mortality rates, it was the presence of "superstition" itself that unnerved medical personnel. In their almost formulaic references to the folk beliefs of the black midwife, it is as if Virginia's medical professionals wanted to convince themselves and the public of their own intrinsic worth as scientists and professionals. Ironically, although white doctors and nurses believed that midwives were "ignorant," superstitious illiterates belonging to a different and inferior culture, they also realized that in the sphere of childbirth, midwives could be, and indeed were, able competitors. Van Blarcom noted, for example that, bad as the midwife is, we are sorry to have to admit that on the whole a patient is probably better off in her hands than in the care of many of the physicians who compete with her (Van Blarcom 1930, 198).

In a manner similar to those of medieval (Ehrenreich and English 1978) and nineteenth-century physicians (Smith-Rosenberg 1985), Virginia's medical personnel reenacted a morality tale in which science and efficiency subdued the disorderly, murky world of the untrained midwife. African American midwives symbolically straddled the domain between womanly superstition/intuition and the alien world of "the Negro." For this reason, they represented, for both male physicians and female nurses, a final frontier on which the new scientific order had to be imposed. After all, "control" and "restriction" were the operative words in Virginia's campaign against midwifery. Furthermore, the routine inclusion of descriptions of the "colored" midwife in articles written by medical personnel no doubt formed part of a general concern with applying the methods of scientific observations to hitherto unexplored cultural domains: observation became the first step in an overall agenda to restructure the social relations of reproduction. Ethnographies of the midwife's mind proved part of the work of imposing authoritative knowledge, and it also proved the impossibility of ever being satisfied that the job had been fully done.

Midwives Teach the Nurse

Ideas about bringing light to the darkness of the midwife's minds expressed the nature of the relationship between the races, as well as between public health nurse and midwife. I have strongly argued for the largely unidirectional flow of authoritative knowledge even though midwives moved between multiple knowledge systems. Here I focus on public health nurses' depiction of reciprocal knowledge flow. Although midwives were never considered the equals of medical professionals, there was some acknowledgment that they had something to offer the nurses who taught them. Often in the secondary literature written during the period, African American midwives were said to have a "spiritual nature" and an ethic of care through which the professional public health nurse got in touch with feelings that had been pushed aside in their quest for professional status and technical competency.

Marie Campbell's *Folks Do Get Born* (1946), written in dialect, is a series of stories about midwives and public health nurses in midwifery education in Georgia during the 1930s and 1940s. Nurses, in Cambpell's work, say that they "learn from the midwives—largely things of the spirit." The midwife is the embodiment of patience, obedience, and good humor. Another nurse remarks on her realization through her work with midwives that "faith is necessary, beautiful, powerful, and practical"; another now knows that "contentment with very little is a very wonderful thing." After an initial intolerance, a nurse comes to defend her midwives, "justly proud of any least improvement they make" (Campbell 1946, 42). The midwife emerges in these tellings as primarily having contributed to nurses' moral development. She is intuitive, self-sacrificing, and nurturant. James Ferguson, in his description of midwives in Mississippi, calls them "natural nurses" (1950, 86). If the midwife could be trained, she offered nurses an image of uncomplaining childbirth practice, while, never, in the nurses' perception, challenging the boundaries of racial segregation.

The interaction between nurse and midwife offered an opportunity for personal transformation. It is revealing, nonetheless, that the domain of midwifery expertise was understood as primarily located in a set of inherent features: the midwife becomes emblematic of the historical image of the "mammy." An idealized figure of the domesticated slave woman, she exists mainly to nurture and give solace to her white charges, who have lost their way. She inhabited an essentially embodied realm of nature, not culture. She was versed in things of the body, not the mind, given to compliance rather than resistance (Hill-Collins 1990; Christian 1985). Ideas about race and gender overlapped in these images: the midwife was the antithesis of professional nursing but at the same time harkened back to prior ideas about nursing being located in the blood and genes rather than being acquired as a set of professional skills (Hine 1989; Reverby 1987).

Patricia Hill-Collins uses the metaphor of the "stranger" to characterize the negative symbology of African American women in American culture. It is an apt one here to describe how the midwife was viewed through racial and professional lenses. "Strangers," Hill-Collins writes, "threaten the moral and social order," yet "they are . . . essential for its survival because those individuals who stand at the margins of society clarify its boundaries" (Hill-Collins 1990, 68). By her very difference, the midwife affirmed the special nature of public health nursing. Because she was African American, she also reaffirmed for white nurses the inherent authority of the hierarchy that placed them at the apex of the nursing profession. And at the same time, being among the "stranger" allowed the white nurse to redefine her own sense of self.

6

The Logic of Prenatal Care

Sheila Rothman heralds the medical gains made as a result of the activities of "educated women [who] instill[ed] in other women a broad knowledge of the rules of bodily hygiene and in this way prevent[ed] the onset of disease" (Rothman 1978, 136). In this positivist vein, it is easy for scholars to ignore the negative manifestations of supposed medical and social advances. Was it coincidental that the national push for prenatal care and "improved" maternal health in the early twentieth century (implemented in Virginia as part of the movement to regulate midwives) occurred at a time when many whites spoke of the fear of "race suicide"—that is, racial "mongrelization" by mixture with immigrant blood in the North and "Negro" blood in the South?

Early feminists such as Lydia Kingsmill Commander believed that the problem would be best solved by white women having fewer, healthier children of greater intelligence. These qualitatively better people would be fitted for the technologically superior nation in the making. Others blamed the situation on racial and ethnic "admixture" and advocated policies to encourage "pure" breeding (Chase 1978). Still others, President Theodore Roosevelt among them, believed that the problem was primarily a quantitative one in which women of pure Anglo-Saxon descent (as opposed to Italians, Jews, and "Slavs") were delaying marriage and having too few children (Chase 1978; Commander 1907). Proponents of this view berated the "family planning propaganda," as one Virginia physician put it, of women such as Margaret Sanger (Baughman 1928). Whatever the course of the problem, however, prenatal care was one means of producing vigorous, smart, and competitive Caucasian

125

stock. From this perspective, any Anglo-Saxon woman could contribute to nation-building by availing herself of prenatal and maternal care.

But what of the African American woman? When she accepted the "gift" of prenatal and maternal care, she was forced to accept the cultural order that relegated her and her offspring to an inferior status. The children of these "inferior, prolific" women were not expected to contribute to the "upbuilding of the American nation" (Commander 1907, 230). Motivations for the insertion of medical authority in the bodies of women differed radically depending on the implied and explicit objectives of the polity and on the social construction of race. When Barbara Duden writes of the twentieth-century construction of the "needy body" that has to be serviced by appropriate health professionals, she describes a process that took many forms and evolved along with the development of industrial capitalism. As she suggests, "the needy body and the productive society fit each other" (Duden 1985, 7).

Virginia's efforts to control and eliminate births attended by midwives may be seen as part of the creation of female bodies dependent on scientific medicine. But the state was also concerned that women contribute more fully to the development of the economy by the allocation of a greater portion of the family's disposable income to reproductive health care, and by a drastically reduced period in which they were removed from the productive sphere after childbirth. Virginia's Dr. Harry Ware Jr. put it succinctly when he reminded his colleagues that the "function of the obstetrician" was "first to deliver the woman of a healthy living child with the minimum of injury to her general condition . . . [and] second to leave her in such physical condition that she may be an economic asset to her family and community" (Ware 1931, 246).

Yet what is already a complex tale about the links between medical science, the body, and industrial capitalism becomes even more complicated when the racial inequalities of American society during the period in question and the intersection of race and gender are added to the narrative. As an example of the complexity of the problem, consider how a seemingly beneficial medical concern with prenatal care in the first three decades of the twentieth century might be subjected to an alternative interpretation.

When a white and an African American woman came into one of Virginia's newly formed prenatal clinics in the middle of the 1920s, both were acquiescing to the authority of medical men, engaged in a reinterpretation of their bodies as "needy"—subject to monitoring and professional preparation for childbirth. In one sense, the focus on woman as responsible for the "production of healthy children" (Rosenberg and Rosenberg 1973, 338; Ehrenreich and English 1978), articulated in the late nineteenth century and still an important ideological concern through the 1930s (Chase 1978; Smith 1984; Wiebe 1977), potentially bound women, regardless of race, to fixed roles based on their shared biology. According to a professor of obstetrics at the Medical College of Virginia, "motherhood" was "one of the most important functions of woman" (Baughman 1929, 849).

The underlying consequences of seeking out prenatal care, however, could be dramatically different for African American and white women and their children. In a society that maintained a racial and economic pyramid where Anglo-Saxons "always rested at the top" and African Americans provided the "innately inferior" (Wiebe 1977, 157) but vital labor force, the new emphasis on prenatal care in the early twentieth century enclosed bitter ironies.

Assuming that prenatal health care was offered on an equal basis to all, which it was not, what were the overall benefits for African American women and their children of being healthier if they would be unable, in the view of the majority of whites, of ever gaining economic or social parity? Such contradictions existed not only in the South or among social conservatives. "We are sure," an otherwise radical northern feminist wrote, "that a negro even though he were educated at Yale, rode in automobiles, practiced a profession, trafficked in real estate or traveled around the world and wrote a book about it would still remain a negro. He would not be a particle the more Caucasian for all his 'white' experiences. It is because of the deep and ineradicable racial differences, that we have in this country a negro problem, Indian reservations and Chinese exclusion" (Commander 1907, 59).

Thus, to extend this argument, even with the best maternal and infant care, whites assumed that African Americans would retain what they had defined as inferior traits. For them, it would be impossible for a "Negro" really to participate in American society, except in the narrow boundaries that had been reserved for him or her. In the case of maternal and infant health care, African Americans received few of the idealized rewards of scientific progress and permanently lost much of that which had helped to sustain them.

While the professionalization of childbirth had resulted in some impressive gains for white women and their children, African Americans still lagged far behind. At base, the programs developed by the state and supported by physicians never really addressed the root causes of poor maternal and infant health—poverty and severely imbalanced access to resources—among African Americans. Donzelot (1979) has argued that in return for control of life processes, the state offered its citizens individual well-being. Yet even this exchange, imbalanced though it may have been for white women, was never completed for most African Americans. They were denied participation in the political process, and at the same time were given few opportunities to fairly compete in order to attain personal and familial health and fulfillment.

Despite this inbuilt inequity, however, my field data and the primary sources suggest that, although relegated to the margins of the social structure, African Americans were part of the audience that the state wished to reach. This presents an interwoven set of circumstances that I do not expect to unravel completely in the confines of this chapter. The administering of prenatal care serves as a good example of the contradictions. On the one hand, the emphasis on prenatal care formed part of the ideology of "race building" among whites; on the other, it was also used to draw African Americans under the authority of the state and medical science. How did this work? For one thing, as I have already argued, at least in the South, the autonomous African American midwife challenged both medical and governmental authority. Prenatal care, the "carrot" for women, served a dual purpose: it offered women the possibility of having perfect, healthy children and safe childbirth, and it was a means by which, physicians believed, the midwife "problem" could be solved. In Virginia, for example, physicians paired their effort to convince women of the utility of prenatal care with the campaign against midwives:

> As to just what sort of prenatal care we are trying to get over; of course what we try to impress on these women is the fact that they must stay away from the midwives, and then we urge them to place themselves under the care of a physician as soon as they discover that they are pregnant (Plecker 1933, 84).

> The solution to the midwife problem is along the lines that the State Board of Health has already started—to try to educate the public as to prenatal care by means of courses of instruction (Baughman 1928, 750).

The reproductive capacities of African American women, and the life processes of African Americans in general, also had to be controlled and regulated. In order to do this, it was important to convince African Americans that scientific medicine was the better moral choice. Furthermore, although they may have initially resisted the insertion of medical authority in the private realm of childbirth, and although my informants in Green River County continue to express ambivalence about this situation, it is also clear that they also believed that the acceptance of medical science was for the individual and collective good.

Thus the efforts to eliminate midwifery was part of an overall movement to gain control of the reproductive sphere. The arguments of Virginia's physicians—that the midwife was primitive, dirty, and potentially dangerous—fit with the new social policies that were being drafted from 1900 to 1950. If African Americans wished to distance themselves from these negative images, then one choice would be to reject the cultural practices and beliefs associated with midwifery. Thus the dominant ideology of racial inferiority could be used to exert control both over the bodies of African American and white women, while appearing at the same time to be providing "equality of opportunity," to use Woodrow Wilson's phrase, through the health care system. Although the intentions of the social feminists who encouraged government intervention may have been worthy, they, too, subscribed to a point of view that contributed to the oppression of African American women.

With their bodies under the care of physicians, African Americans would also share in the benefits of medical progress—or so they were led to believe by the federal government and by medical personnel. At least on the surface, a reduction in the number of midwives could be used as an indication that medical practitioners and the state were making gains in bettering the conditions for all poor women and their children. Paradoxically, between 1900 and 1930, public health officials as well as physicians also realized that medical facilities were unavailable for most African American women. Thus an effective strategy was to retire as many of the traditional midwives as was possible and to replace them with a corps of younger women trained by public health nurses. Without providing the full benefits of medical science, the government could exert control over African Americans in the South. One wonders about the extent to which the intervention of the state in health care during the early-twentieth-century helped to subvert organized protest among disenfranchised and impoverished African Americans.

Certainly the underlying logic of public health programs diverted attention away from structural conditions and toward the individual's role in maintaining his or her own health. In regard to maternal and infant health care, collection of data related to maternal and infant health isolated the causes of infant and maternal mortality. Researchers investigated what they termed the "conditions connected with childbirth." These included studies of housing, economic status, birth attendants, parental attitudes, cultural beliefs, and other explicitly nonmedical variables that potentially affected the outcome of pregnancies.

For example, Julia Lathrop, the Children's Bureau's first director, wrote that "children are not safe and happy if their parents are miserable, and parents must be miserable if they cannot protect their home against poverty. [T]he power to maintain a decent family living standard is the primary essential of child welfare" (Perkins 1937, 15). In research reports, however, the bureau's investigations into the "conditions of child life" found no "direct correlation between industrial, social, [and] economic conditions and deaths of infants in the early days of life" (Bolt 1929, 3).

In the instances where income appeared to be a factor, researchers such as Frances Bradley (1924), for example, a physician who spearheaded the bureau's rural public health service, focused on the negative effects when the mother had to work. Under these circumstances, she believed that "overwork and anxiety" were predisposing factors in infant and maternal mortality. Thus the problem was not poverty itself but rather the negative physiological effects of working on the mother's and fetus's health. By educating rural women about the importance of medical care during pregnancy, and by encouraging rural physicians to practice preventive medicine, the bureau believed that the health of children and, therefore, the nation would be "protected."

Solutions inevitably focused on the ways in which good health care could overcome most problems. The very terms of such research implied that the judicious actions of government working through the sciences (especially the medical sciences) could be used to control what had been previously thought to be natural or inevitable and to modify that which was culturally inappropriate. Thus researchers for the Children's Bureau wrote of the "fatalistic" attitudes of rural mothers who were "ignorant" of "the dangers connected to childbirth" (Meigs 1917, 24). They called for the development of scientific standards of child care that could

be taught to mothers, particularly among the immigrant and rural population.

Giving women greater access to information that could reduce the
risks associated with childbirth was in itself a good policy. A hidden
dimension of the search for causation and control, however, was the
implied assumption that once controls were in place, those who "failed"
to raise themselves out of poverty, to take the advice of experts, to avail
themselves of medical care, or to dissociate themselves with nontradi-
tional practitioners were simply inadequate, "ignorant," or incompetent.
With this in mind, one is able to make greater sense of how Virginia's
medical personnel looked upon prenatal care when it became a health
care issue after the mid-1920s. Women and midwives who "neglected"
this part of the pregnancy had morally, if not legally, transgressed medical
norms that were in effect gradually becoming societal ones (Ehrenreich
and English 1978; Zelizer 1985).

The logic that supported the infant and maternal hygiene movement
led to decidedly unscientific analytic conclusions. In a study of maternal
and infant mortality in Virginia, for example, the researcher found that in
a sample of patients who underwent cesarean section in a Richmond
hospital, the death rate for African American women was four times
greater than for whites. The rate of stillbirths was 24 percent for African
Americans and 2.4 percent for whites. In addition, fewer African American women used these segregated hospital facilities available to them. In
explaining the results, the physician-researcher concluded that "an important factor in this [the figures] may be the indifference of Negro
women to prenatal care and to medical care at the time of delivery. The
stillbirth rate . . . for Negroes is undoubtedly due to the frequency of
syphilis in Negroes and to the indifference of these women to physicians
and hospitals until complications have appeared" (Ware 1936, 83).

The theme of the indifferent or careless African American mother
appeared in medical and public health journals throughout the period
under study, but especially after the 1920s. Once prenatal care had been
established as the cure for high maternal and infant mortality rates, the
continued high rates among African Americans had to be explained. The
failures of the polity's public health programs and of physicians and
nurses were shifted onto the shoulders of the victims. Few investigators
looked beyond this easy remedy; just as the midwife could be blamed, so,
too, could the African American mother.

In the 1940s, the Medical Society of Virginia established a panel of physicians (the Maternal Health Committee) to investigate maternal deaths that had occurred in the state's hospitals. During their investigations, panel members interviewed, when possible, the attending physician or midwife, family members, and hospital personnel. This procedure was the first consistent attempt to critically examine the practice of obstetrics in the state, but often in their classification of "preventable deaths," the review board judged the deceased woman at least partially, if not fully, responsible for her own death or the death of her child. In their case reports, the investigators based such judgments on two criteria: the woman's "failure" to properly interpret and act on the physical "danger signals" of her body, or her negligence in not seeking out adequate prenatal care. Again, the flawed assumption held by the investigators was that these were deliberate or avoidable actions on the part of women who "failed" to take advantage of readily available health resources. As I have argued, few African Americans had access to affordable medical care even after passage of the Sheppard-Towner Act and the lobbying efforts of the Children's Bureau.

Consider the following "selected case of maternal death." It is typical of those highlighted in the *Virginia Medical Monthly* during the 1940s:

> The patient was a 23 year old colored multipara with one previous pregnancy who was seen at home by a physician at the eighth month of pregnancy [and was] in labor for fifteen hours and had been bleeding in excess [and] passing some fairly large clots. She gave the history of having had some painless vaginal bleeding periodically for one week before the onset of labor. After observing the patient for one hour of labor without progress and with continued bleeding, the physician referred her to a hospital. (Maternal Heath Committee 1942, 335)

By the time she arrived at the hospital, the young woman had lost approximately a pint of blood and "about a quart during delivery." A cesarean section resulted in a stillborn infant weighing five pounds. "Though a suitable donor was obtained," she was not given a transfusion, and when such an attempt was made eleven hours after her surgery, "she died before it could be started" (Maternal Health Committee 1942, 345). To what degree was her race a factor in physicians' treatment of this young woman? It is impossible to draw any firm conclusions some forty-five years later. Yet it is obvious that her life was not highly valued by the hospital's medical personnel.

The review panel noted that "the most serious failure on the part of the physician was the failure to replace blood loss by blood plasma, or fluids." The transfusion should have been "done first rather than attempted last." In addition, the panel reported that the "administration of blood or plasma should have continued through the delivery and afterwards until the patient had recovered from the hemorrhage" (Maternal Health Committee 1942, 35). In the view of the panel, this procedure was the "approved method of treatment." Yet my argument here rests not so much on the medical treatment but rather on the panel's final conclusions. Despite the admitted gross errors in medical judgment, the greatest blame seemed to fall on the patient: "This has been classified as a preventable obstetrical death, because of the absence of prenatal care, the failure to seek medical attention at the onset of the bleeding [the sign of danger]. These failures were due to neglect or ignorance on the part of the patient and her family" (Maternal Health Committee 1942, 335).

If we accept the premise that prenatal care was readily available to this young mother, then in some twisted logic the infant's stillbirth may have been "caused" by her failure to take advantage of such care. Even on the basis of this assumption, however, certainly the mother's death was in no way a result of her "inattention" to prenatal care. One need not be a medical expert to realize that she died as a direct result of the tremendous amount of blood lost during surgery.

Even with the distance of time, the injustice of the investigators' conclusion and of the tendency to blame African American women for the high rates of maternal and infant deaths is painful to consider. Regretfully, the literature tells nothing about the anguish of African American women and their families. A trip to the hospital during pregnancy must have been filled with anxiety. It was, given the statistics, a place for dying during childbirth. But lest the focus be shifted to the actions of a single physician in a single case, it is vital to realize that the very structure of health care and the economic system in Virginia normalized the circumstances that led to the death of the "23 year old colored multipara." The ideology of prenatal care—in which "good advice" and "cleanliness" was to solve all the problems faced by rural, poor women—legitimized the racist assumption that African Americans suffered because they were "indifferent" or "bad mothers."

With the virtual elimination of midwives by the end of the 1950s, women had little choice but to use the hospital. In the final irony, physicians found themselves overburdened and incapable of dealing with the influx of new patients, most of whom were poor and African American. In 1966, one physician, in some desperation, noted that "the old-fashioned uneducated midwife is fast disappearing, prenatal clinics have educated the poor who once employed them, and the ease of getting to a hospital where an intern or staff doctor will deliver them has eliminated the granny almost completely in many areas where she was popular even a decade ago" (Jones 1966, 173).

Although he did not wish to return to the era of the midwives' dominance, this doctor wondered with some seriousness if there was "a place for [trained] nurse-midwives" who would attend to indigent cases. Jones portrays himself as the martyr-physician forced to deliver the babies of African American women who, in a revealing merging of categories, he suggests are both indigent and "abnormal" parturients. Such patients stand in contrast to the "private," normal, and, we can assume, white patients who could afford his services and whom he preferred to treat: "A normal parturient is a blessing to her physician: for one thing, she softens the sting of the abnormal ones. Private patients will always be private patients—we hope. But what of the flood of indigent patients who have turned from and will turn from their old grannies and are pouring into the hundreds of excellent community hospitals which are unable to find interns?" (Jones 1966, 173).

In the end, birth for African American and poor women indeed had been transformed into a medical crisis as they found themselves in the emergency rooms of urban hospitals under the care of anonymous, resentful physicians. Here is a frustrated doctor Jones again lamenting his fate: "One month the writer delivered twenty of these women who he had never seen before, most of whom just dropped into the emergency room in labor, without having any prenatal care. Such a load on top of a normal practice plays havoc with rest, to say nothing of office hours" (Jones 1966, 173).

Virginia's public health and medical personnel successfully used the issue of prenatal care and the specter of unhygienic, high-risk births to argue against and eliminate midwives. They were unsuccessful, however,

in replacing them with easily accessible, considerate medical practitioners. But as Jones's complaints suggest, the problem was never formulated in these terms. Instead, the blame was placed squarely on the
shoulders of pregnant women, who were seen as negligent in not seeking prenatal care and perhaps even responsible for their own impoverishment.

In the end, Jones rejected his own call for nurse midwives. From the
thrust of his argument, it seems that these would have been young white
women, nurse graduates as he termed them, not African Americans.
These women would undoubtedly in Jones's fantasy be more malleable
and respectful of science and scientific men than the "grannies" had ever
been. Yet Dr. Jones feared that his proposal was but the "dream of a peri-
odically exhausted obstetrician." One of the major drawbacks of such a
program, he believed, was that "nurses graduate to marriage so quickly
that one often wonders how much point there is in extensive nursing
education" (Jones 1966, 175).

Jones's dismay crystallized the issues that rested beneath the romance
of professional childbirth throughout the first half of the twentieth century. The ideology of prenatal care and of professional childbirth had
ignored the economic conditions at the root of poor maternal and infant
health. Perhaps the elimination of traditional midwives served an important purpose by exposing the myth that they had been the source of
such problems. But this had been a heavy price to pay, and it appears
that medical personnel continue to emphasize narrowly defined health
issues.

In the public health clinic in Green River County, staffed by white
medical personnel, nurses continued to complain about young African
American mothers who did not take advantage of prenatal care programs. This, one nurse believed, was a consequence of these women's
"fatalistic" attitude toward childbirth. The majority of poor women only
came to the clinic in the final trimester of pregnancy so that they would
have the appropriate funding authorization for the hospital. During my
stay in the mid-1980s, a new federal grant had been received to study
and attempt to rectify high infant mortality rates in the county. Yet
"community outreach programs" that invited women and families to
monthly meetings to address the problem were largely unsuccessful.
Few, if any, mothers attended.

As to their avoidance of the clinic, some women with whom I spoke related experiences of rough treatment in the hospital. Nonetheless, although they individually resisted such treatment, they rarely challenged the "appropriateness" of birth in the hospital. They agreed with older women that this was the modern and better way to do things. Midwives had been part of a superstitious past. Few realized that embedded within that now maligned past had been other possibilities that would not have turned the event of childbirth into a battle for considerate and respectful care. Yet given the history of the campaign against midwifery and the larger political and economic context within which it occurred, I, too, struggle to envision other outcomes that would have nurtured African American philosophies of the body and rituals of childbirth.

III

Memory and Experience

7

On Silence and Memory

It must have been the third Sunday after my arrival in Green River county. My landlady invited me to church. At the same time, members of the congregation got the chance to sum me up. I expressed my general interest in the "home remedies" that people used during the time when medicines and doctors were not readily available. I said that I wanted to learn about these things because they were important and valuable. Then, I further mentioned my interest in the midwives who used to deliver babies at home. People nodded their heads in welcome and what seemed to be interest. But although some members of the congregation stopped to talk to me afterwards and invited me to their homes to discuss the "old folk's remedies," no one made mention of midwives or of their experiences with home births.

Eventually, after similar experiences in other churches, I realized that even though I would be later told that most midwives had been devout, Christian women, my discussion of these subjects in a church setting had been highly inappropriate. Even outside the context of church, older residents who were normally enthusiastic when discussing their families, the community's farming past, their illnesses and personal tragedies, or the home medicinals that formerly were an everyday part of their lives skirted the issue of midwives and home births.

Slavery and Past Time

The records in the state archives and at the county courthouse are largely irrelevant when African Americans relate the history of these communities—persons related through church, marriage, and "blood." For most of the elderly with whom I spoke, landownership and worship in their own churches are the important historical reference points. These events signify the creation of independent communities and independent people in the latter part of the nineteenth century. In many senses, it is as if they were people sprung anew in the 1890s, untouched by slavery's demoralization. Informants did speak about the brutality of whites during slavery, but they also suggested that slaves themselves became defiled in the process. Thus slavery was more than institutionalized oppression, it is given the character of a disease or malady that African Americans were forced to endure.

Two views of slavery time parallel each other. County whites declare that their ancestors "freed all their slaves," thus absolving their forefathers and themselves of any guilt, whereas African Americans often distance themselves from the reality of their ancestor's enslavement. "Praise the Lord," one elderly woman told me, "none of my family's blood is tainted by slavery." Both blacks and whites in the county retell the stories of their own communities and families as they would have it be told. A comparative discussion of whites' and blacks' reconstruction of the past is an important part of the story. But it is not one that I am going to tell. Instead, I am interested in the dynamic involved in African Americans' reworking of the past, the more recent as well as the far past.

Older informants would often refer to four levels of past time. "Slavery times" was a period with no clear boundaries but roughly corresponded to the period before the 1890s. Two categories of past time have no specific names. Nonetheless, distinctions were routinely made between what I have termed the "far past," from about 1900 to the 1940s, and the "near past," from the 1950s onwards. These two time spans overlap with the early childhood through young adulthood of older residents who ranged in age from ninety to the early sixties. Comparisons between past and present usually related to these two time periods. In this context, the immediate present, the fourth division of time, was included in discussions of "today" or "nowadays," as in "things are done different today" or "nowadays you can't doctor a child like you used to." In the reconstruction of the past and representation of the present, these categories of time provided the framework on which narratives about transformations in both the medical world and the African American community were discussed and explained.

For many older African American residents, "slavery times" is part of a past best forgotten. It is a past in which, unlike whites who erect public statuary to the Civil War dead and to Revolutionary War heroes, African Americans in the community believe they do not have a stake. This is not to say that slavery time disappears from memories. Rather, it provides a frame of reference for distinguishing between the "acceptable" and "unacceptable" past.

An illustration should clarify this concern. A common response from older residents to questions about aspects of traditional medicine that are now classified as "superstition" would be to say, "Oh, that's only how they used to do it during slavery times." I received such a response, for example, when I asked about the practice of tying necklaces of asofetida or garlic around the necks of infants and toddlers to ward off misfortune. More than six months after our initial meeting, a seventy-year-old woman whose grandmother had provided such necklaces for all her grandchildren confided to me that most children wore these protective amulets, hidden under their clothing, well into the 1930s. Furthermore, children thought to be sickly were made to wear these amulets even after they reached school age. In the schoolhouse, on a winter's day with the woodstove stoked high and windows closed, she recalled that "the room stinked to high heaven" with the combined aroma of garlic and asofetida.

What concerns me here is not the question of historical reliability. I want to point to the different ways in which the past was reconstructed in this community. For those who wish to distance themselves from the tradition of folk medicine that has been greatly devalued by the dominant culture, by health care personnel, and by the younger generation, "slavery times" provides both a means of explaining such practices to the outside world and to themselves. Because these people believe that such information does not reflect well on the county's African Americans, they relegate it to a period of time when such practices came about because "people didn't know any better and couldn't do any better." On the other hand, for others, there is no shame in talking about "the old folk's remedies." But even that statement can be further refined. Home remedies included both herbal treatments applied directly to the body and those whose efficacy entailed the supernatural, the world of things not seen. The asofetida necklaces straddle the boundary between these two categories, for they involved the use of "medicine" but were directed at the nonmaterial, spiritual causation of illness and disease.

For the first category, analogies are easily found in modern medicines:

homemade cough syrups and poultices, for example. The second category of remedies has been most maligned and diverges to a greater extent from scientific medical practice. These remedies are remembered with greater ambivalence and are more likely associated with "slavery times." In either situation, however, people make judgments about what part of their history is to be in the public domain.

The Said and Unsaid

Determining the boundaries of what constituted illicit, secret, invisible, or shameful knowledge, however, was far from a simple task. Neither has it been easy, in writing, to give a name to the dense mix of attitudes and perceptions that characterized the relationship of the members of Green River's African American community to traditional birthing and midwifery. To unravel the ambiguities, or at least to see them more clearly, a distinction is necessary. That is, the reasons for reserve in talking about birth did not mirror reasons for reserve in bringing the history of midwives into the open. Significant areas of overlap were discernible, but these are best understood by examining the different reasons why birth and midwifery belonged to a restricted domain of discourse.

Midwives and Oxcarts: Poverty and Stigma

Midwives were central participants in community life, yet some were perceived as different and perhaps frightening. The conflicting nature of the roles they played no doubt influenced the ways in which knowledge about them was constructed and presented, or not presented, to me. Mrs. Wayne, a woman in her early seventies, told me that "some of the midwives we looked up to, but not all." Another woman argued that safe births at home had largely been a matter of luck, for, as she sarcastically put it, "those midwives didn't know no more about delivering babies than I did." Are such attitudes to be understood as alienation from the past, as a consequence of the discourse that accompanied the rise of obstetrical science in Virginia, or as an expected ambiguous cultural response to such powerful, liminal figures as midwives? The material from Green River County allows for no simple answers.

I am unable to say, for example, whether the woman who referred to midwives' "luck" would have done so in the 1940s when a significant number of children were still being born at home under the guidance of midwives. Was she reevaluating midwives with new eyes or expressing a long-held opinion? Ironically, this woman, now in her late sixties, had used a midwife for three of her pregnancies, while her mother's thirteen children had all been born at home with a midwife in attendance. In other conversations, she acknowledged that her mother's generation knew a great deal about "getting along" and about "doing things for themselves." Her disdain, therefore, may have been less a denunciation of midwives and more an expression of her sense that, because of her poverty, she had been unable to choose between birthing options. In looking back, therefore, she interpreted her experience as having been forced to rely on the "midwives' luck." Such feelings may have been engendered by a particularly painful or frightening home birth. Because the issues are so complex, it is important to describe the variety of people's responses to the subjects of birthing and midwifery, only then will we begin to tease out the layers of meaning and to understand why certain subjects were categorized as restricted while others were not.

Waiting on women during childbirth was the central but by no means the only responsibility undertaken by midwives. They were also the individuals who normally washed and prepared the dead for burial—an activity that other women shunned. Unafraid of the corpse and thought to have spiritual gifts, some midwives also were believed to have the ability to "conjure," which entailed using certain roots, potions, and rituals to influence a person's behavior in one's favor or to cause harm. Their involvement in birth and death, their supposed ability to mediate between the real and supernatural world, and their authority in spheres of knowledge closed off to ordinary persons meant that midwives had been regarded with what might be described as awe. While it is impossible to delineate all the explicit connections, the negative campaign of medical personnel may have overlayered existing ambivalent attitudes toward these women. Conversations about midwives, in the present, often evoked a combination of awe and respect, as informants attempted to situate these women (now rendered powerless) within the context of a changed social world.

I remember sitting in a room one evening with four women (two sisters, their cousin, and a childhood friend) all well past their sixties. We had been talking about home remedies, illness, and recent deaths in the community (one a suicide), all somber subjects, when the conversation turned to midwifery. The women began to generate a list of midwives who had practiced in their part of the county. As they called out names to one another, corrected or corroborated one another's memories, they often broke out into nervous giggles. Except for Ms. Jenkins, who didn't have any biological children, the other women had all been waited on by midwives. But they did not elaborate on this aspect of their experience. There was a sense in which the memories evoked by these women seemed to have been from their youth, before they had themselves borne children:

> *Mrs. Rose:* Aunt Margaret Jameson, now she was a midwife, Louisa Jones, Rubelle White, Olga Perkins, they all waited on women around here in this community.
>
> *Mrs. Wayne:* [*her sister, interrupting*] That's right, Aunt Olga Perkins, and she used to do some conjure. [*giggles*] We was all scared of her. [*more laughter*]
>
> *Mrs. Rose:* [*explaining to me*] See, they were not what you call professionals, but doctors couldn't get to the patient. . .
>
> *Ms. Jenkins:* [*cousin, picking up the naming*] Aunt Dolly Miller.
>
> *Mrs. Rose:* She wasn't no midwife!
>
> *Ms. Jenkins:* I ain't never thought about it. She looked like a midwife. Big full black skirt, a white apron, and she was big, jet black and fat. [*more laughter*]
>
> *Mrs. Wayne:* Who else?
>
> *Mrs. Overton:* [*friend*] Aunt Sula Scott, Aunt Martha Howell.
>
> *Mrs. Rose:* [*interrupting*] Aunt Martha Howell? No, she wasn't no midwife. She was too much of a devil. [*infectious laughter*]

These women did not discredit midwives as a group. In fact, as they named midwives, they were concerned with separating the "good" ones from the "bad." This concern with distinguishing between good and bad practitioners is a vital part of the Afro-Caribbean and African American folk medical tradition (see, for example, Rocereto 1973; Snow 1978; Hall and Bourne 1973; Hill and Mathews 1981; Jackson 1976). For the women in this dialogue, midwives were individuals with differing personalities, strengths, and foibles. Such a view differs from those of the doctors and nurses who wrote in medical journals and represented midwives as a relatively undifferentiated mass. Furthermore, while these women preferred not to discuss their birth experiences, they showed no hesitation in acknowledging that they had delivered their children at home with a midwife in attendance. Nevertheless, despite their relative willingness to remember and talk about midwives, there was a particular edge and excitement to the conversation, especially around the issue of a particular midwife's ability to manipulate the supernatural.

Concerns of a different sort were at play when some informants actively distanced themselves from the history of midwifery because of its association with "backwardness" or because it is now considered to have signified low economic or social status. Admitting to either having knowledge about midwives or having used their services was perceived as somewhat shameful. Some descendants and clients of midwives completely avoided discussing their relatives even when they willingly spoke to me on other matters related to the community's past. In the county, home births attended by midwives came increasingly to be seen by members of the African American community as lower-status care rather than the normative choice of the majority of families. To admit to having used midwives, therefore, hinted at a failed morality on at least two levels. First, it suggested that one's family had been too poor to call a doctor. Second, and perhaps more damning, it implied that even when offered a "better" alternative, some woman and their families had continued to rely on attendants who had been categorized as inferior by medical personnel.

Being poor had not always been seen as a shameful condition. When speaking about their childhoods, people would invariably comment that "we didn't even think of ourselves as poor because everybody else was going without." Yet that way of life now carried a certain stigma, the dimensions of which were never made fully clear to me but in part encoded a set of assumptions about "laziness," "absence of ambition," illiteracy, an inability to manage resources or to curb one's sexuality so as to limit family size.

Although the association of poverty with moral failure was not wholly accepted, many individuals nonetheless selectively filtered out references that might suggest that their families had been impoverished. This process of selection varied, but there were shared references across narratives. Commonplace activities or objects took on symbolic meaning; they became culturally shared signs that marked the distinction between the acceptable and the unacceptable past—what was appropriate and not appropriate to publicly remember.

Like the midwife, the oxcart, for example, often appeared in narratives
as a sign of shameful poverty. Older residents easily remembered that
oxen were used as plow animals. Yet they characterized as low status and
undesirable the use of these animals to transport people. The process by
which this particular use of oxen took on a discredited place in the
memories of residents is outside the immediate domain of the chapter. In
conversations, however, oxcarts and midwives were treated similarly, as
were other past practices that my informants now classified as shameful.

Usually, the nature and content of what was acceptable and not acceptable to remember about the past emerged in group conversations rather
than in dialogues between myself and a single informant. In the following conversation, for example, there is contestation about the use of
oxcarts. The exchange occurred between three elderly sisters who were
born and raised in the county. They were all gathered at the home of
the eldest sister's daughter, who was very ill. I visited one early after-
noon, and our conversation turned to the early childhood of these three
women—Louise, the eldest at seventy-eight; Josephine, seventy-two;
and Ruth, seventy. The two younger women had worked in New York
before retiring to the country a few years earlier. It was clear, however,
that despite their experiences in the city, they deferred to Louise, who
had, as they characterized it, "helped Mother to raise us" after their
father died when the youngest was only two.

> *Louise:* Before Papa died, we were in right good circumstances. He
>   always had two horses.
> *Josephine:* [*interrupts with laughter*] Yes, but some people used to
>   have oxcarts. They would hitch up the ox that they used to plow,
>   you know, put them up to a cart and use that to come to church on
>   a Sunday.
> *Louise:* [*a bit annoyed*] We never knew any oxcart. We never had any.
> *Josephine:* Right, my father always kept two horses. But I am just
>   saying that I knew people who had them a lot of people don't
>   remember, that's all. They used ox to plow the ground too.
> *Ruth:* We never had any oxcart. I never was in one myself. But some
>   people did. Papa always had two or three horses.

The hesitancy expressed by informants in speaking about traditional
midwifery was related to the midwives' connection with the intimacy of

childbirth. But without disregarding the specific nature of home births and midwifery as belonging to a restricted field of discourse, it is also true that in the more general reworking of individual and family history, some informants were quite reluctant to introduce explicit references that might have suggested that they had somehow failed to "uplift" themselves. Thus, even as they acknowledged that being poor in the past had not carried the moral stigma that it does today, individuals often denied firsthand knowledge of any beliefs or activities that might be construed by others as low status or practiced primarily by those who did not have other options.

At the second level of interpretation, use of the midwife bespoke another type of moral deficiency: the failure to make the suitable choice of birth attendant. In this view, those families who chose midwives when doctors and hospitals were available were "superstitious" and "backward." They had rejected medical progress. "Progress" was perceived as positive, and if not always welcome, it was an inevitable part of living. The past had to be abandoned (to be forgotten?) in order to accommodate the benefits of the present. Michel Laguerre (1987) writes of a similar set of attitudes among post–World War I African American migrants to California. He found that they actively decided to cease the transmission of folk medical practice to their children, most of whom were born in California. He writes that first-generation migrants, because of their trust in modern medicine, failed to share their medical traditions with their children. They believed that educated persons should not practice folk medicine. The use of folk medicine was seen as a remnant of a distant past, the practice of uncivilized persons (Laguerre 1987, 47).

In Green River County, those who linked midwives to poverty and poverty to moral failure believed that to remember midwives was to unearth a part of the past that reflected negatively on individuals as well as on the community. "What do you want to know about that old stuff for?" I was asked by Mrs. Simpson. Her question carried multiple meanings. She viewed the suggestion that older approaches to birth could be the subject of academic inquiry with skepticism. This wasn't history. If I wanted to know about the community, it would be more appropriate to focus on the establishment of churches and on the achievements of those who had been successful. Because images of African Americans in the media were invariably derogatory, it was important to provide a corrective. In this woman's view, such a balance would not be provided by calling attention to medical belief systems that were now defunct and discredited.

Furthermore, information about traditional midwifery was not useful knowledge, and if such knowledge was without value, then how would I give it value in order to market it? She was familiar with the tabloid newspapers sold at supermarket check-out counters and with investigative news programs on television. Perhaps she feared that once I had been given access to knowledge about all that "old stuff," I would expose secrets or somehow sensationalize or deride the community's past.

Known for her outspoken character, Mrs. Simpson listened to my explanations about the need to understand how people had survived and taken care of themselves in the past and granted that this could be important. Yet she had expressed a concern that was more subtly voiced by others. It was unwise to accentuate past cultural beliefs and practices and ways of living that fell too far outside the normative standards of what would be considered appropriate cultural and social behavior in today's world.

Sheila Kitzinger (1982) notes a similar concern on the part of "middle-class" Jamaicans, for whom "nanas [traditional midwives] are evil old busy-bodies who kill almost as many as they help and who are opposed to every benefit conferred on Jamaica by science and medicine" (Kitzinger 1982, 189). For this social class, Kitzinger argues, midwives are "embarrassing symbols of customs associated with slavery and subjection." I hesitate to attribute such attitudes to a specific social class in the Green River situation. Rather, ambivalence about the history of midwifery occurred across apparent socioeconomic divisions. It is more useful in these circumstances to refer to the shared cultural ideas about progress and a collectively endorsed representation of the community's past.

From this perspective, midwifery is not necessarily spoken of in a pejorative manner. Rather, at issue for many people is that the "audience" (whites, outsiders), with an already prejudicial mind-set, will misunderstand and falsely judge these customs. For many informants, therefore, my expressions of interest in these subjects constituted a threat to their public representations of self and community. As in the case of early-twentieth-century physicians, older residents in Green River also worried about leaving an impression that the South—their South—was backward.

Marking Off Terrains of Speech and Silence

An exchange between myself and Mrs. Powell, a sixty-six-year-old retired schoolteacher and active church member who also held positions of authority in a number of women's organizations in the community, illustrates one way in which older women marked off the terrain of their memory/knowledge. Mrs. Powell immediately established that because she had used a doctor for her pregnancies, she would be unable to tell me anything about "those old midwives." Indeed, because both she and her husband were teachers, the Powells would have been able to afford a physician. Furthermore, use of a midwife was clearly associated with families of lower status or with those "who didn't know better." Teachers were expected to be at the vanguard of progressive change in the African American community. Thus despite her desire to provide expert information, Mrs. Powell did not wish to be perceived as having direct knowledge about such matters as midwives and traditional birth rituals: "I have a friend. She's older than I am and she might be able to tell you because she had her children by a midwife. Now, she might be busy hanging out her clothes today but maybe I can call and maybe even if we couldn't go over there you could ask her the questions you wanted to ask her over the phone."

By introducing the possibility of a "phone interview" over my somewhat ineffectual protestations, Mrs. Powell ensured that she would be present to mediate the transmission of information while maintaining a certain distance. She nevertheless allowed some room for maneuvering out of the situation by emphasizing that her friend might be "busy." As our three-way conversation reveals, however, Mrs. Powell brought considerable pressure to bear on her supposedly older friend.

> *Mrs. Powell:* Hello, Dee, the girl is here that I told you about. She is interested in the midwives and since I knew you had yours with one maybe you can tell her. [*I have not yet been given the phone, but Dee obviously protests. Mrs. Powell cajoles.*] I am going to give the phone over to her, because you know we have to help out our

own. [*She hands me the kitchen phone and runs to pick up the bedroom extension.*]

Gertrude: [*after introductions and explanations by Mrs. Powell*] I certainly appreciate you talking with me. I am very interested in hearing about midwives and about the home remedies that they used.

Dee: Well, I don't know nothing about this.

Mrs. Powell: Go on ahead and tell her, all right? Because she wants to know. Didn't they [midwives] stay on afterwards and cook and wash and such to help out the mother?

Dee: Well, a lady in the neighborhood waited on me. She was kin to my mother-in-law. She was a nice lady. My husband went after her [brought the midwife to the house when it was time]. But she didn't stay afterwards to help out or anything because I was living with my mother-in-law at the time. And she [the mother-in-law] generally did all that.

Gertrude: [*Uncomfortable, I want to express interest while at the same time letting Dee off the hook.*] So the midwives helped out sometimes after the baby was born?

Mrs. Powell: [*interrupting to explicate*] Dee, now she doesn't necessarily mean if your actual midwife stayed with you, but if in general they helped the mother out.

There was continued verbal sparring between the two friends, mutually denying any knowledge but also giving each other permission to talk about these subjects to me. Mrs. Powell had implied that Dee's age made her more knowledgeable about midwives. In fact, only a year separated the two women who had been childhood friends. As we talked, I realized that they shared similar childbirth experiences and both knew about midwives. But it was important, nonetheless, for Mrs. Powell to present herself as being as uninformed as I was about these matters.

During the phone conversation that lasted about twenty minutes, Mrs. Powell often "directed" me to ask certain questions to which Dee gave detailed responses, about, for example, the length of time before mothers were allowed to take baths or wash their hair, about the treatment of the baby's umbilical cord, foods that could and could not be eaten, and so on. In this preliminary exchange, while it was obvious that Mrs. Powell knew a great deal more than she was initially willing to admit, it was also clear that some areas of midwifery practice were easier to talk about than others.

Mrs. Powell: [*to me*] Ask her about the smoke, if the midwife used smoke.

Dee: [*laughs and then addresses me, with a hint of sarcasm in her voice*] I thought she said she didn't know anything about all this. I don't know nothing about no smoke.

Mrs. Powell: [*slightly embarrassed*] Oh, I thought it was you who had told me about the smoke.

Even in our subsequent face-to-face conversations, Dee preferred not to speak about the use of smoke during and after childbirth. But later I learned that as a remedy for long or difficult labor, the midwife surrounded the mother with smoke (usually from a burning piece of firewood, feathers, or piece of cloth) in order to hasten contractions and stimulate the movement of the child down the birth canal. Variations on the practice and timing of "smoking" during childbirth and the postpartum have been described for Virginia and in other southern African American communities. In Green River, however, women preferred not to elaborate on the reasons for or methods involved in "smoking."

Women marked off the terrain of their knowledge. They were initially more willing to talk about, or to elaborate on, those aspects of midwifery that they judged to fall inside the realm of the natural (or medical). In the preceding conversation, for example, both Dee and Mrs. Powell explained that women were not supposed to wash their hair because "open pores" provided an entrance for germs. Indeed, the woman's entire body was said to be more vulnerable after childbirth, hence the need for confinement. Women were more comfortable discussing those aspects of midwifery practice that had, or at least seemed to have, correspondences in scientific medicine. They were more reticent to give details about "smoking" and other dimensions of the midwives' practice that they now felt to be connected to the nonscientific, supernatural realm of meaning and explanation. When I was given such information, the speaker often dropped the volume of her voice to just above a whisper. Drawn into the rhythm and atmosphere of conversations, I initially failed to notice the contextual shifts in speech. When I reviewed taped conversations, however, this pattern clearly emerged.

In a previous chapter, I have argued that the recourse to the law to restrict and manage midwives shifted the balance of power considerably in favor of medical personnel. This element of coercion, especially the punishment meted out to women who practiced midwifery without a license, emerged as a subtext in informants' recollections. Responding to a direct question about midwives, Mrs. Wood, for example, an eighty-four-year-old mother of four, recalled that "the doctor delivered all except one of my children, and the midwife delivered one because the doctor was sick." Later in her retelling of her birth story, the physician played only a peripheral role. He arrived well after Mrs. Wood's grandmother had successfully assisted her: "My first child labor started in the evening. The first was the worst, but I got along fine with the rest of them. But the first is always the worst. Now, three of my children were born before the doctor got there. My grandmother was with me at the time. She took care of me before he [the doctor] got there. And my mother said I was the easiest mother she ever knew . . . no wailing or anything . . . I got along fine."

Besides delivering these children, the grandmother also "waited on" other family members and was considered the authority on birthing, sick children, and "home remedies." Yet the family did not consider her a midwife—or it would be more accurate to say that when Mrs. Wood spoke about her grandmother, she considered it vital to assert that she had not "really" been a midwife.

Mrs. Wood's children were born in the mid-1920s and early 1930s, in the years when Virginia's legislature and public health officials instituted the first vigorous campaigns to restrict midwifery. Thus the physician, while not directly involved in the birth, legitimized the proceedings. Perhaps the family reasoned that his presence protected the grandmother from being legally charged with attending birth without a license. It is very likely that the readiness with which some women asserted that they had used physicians is related to the intrusion of the law into the birthing room. With fine or imprisonment a possibility for those who ignored the new rules, families may have continued to depend on their traditional sources of birthing support while explicitly seeming to rely on the medical practitioner. Midwives without permits may have just not called themselves by that name. By law, a woman could attend births without need of a permit if she did not take any pay. Mrs. Wood's grandmother might have fit into that category.

The shadow of the law loomed large when conversations turned to the prohibition against midwives introducing their hands or any instruments into the birth canal. As discussed earlier, nurses and physicians focused much of their monitoring activity on enforcing this rule. Hygiene was an explicit concern, but, as I have argued, the battle over defining and maintaining professional terrain was also played out in the distinctions created between who could and could not enter into the woman's body. Intriguingly, the injunction against midwives entering the birth canal was the only dimension of public health policy of which informants who were not themselves midwives seemed to have been explicitly aware. That this should be so speaks perhaps to the intensity of the struggle waged over the parameters of the midwife's role during childbirth.

In the case that it became necessary to introduce an instrument, or more likely a hand into the birth canal, a midwife may have expressed considerable anxiety. Should a doctor be called? Did the situation warrant waiting on a physician if one was at all available? What constituted an emergency? Could the midwife depend on the silence of her patient and relatives if she broke the rule on her best judgment? Both women who were clients of midwives and individuals with midwives in their families may have participated in discussing, or actually experienced, the practical and philosophical difficulties posed by life-or-death decisions.

If found guilty, or even suspected, of entering the birth canal, a midwife could have her license permanently revoked. In archival research, I have not found any evidence that such an offense was classified as a felony, in which case the woman could be imprisoned. Nevertheless, some informants spoke with such fear about the sanctions brought to bear on those who transgressed this rule that I suspect that they were made to believe that the offending woman could be thrown in prison. E. R. Hardin's (1925) recommendations to his southern physician colleagues that they instill a healthy fear of the law in their midwives seems, in this context, to have been far more than a figure of speech.

Discussions of situations where the boundaries established by public health personnel may have been actually or potentially overstepped were bracketed with references to the singularity of the occurrence, to the extenuating circumstances, or to strict compliance with the law. A classic story of a good samaritan coming to the aid of a neighbor was transformed instead into a cautionary tale when Mrs. Rawling (seventy-one) recalled her involvement in an unscheduled birth. The events occurred sometime in the late 1950s. Mrs. Rawling remembers being awakened by her young neighbor's husband. His wife had gone into labor with the couple's first child, and they were without transportation to get them to the city hospital or a telephone to call for the local taxi. Mrs. Rawling sent her teenage son to alert the nearest neighbor who owned a car and volunteered to accompany the couple to the hospital. In detailing the events, she emphasized that as a Christian woman and as one who had three children of her own, she had little choice. En route to the hospital, the baby "couldn't wait any longer," and Mrs. Rawling coached the new mother through her delivery in the back of the car.

Although we were alone, she whispered when recalling what happened. She had not actually handled the newborn while it was engaged in the birth canal but had simply "caught the baby" as it emerged: "No sir, I wouldn't touch that child. They [the authorities] didn't want for people to do that. Those judges they was hard. I kept out of trouble. I knew how to do it [check on the baby's progress while it was engaged]. But all I did was . . . , I put my hands under and catch that child." Mrs. Rawling's insistence on the propriety of her actions in this emergency became a dominant theme, repeated throughout her narrative.

On listening to this story—one that must have been told many times before—I was struck by the disproportionate attention given to the "catching" of the baby and by the muting of what at first appeared to be the central drama—the excitement of the unorthodox place and manner of the birth. Only later did I fully realize that the sense of risk for Mrs. Rawling, as events unfolded, was tied to her fear that the authorities might have accused her of breaking the law. Thus her heroism had to be underemphasized in order to avoid blame or punishment. (She was, after all, neither a midwife nor a physician.)

Given the circumstances, Mrs. Rawling may indeed have aided the birth more actively than acknowledged in her narrative. It would have been important, if this had been the case, for both women to keep silent on this matter. Or in another reading, the creation of a narrative that emphasized the passivity of her involvement may have been an attempt, on Mrs. Rawling's part, to quickly establish her innocence should there have been complications. Whatever the reasons, more than a quarter century later and despite the happy ending (both mother and child were healthy), the specter of the law and its power continued to dominate the retelling of Mrs. Rawling's story. I, too, had to be convinced that she had stayed well within the bounds of what was allowed.

Such caution also erupted during a conversation with Mrs. Harris, the last of four generations of midwives in her immediate family. I wanted to know the techniques, if any, used by midwives in Green River to deliver breach presentations or to extract a placenta. "Were there times," I asked, "when a midwife had to put her hands in the birth canal, or turn a baby or . . ." I was immediately interrupted: Mrs. Harris's response was pained. I have attempted to indicate the tone of her answer. This, more than her articulated response, suggested the nature of the dilemma she faced in close to sixty years of practice and interaction with physicians, nurses, and the law and now in talking to me.

> *Mrs. Harris:* No! No! No! You not supposed to.
> *Gertrude:* I know that today midwives wouldn't do that, but can you remember if in your grandmother or great-grandmother's time, if sometimes they had to . . .
> *Mrs. Harris:* [*rushing, raises her voice again in agreement*] They did. They did. They knowed how. [*pauses, a bit softer*] Ahhmmm, I know how too. But I am not allowed to do it. [*emphatically*] And I wouldn't do it for nothing cause its against the law.
> *Gertrude:* But in the time when they didn't have a doctor . . .?
> *Mrs. Harris:* [*interrupting*] And couldn't [*draws out this word*] get a doctor. [*angrily*] They had to do these things. They had to.
> *Gertrude:* So the old midwives had to know, ahhh . . . , how to go into the birth canal?
> *Mrs. Harris:* [*silence, hesitating*] I think my grandmother did, but my mother she always called for a doctor. But my grandmother and great-grandmother, they did not have a doctor. Because when my great grandmother went around, my mother said she went on a oxcart with the ox.

Understandably, because she still occasionally attended a birth, Mrs. Harris wanted to clearly establish that she abided by the rules. Furthermore, her response to my question with the emphasis on her obedience clearly set the terms of the relationship between herself and the law. "They did not allow" midwives to enter the birth canal, so she did not. She knew the necessary skills, however, having learned midwifery alongside her mother and grandmother. Although she never elaborated on the nature of her knowledge—had she herself turned a baby or simply watched?—Mrs. Harris wanted to convey that she was constrained in what she could tell me. I would have to read between the lines.

Part of the hidden message related to whether her mother had been in situations that required entry into the birth canal. Toward the latter part of her mother's career, the rules defining the limits of midwifery practice would have been well established. Mrs. Harris, therefore, asserted that her mother always called a physician. Thus she protected her mother's reputation. Given the distance from hospital or physicians in the part of the county where Mrs. Harris's mother lived and practiced, however, it was likely that she performed inversions and extractions of impacted placentas. And it is also likely that she taught her daughter these skills. During the lifetimes of both Mrs. Harris and her mother, however, such knowledge came to be represented as immoral and illegal by the medical profession.

It is only with great caution that Mrs. Harris acknowledges existence of these midwifery techniques. Not only does she skip a generation to ensure that no stigma is attached to her mother, but the stigmatization of these skills, when practiced by midwives, leads Mrs. Harris to provide some "justification" for her grandmother and great-grandmother, to explain why they had to enter the birth canal. I use the word "justify" purposely to point to the manner in which Mrs. Harris felt it necessary to tell me that these women had no choice but to aid pregnant women as best they could in the absence of doctors. It was as if she wanted to convince me of the extenuating circumstances. The tone as well as the content of Mrs. Harris's response took on, to some degree, the character of a legal defense: "They had to do these things"; "They couldn't get a doctor." Thus fear of the law and its construction of reality stretches back to a time (the 1800s, when Mrs. Harris's great-grandmother would have practiced) well before the rise of scientific childbirth.

For Mrs. Harris, in particular, fear of the law continues to be a lived reality. For most of her career as a licensed midwife, she went to the homes of her clients. More recently, as her few clients tend to be spread out across the county, she began to have them come to her house. But, she said, this practice had to be severely curtailed "when the doctors got in the wind of it in Lincrest [the closest town with a small hospital and clinic]. And you know they want to run me up a brick wall 'cause of delivering babies here in my home. Yes, indeed, and they had the judge to write me a letter . . . No more delivering . . . I can deliver one per year if it's not any relation to me, and after that no more. Oh yes! the doctors don't like it at all."

Potential clients were also discouraged from using Mrs. Harris's services. Women informed her that when they went to the public health clinic for prenatal care, nurses expressed disdain for the traditional midwives: "And the people when they go to the clinic, they [nurses and doctors] just lay the midwife out [put down the midwife/speak negatively of home births]. That's what they [pregnant women] tell me, and they have to have a statement saying that it's OK for me to deliver their babies." Dougherty (1978) writes of a similar process in Florida, where the public health clinic determines which women can and cannot use a traditional midwife. Dougherty notes that the midwife, too, becomes a client as the public health clinic mediates between pregnant women (usually poor women) and the birth attendant. Eventually, as Mrs. Harris was well aware, the law is the final arbiter, ostensibly protecting women from health risks but also intimidating the midwife as a means of curtailing her activities.

DeVries (1985) discusses the contemporary confrontation between midwives and the law. What I want to emphasize here is the inscription of the law and its authority into the conversations and narratives of older residents. The fear expressed was real, not merely the recounting of a story about "how midwives were forbidden to enter the birth canal." My informants were afraid to talk. Could people still be prosecuted if they revealed information about long-ago instances in which a midwife put her hands in the birth canal or even if they only told me that midwives knew how to extricate a placenta or help to turn a baby? Was I to be trusted? During conversations, older residents tested my stance before deciding how much to reveal. And when they did break silence, they often used the conventions of legal discourse (defense, justification, proving innocence, denying guilt) to explain their behavior and that of midwives during emergencies.

Birth as Private Matters

What of the culturally prescribed rules about restricting public discussion of childbirth and its rituals? These, too, played a part in the content and style of narratives about traditional childbirth and midwives. At the time in which midwives were the primary birth attendants in the county, silence, euphemism, and coded references were used to avoid any direct conversational references to pregnancy and childbirth. Although she was a teenager at the time of her mother's later pregnancies, Mrs. Hill (eighty-five years old) recalled, for example, that she was never informed of any impending births. To directly refer to the unborn was in some manner to jeopardize a healthy outcome for mother and child.

When women visited the household to exchange news, especially in mixed company or in the presence of children, they spoke in a veiled language about pregnancies in the neighborhood. As Mrs. Hill told me, "Oh, they didn't talk about such things like that. If they wanted to say something, they'd say, 'Oh, I heard so-and-so is going to New York,' or otherwise, 'I think so-and-so broke her arm.' That way you would know what they were saying, but they didn't say it directly." Older women in Green River expressed disapproval of the public display of pregnancy by younger women today who wore maternity tops, popular in the 1980s, that read UNDER CONSTRUCTION or I AM NOT FAT JUST PREGNANT. Birth had been considered perhaps the most intimate event in a woman's life, to be shared with a midwife and a few female friends and relatives. Few understood the motivations of those white middle-class women, seen on television documentaries, who allowed their husbands to watch and film the birth, or who permitted their younger children to be present. This exposure had come about, they believed, because women today were essentially different in sensibility and physiology from older generations of women. Thus the guarded intimacy that had characterized birth in the past had been replaced with loud, public, and even televised display.

Privacy for the mother's sake was but one of the concerns necessitating this approach to childbirth. At issue was the question of etiquette or cultural manners. Without making any direct criticism of drastically different modern practices, Mrs. Franklin (age seventy) emphasized this point: "I was raised the old-time way. My grandmother said she didn't like to see the mother out in public soon after birth. She didn't think it was decent. I stayed inside about one month."

It is important to note the stress placed on the authority of an older woman (the grandmother in this case) in ensuring that younger women conformed to these standards. As such, Mrs. Franklin acknowledged the importance of this behavioral norm while not necessarily implying that they were of her own making. She obeyed out of respect, without question or rancor. Other women of Mrs. Franklin's age spoke similarly of the "rules" regarding the privacy of birth: "The women had to stay in that room [birthing room]. And my mother-in-law, she went by that rule, and so I stayed in until the baby got to a certain age." This I was told in another instance, but here again we must be aware of yet another message—that now that they are themselves grandmothers and mothers-in-law, these women are conscious of the usurpation of their authority. The rules no longer apply. Women of the younger generation neither listen to nor take their advice. Confronted with the disinterest of the young in hearing about the way "things used to be" and faced with the impotence of traditional authority, one response is to withdraw into silence. Some older informants choose this path.

With these overlapping attitudes toward childbirth rituals, midwives, and midwifery, it is no wonder that my interest in these subjects was problematic for many older African Americans in Green River. On the one hand, people wanted to help me in my "project": many were justifiably proud of the accomplishments of relatives who had been midwives. On the other, however, in the presence of an educated stranger, they preferred to present themselves as forward-looking and progressive. Women in these instances did not necessarily want to admit that they had depended on midwives, or that in fact they had any knowledge of birthing rituals that were now discredited. I was also unmarried, childless, young, and an outsider. They were undecided, therefore, about the ways in which they wanted to represent their experiences and knowledge.

The reserve, silence, and distancing on matters related to midwifery knowledge and the birth experience proved initially disturbing because I wanted to hear, know, and understand. This was why I had come to Green River County. Furthermore, it was, I believed, through talking about midwives that the past could be reclaimed and the ideological oppression of science and the law challenged. Sharon Thompson admits to a similar "missionizing" impulse when she conducted interviews with adolescent and preadolescent girls on the subject of puberty. She writes, "Pubescents exercise their right to remain vague, amorphous, unshaped and unlimited by words, concealed: if not to repress, then to keep private, personal, their own. Their silence struck me as an act of self-possession and I admired it, but I was nevertheless convinced at the time that liberation lay in the public direction: in sharing secrets and in shaping them rather than, through silence, accepting pre-existing molds" (Thompson 1984, 350).

Eventually and somewhat "half-heartedly," Thompson, relying on

Michel Foucault's insights on the discourse around sexuality, realized that she may have been just "another dupe of the system that enthralls by causing one and all to obsess and confess ad infinitum." In the process of talking to older African Americans, I came to a similar realization. At the least, I have a firmer understanding of the nature and reasons for the silences of older residents.

Drawn as I was to the differences between my approach to the past and that of my informants, only much later did other possibilities present themselves to me. The opposition between silence and verbalization ("speaking out") need not be analyzed solely from the perspective of nonresistance or resistance, although this approach has proved invaluable in my work. When informants expressed opinions about the changes in community life and their effects on social relations and on the care and treatment of the body, they were involved in a process of giving meaning to their own history. No longer are former ideas about the body and its relationship to the social and natural order taken for granted.

As a part of this process, ambivalence about the rituals of midwifery and home births reflected a belief that one had to put aside the past in order to better accommodate the present. From this perspective, silence was neither a form of alienation nor withdrawal; it was, rather, an integral part of the way that older informants perceived and understood the interaction between scientific medicine and older ways of knowing and treating the body—between past and present. In their own way, my informants had come to terms with the force of authoritative knowledge. The ways in which they carve out areas of reserve legitimize the dominant forms of negative discourse about the midwife, but at the same time this silence is a way of calling attention to an issue. Older residents could be drawn out to speech, but it took some work, and by this effort they pushed me to recognize the import of their silences.

A sense of the uses of "silence" in this regard comes from Dell Hymes (1980). He writes of the "narrative view of life" in which

> incidents . . . have pervasively the potentiality of an interest that is worth retelling. The quality of this is different from gossip, or the flow of talk from people who have nothing but themselves to talk about— their illness, their marriages, their children . . . Not that the difference is in the topics. The difference is in the silences. There is a certain focusing, a certain weighting. A certain potentiality of shared narrative form, on the one hand, of consequentiality, on the other (Hymes 1980: 135).

Ironically, it is precisely the topics that Hymes regards with a touch of disdain—sickness, children, and so on—that capitivate me. Leaving this aside, Hymes makes a crucial point. Silence is woven, he writes, into his Native American acquaintances' narratives about everyday experience. What is left unsaid may be later voiced in future retellings. Alternately, the areas of silence are assumed to be generally known by the audience. Or from another perspective, one is expected to fill in between the lines.

The weight given to certain parts of a narrative may at once indicate its importance or, under other circumstances, act as a decoy to draw attention away from the issue of real significance to the narrator. Leaving things unsaid may also reflect a view of the way the world is ordered. Narratives from Green River County, for example, reflected a view that, though painful, it is sometimes necessary to lay aside the past—leaving things unspoken—in order to take full advantage of new realities and opportunities. This view, then, becomes part of the narration of the sequence of events or circumstances. Such a complex telling clearly emerged when older residents discussed the erosion of ordinary knowledge about the body and its replacement by the expertise of scientific medicine.

The contestation about what is acceptable to talk and remember about the history of birthing and midwifery in Green River County's African American community may appear bewildering to our modern sensibilities. How do we understand the nature of the ambiguities that confronted these older African Americans when they recalled the history of birthing in their community? Their silence and reserve run counter to contemporary birthing movements that focus on verbalization as empowerment.

8

Changed Bodies,
Changed Communities

I have seen my mother make baby clothes. Like she had to deliver a
baby and the people was kind of up against it [poor/desperate]. . . She
would make clothes and carry with her. But now if you don't have it it's
a shame. But those days people had more tender feelings than people
do of today. And I heard one midwife say she's been to a home, and after
the baby come she'd sew and make clothes for the baby to dress it, so
you know that was sad [that the family couldn't even afford clothing for
the newborn].
I never known a midwife to refuse a case, no indeed, even if they owed
her from the last baby she would go. Those midwives would go. But the
doctor won't. You got to pay them in advance. And now in the hospital
it's gone from two thousand to three thousand dollars. Just depend on
what they have to do. And you have to pay for everything even if you
take a aspirin or whatnot. You got to pay for those things . . . Everything is extra, even using the room and pay the doctor.
—Mrs. Harris, fourth generation midwife, eighty years old

Within the past decade or so, feminist scholars have insisted on the
importance of exploring the ways in which individuals in Western and
non-Western cultures experience and give meaning to transformations
in cosmologies of the body, about how it works or ought to work, and
about what can and cannot be done to it (Behar 1991; Duden 1985;
Davis-Floyd 1992; Martin 1987, 1994; Rapp 1979; Ginsburg and Rapp
1995; Scheper-Hughes and Lock 1987). In this chapter, I take up this
issue by focusing on the voices of older African Americans in Green
River County. How, if at all, do they talk about their experiences of the

163

eclipse of traditional midwifery and the rise of medicalized birth? To answer this question, one is inevitably drawn into a much greater discussion about changes in personal, family, and community life, and about the meanings given to former ways of being and knowing.

Gift Giving and Social Change

African Americans in Green River County held definite, though by no means homogeneous, views about the waning of what they termed "home remedies" or "home doctoring," and about the disappearance of the midwife, once a central figure in the life cycle of community members. But even if they disagreed about the relative benefits of progress, most older informants concurred that in the past there was greater collective interdependence and individual self-reliance. The concepts of church and neighborhood lie at the root of this mutual reciprocity.

Even if they were not regular churchgoers or had lived away from their home church for years, individuals considered themselves members of the congregation into which they had been baptized. Mrs. Lewis, for example, was born in 1904 and as a teenager attended the church closest to the home of her widowed mother. Yet she insisted that this was not her "real" church: "Papa died when I was twelve. He used to take us to Bright Hope, which was our church. But after he passed, the superintendent of Sunday schools told mama to let the kids go to Mt. Calvary since it was closer. And we've been going ever since. But by right our church was Bright Hope. And sometimes we still go there for services."

Thus when older informants spoke of community, they referred to an overlapping network that included members of the same church and persons, usually related by marriage and blood, who lived near one another. From 1900 to 1940 and to lesser degree in the following two decades, these networks of individuals were relied on in times of illness, during childbirth, and when a death occurred. It is somewhat specious to try to separate the memories that related to medical transformation from those concerning the changes in communities over time. These subjects are inextricably connected in the narratives and reminiscences of older African Americans. Furthermore, the body, the mind, and the self are conceptualized as having evolved or been altered from one generation to the next.

The movement of birth from the domestic sphere occurred at a time when increasing numbers of families were abandoning any effort at subsistence farming in Green River County. The ability to provision the family without relying on store-bought food had once been the norm, and the old speak of this self-reliance with pride. Yet they do not explicitly lament its loss. They describe the passing of midwives and the eclipse of a time when mothers "doctored children at home" as phenomena that are best explained with reference to the natural and spiritual world over which human beings' control is at best ephemeral. They also speak of the moral and physical bankruptcy of the younger generation, who despite their privileges don't know how to "do for themselves." Still, my older informants say that such changes are inevitable and not necessarily detrimental. Children "nowadays" are more precocious, less willing to be submissive to whites, and more aware of the world outside the county. Like the older residents of an Ulster farming community described by Henry Glassie (1984), elder African Americans in Green River County believe that "things get better, and they get worse."

Education is greatly valued in Green River County. It was generally expected that the young would seize every opportunity to "get that education." Yet, according to informants, there was a downside of depending too much on knowledge only gained in the classroom and through books. The younger generation, I was often told, did not have the common sense of their parents and grandparents. My informants would marvel at their grandchildren's intellectual precocity, but at the same time they would comment critically on the youths' inability to perform basic household tasks or to take care of themselves without supervision. Mrs. Waters, who was only ten when her mother died, recalled that she was expected to help her father care for four siblings while working as a maid's helper in the household of a local white doctor. She doubted whether her eighteen-year-old grandchild would have been able to handle half these responsibilities under the same circumstances. In another instance, a man who planted a small garden in accordance with the moon's phases, as his father had in the 1920s, explained to me that his common sense allowed him to do this. Yet his sons, he believed, didn't garden because they did not know when and how to plant. "Why didn't you teach them as youngsters?" I asked, to which he replied that "they simply didn't have it in them to learn." In a pattern reminiscent of the process for the nation as a whole, as described by Viviana Zelizer (1985), children in Green River County no longer are held responsible for contributing to the household economy. Their value is now measured in terms of the affective bonds between parent and child. Looking back on their childhoods, informants commented, sometimes critically, on these changes. Yet they largely believed that such changes are a mark of achievement, a permanent escape from the oftentimes harsh lives that they experienced as children in the first three decades of the century.

Such ambivalence is familiar to those who have listened to the voices of people who live between two worlds—people who, unlike their grandparents, know with certainty that their grandchildren's lives will be radically different from their own. How do older African Americans in Green River County explain the eclipse of "home remedies" within their lifetimes? Where do they locate the factors that have caused the younger generation to be so different from their elders? In the view of my older informants, the community has changed corporally as well as socially and economically. Things are of a piece. Home remedies no longer work because bodies are different and illnesses no longer respond to traditional remedies. In turn, bodies are different because the community members' relationship to the land, to God, and to previously established norms of behavior has been irretrievably altered.

When older women spoke about their experience of childbirth, or when both men and women remembered midwives, discussed home remedies, spirits, family, or their life histories, there was an ongoing dialectic between the acceptance of modernization and all it entailed and the assertion that "things were better back then." The existence of this conflict between acceptance and rejection of the dominant ideology of scientific progress constituted a form of resistance.

Yet part of the power of the ideology of science rests in its invalidation of other systems of belief and explanation. This process of invalidation can occur even in a context of contestation and resistance. Older African Americans in Green River struggle to give meaning to the drastic alterations in community life and in the treatment of illness and health in particular. In doing so, they question—indeed, they are forced to question—to become their own ethnographers in a sense, to make exotic those forms of knowing and doing that had once seemed familiar and appropriate. They do not deny the efficacy and worth of medical science; rather, they attempt to explain and justify the disappearance of the medical beliefs and practices that had sustained their parents and grandparents.

This is part of the process that Immanuel Wallerstein refers to as "universalism" and Bridgette Jordan calls "authoritative knowledge" (1983; 1991). Wallerstein writes of the cultural dominance of the ideology of "universalism" that "has been the keystone of the ideological arch of capitalism." As Wallerstein characterizes it, universalism is "a set of beliefs about what is knowable and how it can be known. The essence of this view is that there exists meaningful, general statements about the world—the physical world, the social world—that are universally and permanently true, and that the object of science is the search for these general statements in a form that eliminates all so-called subjective, that is all historically constrained elements from its formulation" (Wallerstein 1983, 81).

From this perspective, the gift of medical science required in return a dismantling of other previously accepted systems of treatment. Jean Comaroff's discussion of symbolic healing among the Tswana explores the nature of this predicament (1981). Even as it appears that greater choices are made available to modern Tswana, the elemental contradictions in ideology and practice between traditional healing and medical science actually create an either/or situation. Comaroff writes, for example, that although middle-class Tswana individuals may opt to consult indigenous healing, "they are inevitably compelled to 'choose' adherence to Western bourgeois ideology" (Comaroff 1981, 375). As a consequence, the perception of alternatives do not "in fact resolve the contradictions inherent in the modern predicament, for they [late-twentieth-century Tswana] are caught up in the dialectic between Tswana culture and social relations and the wider world beyond them" (Comaroff 1981, 375).

The dismantling of former approaches to birth and healing in Green River County occurred as the older generation became increasingly self-conscious of the limits of their moral and medical authority over the minds and bodies of their children, grandchildren, and great-grandchildren. Having acquiesced in the breakdown of the transmission of knowledge, people can still express suspicion of the "new ways." But this does not effectively challenge or usurp science's incursion in domains previously closed to its authority. In the conversations of Green River's older residents, therefore, one is always aware of an implicit standard against which former systems of belief are compared and judged.

This process of evaluative judgment, however, did not necessarily lead to a hierarchical model in which "home doctoring" took the inferior position. Rather, older residents constructed two parallel worlds within which they explained the shift away from former modes of treatment and knowledge of the body. They argued that just as the community had changed and become more modern, so, too, had the bodies, minds, and sensibilities of the younger generation for whom older medical rituals, treatments, and forms of knowing have no power to influence, heal, or inform. Especially in the philosophy and praxis of childbirth, older residents forcefully made this point.

Changed Minds and Bodies

The belief that scientific birth is more appropriate for modern bodies was not necessarily based on judgments about its intrinsic merits but on a set of assertions about its suitability. Traditional birthing and healing practices were similarly discussed. Some women recounted instances in which they disobeyed the injunctions of midwives and became seriously ill. During the postpartum period extending between two weeks and a month, for example, women were expected to refrain from eating certain categories of foods that were believed to "set back" the body. Midwives monitored new mothers to ensure that they did not inadvertently or purposely eat any foods that would retard the healing process. After the birth of her second child, Mrs. Earling recounted that she had sneaked a plate of butter beans "that almost like to kill me." Having once suffered when she attempted to "get around" the midwife's rules, she was forever convinced of these women's wisdom and power.

Weighing her experience against that of younger women, she wondered how they were able to eat just about anything they wanted without being troubled by any side effects. She supposed that the bodies of younger women either reacted differently to foods or that store-bought foods were not as "strong" as home-grown ones: most of the foods she ate during her childbearing years had been grown on the family farm.

Here as in other instances, Mrs. Earling emphasized that the shifts in approach to childbirthing behavior occurred at the same time as physiological changes in the body and even in the nature and source of the food supply. She did not expect, therefore, that the rules by which she experienced childbirth would have salience for the younger generation. Mrs. Billson made a similar point. She asserted that the long postpartum seclusionary period was absolutely essential for the good health of mother and child. By contrast, modern women emerge from the hospital after a few days and seem none the worse for the experience. Yet, as suggested by her reference to the "good care" given by midwives, Mrs. Billson intimated that the brief stay in the hospital that was now the norm shortchanged new mothers who had to be up and about immediately after giving birth.

If Mrs. Billson voiced two views about modern childbirth—women's bodies had changed, on the one hand, and on the other, the abrupt care offered in the hospital was inappropriate even for today's women—she was certain that the physical development of the newborn was drastically different when she was having her children in the mid-1920s. Besides allowing the mother's body the time to heal, one of the reasons midwives had insisted on the long postpartum rest period in a darkened room, she recalled, was to give the newborn's eyes the time necessary to mature fully. Newborn children were not to be exposed to any bright light, as this could permanently damage their eyesight. Molly Dougherty reports a similar belief among African Americans in Florida, where a lay midwife recalled that seclusion in a darkened room "was on account of the eyes, the baby would go blind, it couldn't have no light in it eyes" (Dougherty 1978, 162). Dougherty does not indicate whether people discussed the effect of light on the eyes of present-day infants.

Mrs. Billson drew an analogy between the eyes of infants and newborn kittens, who were born blind and then slowly opened their eyes and grew accustomed to their surroundings. Such was the case with human children in the time when home births were the norm: "The baby didn't open its eyes for about . . . until I think about two or three weeks old before the baby would be able to see. They would just sleep you know . . . didn't even open their eyes. And now they born you know . . . They born with their eyes wide open." Other informants remarked on this essential difference between today's children born in the hospital and those born at home in the first half of the century. Such alteration in newborns' eyesight was discussed not so much as a consequence of new medical techniques but rather as a developmental change in the body.

The fully functioning eyes of newborns could be said to stand in some synecdochic relationship to the rest of children's minds and bodies, which, according to older residents, seem to mature faster and along different trajectories than they had ever imagined possible. Children's eyes, women's fast recovery from childbirth, the food taboos that were no longer necessary—these were all proof that the natural world in which midwives had learned and practiced their calling no longer existed.

Rarely, if ever, did older African Americans critique the methods of obstetrical childbirth (though the actions or attitudes of specific physicians or nurses did receive negative and positive commentary). Acceptance of the medical approach to birthing, however, did not necessarily lead to a negation of the value of older childbirth practices. While beneficial to women of an earlier generation, the midwife's ways no longer applied because women's and infants' bodies had somehow changed. Often conversations about intergenerational experiences of pregnancy, childbirth, and the postpartum period were punctuated with the assertion that "women [or children] are different nowadays."

The movement of birth away from the home and out of the midwife's hands was deemed necessary and appropriate. Yet older women, in particular, continued to express dismay at the dismantling of the expected set of childbirth behavior that had accompanied home births attended by midwives. The irony of the situation was brought to my attention in a striking manner by a woman in her sixties who accosted me one morning after church to describe with horror the decision of her daughter, living in New York, to use the services of a nurse midwife and to have the future father present in the birthing room. Here, in a slightly different version of a familiar argument, the mother seemed to suggest that her daughter's actions betrayed the progress that the family had achieved. Even more disconcerting was the fact that the daughter could have afforded the best hospitals and physicians.

Perhaps the most remarkable part of her daughter's behavior, in this mother's view, was her insistence on having her husband aid in the birth. As my informant characterized it, this break with the previous norm of completely excluding family men (as opposed to male physicians who occupy a separate, perhaps neuter, category) from any participation in birth was completely alien. It bespoke an almost incomprehensible shift in sensibilities. Paradoxically, the use of a midwife had, from the daughter's perspective, returned her to the cultural roots of traditional African American home births. To the mother, however, such a juxtositon of modern and traditional bordered on the obscene.

When they explained the shift from a reliance on ordinary to expert knowledge about the body and its functioning, older African Americans also spoke about the waning efficacy of home remedies. They refused (sometimes expressing this as being afraid) to treat their grandchildren with older medicinal herbs and techniques because, they argued, younger bodies did not work according to the principles with which they were familiar. The breach in their authority over the young was discussed as both physiological and social. According to Mrs. Sullivan (age seventy-two), "Used to be everybody could correct [discipline, advise on inappropriate behavior], but now you're afraid to correct a child. . . Seems like they know so much more. Children are raising themselves nowadays." Aside from these changes, there were changes in the spiritual world. "It seems to me," a woman in her late sixties reasoned, that "you used to have more ghosts and such back then, and I know for certain that there were those that used them [to influence events among the living]." Speaking on this same issue, Mr. Crawford (age seventy-five) linked the disappearance of supernatural beings to modernization: "Well, as you add on new stuff then you don't have no trouble with the spirits. . . Seems they don't bother round or something. But way back it used to be 'see this, see that' [frequent sightings of ghosts, spirit animals]."

Land and the Social Body

The increased authority of medical science was also described as a result of the diminished capacity of African Americans to heal themselves, to handle birth and death in the home, and to identify, harvest, and compound the herbs and roots required for the remedies used by the previous generation. Reflecting on the seeming unavailability of the herbs and roots used by their parents and grandparents, informants believed that the land itself had changed and no longer produced these medicinals. In one version of this process, related to me by seventy-year-old Mr. Rogers, who had farmed until the 1950s and then worked in a factory in the city until his retirement in the early 1980s, the healing plants had disappeared from the land. Mr. Rogers explained that even if people wanted to use the old remedies, some of which were better than what the doctors offered today, it would be impossible.

Mullein, for example, was a plant that his mother used to cure "lingering colds" and headaches. But this plant only grew on land that had been cleared and burned in preparation for farming. Now that people no longer farmed, mullein had become extinct. Mr. Rogers's ecological explanation is intriguing, for it supports the view that changes in treatment of the body were inevitable and to some extent an extension of natural law. Yet on walks through the woods or their gardens, at least three persons pointed out the mullein plant to me. It still grows, but, in a complicated conjunction of transformations in medicine and in economic and social life, it has lost its use value and even become invisible to some residents.

If the land had not changed, then the people themselves had lost the capacity to harvest the "right" plants. When I asked why most people didn't use home remedies as before, Mrs. Corven (in her late sixties), who still prepared her own cough syrup, made a connection between the disappearance of medicinal plants and knowledge about them: "There was a plant that grew on our farm and that was good for loose bowels. But now it doesn't grow anymore. Look like it just died out. People didn't plant any of these things; there was always plenty of them growing in the woods, and the older people knew them because their people used them. See, they taught them how to use the roots and such. But now since people stopped using them, most of those things, I guess, they just stopped growing."

Another individual who continued to "see" the medicinal roots and herbs explained their fall into disuse in other terms. The availability of modern medicine and physicians, according to Mrs. Robinson (late seventies), had caused people to lose their knowledge of and need for home remedies derived from plants. "They are still growing," she reasoned, "but I don't think people use those things now ever since antibiotics come in. They have antibiotics for everything now." Antibiotics had been the key. But Mrs. Robinson also referred to the breakdown of the once normal exchange of information about the body and its treatment between young and old. "It all started," she argued, ". . . when they had more doctors to tell them [younger generations] about the medicine. See, the older people knew what to do. They had done it so long that they just knew what to do. They didn't even bother with the doctor. Then the younger people went to school. Then they started to say, 'Oh, we don't do that anymore.'"

The unraveling of the shared links between the old and new touched all spheres of life. I was told, for example, that the strong emotional ties between close kin and neighbors had disappeared. Even though she had been long married, with children of her own, when her mother died in the 1940s, Mrs. Morehead recalled the intensity and long duration of her grief. Her belief that "people don't mourn the way they used to" was a sentiment shared by others. When explaining the disappearance of non-monetary, reciprocal relations between neighbors, informants similarly spoke about the loss of "tender feelings towards one another." Just as the community had turned "colder," so, too, it was argued, had families. According to informants, the world of past social relations had disappeared.

Speaking of the disjunction between past and present, Mrs. Lowell, a sixty-five-year-old retired domestic and grandmother, commented that children no longer "knew who they were": "Now you can ask a child and he won't even know who his grandmother is. . . If you ask, 'Who is your grandmother?' sometimes they don't even know. I mean, unless you say directly, 'Is Mrs. So-and-So your grandmother?' But when I was coming up you knew your grandmother on both sides and all your great-grands, cousins, who married who, and how they were kin. You knew who was kin to you."

Even persons who otherwise saw little value in the "old ways" returned to this theme in their conversations. The individual was a part of a web of blood and conjugal kin, and it was from these networks that she derived her primary social identity and related to others. Just as Mrs. Lowell attempted to interrogate young children about their family ties, in a story about his youth and the rediscovery of family, Mr. Jackman (age sixty-three), who had been raised by his grandparents, remembered an older woman's scrutiny when he took a trip to an adjoining county in the late 1930s:

> I think I must have been seventeen or eighteen. I used to work on these jukebox, what you call pinball machines. And on account of that work I used to move around a lot. And I went to a place up in Beaver County. This lady had two daughters . . . Well, the two girls was . . . well, you know . . . you know how boys will see . . . Well, anyhow I told the girls I was gon date them, you know. So this lady she asked me . . . You know at that time they would ask you, "Who were you?" "What's your people's name and your background?" So I told her, you know. I told her my grandfather's name and where he was from and all. So she says, "Well, I think I kin to you." She said, "Don't you come back here no more until you bring him [his grandfather]."

Narratives about past and present may have somewhat romanticized the former "closeness" of families and communities and exaggerated the current shallowness of relationships. But here I am not particularly concerned with judging historical validity but with the opposition created between the interdependent, warm, kin-based communities within which midwives played a central role and that of the community "nowadays," wherein people are no longer tender toward one another, relationships between neighbors and kin are more fragmented, and birth takes place among strangers.

Even Mrs. Harris, who was well aware of the pressures placed on midwives by physicians and nurses, subscribed to this view. In anger coupled with bewilderment, she stated that "doctors can't stand a midwife. They just can't bear to have a midwife around. I don't know why." Yet when I asked her why younger women (including her daughters) had not taken up midwifery, she focused on the shortcomings of women who had lost their Christian ways and the desire to serve others. The disappearance of the reciprocal communal and family relationships that had been the foundation of community during the childhood and young adulthood of older residents formed a backdrop whenever people discussed the "dying out" of midwives, home remedies, or ordinary knowledge about the body.

More than a secular craft, midwifery was part of a moral and spiritual set of relationships between God, the midwife, the pregnant woman, the family, and the community. Informants argued that midwives disappeared because these links were broken. They focused on the natural rupture in the transmission of practical and spiritual knowledge. In the same manner that herbs and plants ceased to grow as people stopped knowing how to use them, so, too, did younger women stop receiving the call and lost their knowledge of birthing.

Why did the notion of the gift figure so strongly as the way to explain midwifery's disappearance? I would argue that the medicalization of childbirth, the rising authority of physicians, and the shift toward wage labor and away from subsistence farming was most dramatically experienced as an erosion of the commonly held assumptions about reciprocity and gift exchange. Thus, rather than focusing on the actions of public health personnel to discourage home births, older informants inevitably returned our conversations to the disappearance of interdependency and mutual help and by extension to the break in the previously close relationship between human beings and God.

Allusions to the "devilishness" of certain midwives, for example, provided a counterpoint to the emphasis placed in other contexts on the unbounded altruism and commitment to caring of most of these women. In part, the problem for Mrs. Wayne and her peers in the dialogue reported earlier, for example, was that there were some individuals who used their "gifts" inappropriately. The notion of the gift and the circularity of its exchange informed people's discussion of social childbirth. In this chain, God gave the spiritual and practical "gift" to midwives, who in turn then passed it on to the women and children she attended. They in turn were expected, in the daily course of living, to offer help and support to kin and neighbors. The nature of the midwifery gift was such that even if the woman and her family failed to offer payment in cash or kind, it was incumbent on the midwife to offer her services yet again if the need arose. Neither could a woman refuse the supernatural call to become a midwife without incurring potential harm to herself or her family. By contrast, doctors will only offer their services if they are paid. This was a point brought out by Mrs. Harris as well as other women who had not been midwives but who had been patients in the hospital or visited ailing friends or relatives or used a private physician. The hospital and doctor bills with their itemized expenses were a source of spirited commentary in conversations with families recently experiencing a death or illness.

Furthermore, these services come in the form of fragmented care. While some older persons experiencing the failures of the body—heart conditions, high blood pressure, failing sight, diabetes—told me with some pride that they had to see a "specialist" to treat their particular ailments, others were bothered by the fact that it was necessary to have a different doctor for the different illnesses and parts of the body.

Each aspirin and each procedure, plus the room, the television, the food one eats, comprise the product for which one pays. On the other side of the equation, people only rarely establish a relationship with their caregivers. Especially with reference to childbirth, older as well as younger women complained that the prenatal nurse at the clinic did not accompany the woman through the other stages of childbirth. In the hospital, another person checks you into the hospital, different nurses monitor and prepare you for childbirth, and the physician on duty is likely never to have had any previous meetings with the laboring mother. Although they never expressed their feelings of frustration in these terms, certainly these women, young and old, were responding to the fragmented care that they or their children or grandchildren received. As I noted in Chapter 4, there is anger about this situation, and in many instances the creation of narratives provided the only form of direct protest.

Once people knew I was interested in these issues, young women wanted to talk to me about their experiences. Older women did not. Instead, they offered narratives of a different sort—ones that attempted to explain how different these young mothers and their babies were. "Nowadays" newborns acclimate themselves immediately to their physical surroundings, just as mothers quickly reintegrate themselves into the world of work and home. In the opinion of my older informants, such a new world requires new and different bodies and sensibilities. Their narratives are made coherent by the emphasis on the biological suitability of the younger generation to the kind of medicine that they receive.

Noting the persistence of reciprocity as a central ethic in the treatment and diagnosis of illness among African Americans on the island of St. Helena, South Carolina, Daniel Moerman (1981) provides evidence of a markedly different response to similar socioeconomic and political conditions. St. Helena islanders, whom he terms "masterful marginals," continue to rely primarily on folk medical practice rather than on biomedicine, even with their greater incorporation into a wage economy. According to Moerman, St. Helena islanders do not have individuals who are marked as specialists in folk medicine. Instead, treatment and diagnosis is "personal and within the family." He sees this as a conscious rejection of the commodification of health care: "The locus of [the] popular medical system, embedded in the family system, and its personal, non- or even anti-professional character, were the response of a marginal community to one aspect of the wider society. The system was designed to separate medicine from the wage-system, to get it out of the money economy. Hence there was no role for a popular medical specialist who would have needed to be compensated for his services—precisely the problem with professional medicine" (Moerman 1981, 288).

Given their geographic and cultural isolation, St. Helena islanders may have been well able to resist the commodification of the body and the social relations of health care in this manner. Green River County, however, is and was not similarly isolated. Thus even though older residents expressed admiration for the interdependence, self-reliance, and closeness of previous generations, they equally value the access that they and their children and grandchildren have to biomedicine, to the cash economy, and to the wealth of consumer goods and services. In their narratives about the eclipse of midwifery and the ties of kin and neighbor, they constantly weigh and evaluate the trade-offs.

Memory and Social Inequality

The ways in which the history of reproduction and the histories of bodies are remembered by African Americans in Green River raises questions about the nature of what was being remembered and about the uses to which these memories were being put. One reason for making distinctions between the world of midwives and home births and that of doctors and hospital births was to satisfy the anthropologist's curiosity. I interpreted these reproductive and community histories with an analysis that foregrounded their folk and metaphoric function, and I have further opposed this analytic perspective to that which emphasized the social facts of the transformation in reproductive health care in the South. Such a dichotomy has taken me this far in the text, but it is in this case murkier than I have posed it. The meanings given to the shifts in social and reproductive life provide commentary on both the world of symbols and that of the social, and these meanings only become clear when we are willing to see how the two worlds are intertwined.

It has been useful, therefore, to examine the categories and sets of meanings that emerge in the experience (or the narration of the experience of) transformations in birthing rituals. Talking about the relationship between past and present, however, was not only an exercise for the inquisitive outsider. Older African Americans in Green River also seemed to be concerned with giving order to their individual and collective histories—histories that had not been entirely shaped with their interests and preferences in mind. The transformation from midwife-attended home births to physician-attended hospital births did not entail much choice on the part of my informants, either in the form or the pace of change. Contemporary home-birth movements, by contrast, are characterized by the focus placed on a woman's and her family's freedom of choice.

Choice, as an ongoing opportunity to pick from a series of options, did not figure much in my informants' discussions. They believed that neither individual women nor the community had any control over the decline in midwifery. The medicalization of childbirth was, on the whole, seen as a positive occurrence—good for women, their families, and the African American community. This viewpoint was not unexpected given the history of segregated hospitals and inferior health care that southern blacks had endured (Savitt and Young 1988; Beardsley 1990).

Yet because its practitioners worked well into the twentieth century, the African American midwifery tradition is close enough to touch. It has become, therefore, a potent and complex symbol, not the least because it counterposes authentic, natural nurturance with the unnatural, technologized management offered by the biomedically trained obstetrician. For me, the history of midwifery in the South also evokes a certain nostalgia for the lost possibilities of an autonomous African American community, rooted in its own kin-based institutions. Just as my informants imbue the disappearance of the traditional midwife with meanings well beyond the intrinsic concern with reproductive health, so, too, do I, and so do those scholars who support the demedicalization of childbirth.

Interest in the African American midwife and her history is connected to the emergence of theoretical and practical critiques of the hospital-centered, medicalized obstetrics that have dominated and continue to dominate reproductive health care in the United States. The responses in Green River suggest that the crucial issue had not revolved around resisting medicalization. Instead, reproductive change signalled African Americans' symbolic, if not fully realized, inclusion in the field of vision of a health care bureaucracy that had until then largely ignored their health needs. If this meant giving up the much-valued midwife, it could also lead to being a part of the "public" in public health. Our own enthusiasm for the recuperation of the midwifery arts should not obscure the race and class issues that led African Americans to welcome modern bodies and modern minds even at the expense of the traditional values and knowledge that they had so respected and valued. Close ethnohistorical studies constantly remind us that local perceptions and historical experiences must be taken into account even as we chart and reveal the politics of reproduction writ large.

On the basis of the accepted measures of wellness, whites in the South are healthier and blacks sicker. This disparity is a historical fact, with programs to improve health being targeted at generalized groups (such as the poor or mothers and children) rather than toward blacks. Furthermore, the overall economic and social differences are not usually addressed in health policies (Hill 1992, 35). In light of these disparities and the long history of compromised health care for southern African Americans, the narratives told to me in Green River also represent a history of the accumulated observations of older residents about the inequities in the system. Under these circumstances, the midwife, with her close supervision and strict attention to the mothers' and infants' postpartum care, used her empirical and folk medical knowledge to mitigate the deleterious effects of compromised nutritional and health status. At the same time, however, even as they acknowledge the advantages of deseg-regated, hospital-based care, and of the greater choices available to the young, my informants voice a strong concern that mothers and children now operate in a health care and social system that offers less nurturance and that has ruptured the links between family and community mem-bers, and between young and old.

The contradictions that develop are nonetheless insufficient to suggest to my informants that losses outweighed gains in the community's en-counters with scientific medicine. Indeed, the perceived material trans-formations in the bodies of infants and mothers offer legitimacy to the health care initiatives that had accompanied the midwifery control cam-paigns. Hospital births are desirable and in some senses natural for the bodies of young women. Hospital care becomes problematic, then, only in those instances when medical personnel are perceived as having treated black women differently. A number of women in Green River who gave birth in the hospital were particularly concerned that the with-holding of anesthesia from poor, black women was an act of discrimina-tion.

Margaret Nelson (1986) raises a related issue in her study of middle- and working-class women in Vermont who gave birth in the hospital. These two groups have very different expectations for the childbirth "experience." Indeed, her study suggests that the very stress on the expe-riential over the medical nature of the childbirth experience is framed by class and cultural considerations. Focusing on a sample of women who had children in the hospital, she found that "middle-class women wanted births in which they could actively participate while avoiding intervention; working-class women wanted quick and easy births with as much intervention as they perceived to be required to bring about this end" (1986, 168). Nelson cautions against the reinscription of a unitary model of what constitutes the best childbirth experience.

In making this critique, however, we must be willing to double back in order to reexamine what, as academics, we have at stake in creating cultural narratives about natural or autonomous reproduction held in women's hands and serving women's interest. I, for example, saw and knew the erasure of the traditional midwife to be a tragedy of immense proportions because of the racist and faulty assumptions that guided the southern health care establishment's campaign against her. By contrast, elder African American residents of Green River County spoke in terms of the benefits of reproductive progress and of health care equity that had come with increasing access to hospitals and obstetrical technologies. Furthermore, where I had imagined a reproductive present in which African American midwives could participate in obstetrical care, my informants spoke of the material changes in the female body that had rendered midwifery practice obsolete.

The task of setting out these points of view was complicated by the ways in which the call for natural childbirth and increased control over birthing has been linked to social critiques of medical hegemony. That call has primarily been analyzed by examining how gender and class struggles have historically underpinned the medicalization of childbirth. The refusal of residents of Green River to speak of midwifery's disappearance as a bad thing can be falsely read, then, as an instance of accommodation and an absence of resistance. Our intellectual project, on the other hand, can begin to feel too much like a missionizing venture to expose the oppressive dimension of what passes for scientific reason and progress.

When they reflected on their experience of birthing and community history, Green River residents did not speak in terms of oppression. They did not mourn the midwife's passing. They spoke instead of compromise and of what had been gained.

In exchange for progress, one must expect to offer something in return. Yet the nature of the gift cannot be decided by those receiving it. Instead, one must learn to adapt and to compromise. There is, in their view, little room for the coexistence of past and present: the invisibility of the past is part of the cost that must be borne. With only a poorly developed sense of the nature of such a sacrifice, I cannot help but interpret these narratives as tragedies.

It is impossible to deny the presence of a strong undercurrent of regret for all that had been eclipsed in the transition to hospital births and away from midwifery care. Caught in this conundrum, I am drawn to memory and to the details of narrative. Stories about midwives, the birthing experience, and community work by giving meaning to the past, even as modernity and progress are heralded.

9

The Social Context of Midwifery

Many African American midwives were illiterate or minimally literate. They did not participate in the official debates about the medicalization of birth. Occasionally, we are able to glimpse in the texts the existence of a dialogue, albeit imbalanced, between midwives and the medical bureaucracy. Yet these are rare. And when they do appear, they are set in the interpretive framework of white physicians and nurses. The insertion of the voices or written words of African American midwives into medical articles served only to emphasize the cultural and professional distance between these women and those who practiced scientific medicine.

This chapter shifts away from the perspective of Virginia's medical personnel and turns to the perceptions of midwives. I offer no strict exegesis of the differences and similarities between politico-medical as opposed to African American constructions of midwives, midwifery, and the body in Virginia (specifically in Green River). Rather, my underlying intent is to juxtapose the two worlds of meaning—one textual, the other oral; one about regulation, the other about experience—in order to understand their interrelationships.

Women who were attended by physicians during the first half of the century were eager to establish that they could and did use the medical professional. Yet having done so, if they then described their experience of birthing, they tended not to focus on what the physician said or did but on the interactional dynamics of family and community members (mothers, grandmothers, neighbors) or the postpartum experience. These aspects of birthing generated the greatest detail. Such an emphasis was certainly influenced by my interests in these aspects of women's experience. But not completely.

When asked directly about the physician's role at childbirth, women responded with shorter, less elaborated answers. Perhaps informants assumed that this sphere was one with which I should be familiar or that the doctor's role did not much vary from woman to woman. Whether they relied on a physician or a midwife, the compelling drama for these women centered on their active involvement in a web of communal and family relations that further centered on childbearing and childbirth.

Am I caught in a hopeless contradiction? On the one hand, I have argued that informants were hesitant to speak about midwives and traditional childbirth rituals, and on the other, I have shown that these subjects generated detailed narratives. What seems inherently at odds is in fact at the heart of the process that I have attempted to describe in this work as a whole: silence counterbalanced with the creation of detailed narratives, the privacy of birth up against the communal involvement of family and neighbors, the devaluation of traditional midwifery alongside an affirmation of its power.

My approach, born of necessity as well as of concern with different sets of issues, diverges to some extent from that taken by scholars who have written about the southern African American midwife. Beatrice Mongeau (1973), for example, a nurse and sociologist, conducted fieldwork with lay African American midwives in a North Carolina county during the early 1960s. Her findings were subsequently published a decade later. These women were the last generation of active practitioners. Mongeau observed midwives in attendance on women in labor, followed them on their pre- and postnatal visits, and documented their ultimately failed struggle to carve a niche as birth attendants in an openly hostile and racist local health care bureaucracy. One is often taken aback by Mongeau's own narrow conceptions of African American culture and of these women in particular. Her study is nonetheless invaluable for its detailed description of traditional midwives as members of their communities and in the process of pursuing their "calling." Regrettably, any opportunity to do similar participant observation in Virginia is well past.

Midwives as Mythic Heroines

Those individuals who were most willing to speak to me about the midwife or midwives in their families had generally positive and warm memories of these women. Though somewhat idealized portraits, they do tell much about the cultural standards used to define midwives as ritual and medical experts in the arena of childbirth and healing. Talk about midwives by family members—what they said, how they acted—is helpful in providing a frame of reference so that we will be able to explore midwives' relationships with women in childbirth and, on the other side of the equation, understand the communal and individual experiences of women who gave birth in the first half of the century. Finally, but perhaps most important, stories about midwives and the experience of childbirth break the confines of their subject matter in that they offer commentary on the past and the present as understood and expressed by older African Americans in the county. I hope to show that these commentaries eventually lead us back to broader issues having to do with questions of power and authority in the treatment and conceptualization of the embodied self.

Once I did archival work after my field research, I may have in retrospect juxtaposed the negative image of the midwife discovered in medical journals with her positive portrayal in these narratives. Nonetheless, stories about the midwife do seem to have been cast, to some extent, as a defense of these women. When relatives, clients and friends reminisced, they marveled and expected me to marvel at the ingenuity of people who made the best of what they had available to them. Though generally silent on the elimination campaigns and on the pressures brought to discourage home births, informants, in these narratives, indirectly provided a counter argument to the official discourse.

To place the African American midwife in context, a story told by Mrs. Harris proves invaluable. Her story is akin to that told by Mrs. Rawling in the previous chapter because it focuses on an unusual birthing event. Herself a midwife (the last actively practicing in the county), Mrs. Harris evoked a memory of an atypical birth attended by her mother. Although she never specified an exact date, she recalled that she had not yet begun to "follow her mother" around as a young apprentice: thus Mrs. Harris was a young onlooker rather than a participant. These events probably occurred sometime in the 1930s, "years and years ago," as Mrs. Harris characterized it.

Her narrative is mythic. Told in its "proper" sequence, the retelling of the story about her mother's heroism situated Mrs. Harris in a longstanding family and community tradition. Apart from its intrinsic historical value, her narrative shared themes with those told by other in-

formants. First, it is a narrative of epiphany as a young child first becomes aware of her desire to attend other women in childbirth and a
source of affirmation as a now elderly woman examines her life in retrospect. It is also a family narrative—perhaps told and retold over the
years, simplified at times, elaborated on in other instances. It is also a
communal narrative about the character and versatility of the traditional
midwife set against the shared hardships of rural life for both black and
white women.

This version was recounted during one of our first conversations. Mrs.
Harris ostensibly began to relate her life history: "I was born in a Christian home." But then, as if her sense of the orderly sequence of events
had been violated, she stopped: "I'm getting ahead of the story, I believe,"
she remarked, and then began again:

> One experience my mother had, I remember. It was a lady, on the same
> road that leads here . . . because I'm a little way up from where I was
> born on the same place . . . And it was a lady, a white lady traveling to
> go and see the doctor. And, ah, she taken sick [started labor] . . . not far
> from my mother's home. And it was a horse and buggy in a muddy
> road, it was very muddy. And a neighbor called my mother and told her
> the lady was sick and needed somebody. So my mother taken her a
> quilt, I remember that, and went down the road where this lady was sick
> and, ah, she had the lady to deliver the baby on the quilt in the road and
> then she brought this lady to my aunt [sic] house which was the closest
> house to the road and there she stayed a month in my mother's care.
>
> Her husband was with her. That's been years and years ago. They
> thought they could make it, I guess, to Lincrest [nearest town] to see
> the doctor. That's where the doctor was. I'm sure they started early that
> morning going to the doctor. But they got stuck in the mud. And after
> delivering a baby you can't go but so far, so she stayed at my aunt house
> for close to a month, and my mother looked after them [mother and
> child].

The white woman is remembered to have been on her way to the
physician in the nearest town. Lincrest is less than fifteen miles away
from the location of Mrs. Harris's family home. But in a horse and buggy
during what must have been winter or early spring, this was quite a
distance. The white couple's decision to start out for the doctor, despite
the condition of the roads, was likely connected to the emerging emphasis in the 1930s on the risks involved in home births, particularly if they
were attended by African American women.

Paradoxically, such a trip placed this woman at greater risk, and in the end she had to rely on the expertise and good graces of an African Amerian midwife. The mention of the quilt laid on the muddy road and our imagined reconstruction of events with the white woman in labor aided by the hastily called midwife recalls public health nurses who railed against "dirty quilts." Somehow the quilt represented the African American midwives' inefficiency and uncleanliness (*Virginia Health Bulletin* 1951, 10; Bennett 1925; Van Blarcom 1930). Abhorrence of the quilt among public health personnel extended beyond whether it was clean or dirty. Some midwives spread a quilt on the floor so that women could deliver from a kneeling or stooping position. Public health nurses preached against this practice. No doubt they believed the floor to be unhygienic and primitive. The quilt, therefore, came to symbolize all that was unseemly and undesirable about African American midwives. By contrast in Mrs. Harris's narrative, the quilt is a sign of succor, warmth, protection from the mud and a surface to receive the newborn.

Having been delivered in the road, on the outside, away from the acclaimed sanitation of the hospital, the white woman entered into the home of a black family for an extended period of time. This, too, is revealing. While the white couple may have initially sought out the scientific care of a physician, they nonetheless appeared to have shared in or acquiesced to the customs governing birth in the African American community. The health of the newly delivered mother and the infant was believed to be endangered unless they remained indoors for a specified period of time. During the 1930s, at the period that Mrs. Harris's mother practiced, postpartum seclusion lasted for approximately one month.

Mrs. Harris in other conversations mentioned that this period was shortened by the time she started to practice in the early 1940s and in the latter days of her mother's career. Other informants also indicated that the time required for "healing" and seclusion had been shortened over the years. Nevertheless, when she recalled this story, Mrs. Harris spoke in the present tense: "you can't go but so far" immediately after childbirth. Although she learned to compromise that dictum, she still held to the validity of its basic premise. For the woman giving birth in the road, therefore, the midwife's authority on this matter probably went unchallenged.

As a historical account, Mrs. Harris's story provides a glimpse into the pivotal role that midwives continued to play despite the explicit desire of medical personnel and the state to bring birth completely under the authority of physicians. Given such variables as the disparate settlements of households, impassable roads (especially in winter), restricted mobility, and the reluctance of physicians to take "charity cases," midwives provided an essential service for white and black women well into the 1940s. They lived close at hand, ready to be summoned by a neighbor, or more typically the husband of the laboring woman. They offered help with housework, if necessary and, follow-up care for mother and infant.

According to Mr. Jackman, it was not unusual for his grandmother to deliver white women. She worked as midwife in the lower end of the county for a period overlapping that of Mrs. Harris's mother and roughly contemporaneous with that of her grandmother (1890s to 1930s). He recalled that "she used to have the white and the black." Other individuals who were related to, or knew, midwives also commented on their attendance on black and white women. Midwives crossed racial and class boundaries in ways that other people could and did not. In the case of the events described by Mrs. Harris, for example, the presence of a white woman in the home of a black family for such an extended period of time during the 1930s was probably unprecedented in the county.

Whether any white midwives practiced in the county during this time is hard to say with certainty. Mrs. Stewart, a white public health nurse, recalled that all the midwives in the county were and historically had been African American. Similarly, informants ranging in age from late fifties to early nineties do not remember any white women practicing midwifery. People were emphatic about this point.

In other areas of Virginia, particularly in the mountains with a negligible African American population, white women were midwives (Plecker 1925; Bennett 1925). In Green River County, however, midwifery was a gender- and racial-specific craft. Because of its associations with African American women and with slavery, it may well have been perceived as an inappropriate craft for white women to pursue (Robinson 1984; Mongeau 1973; see also Savitt 1978 on midwives in slavery). Allusions to that possibility include a historical prologue in the *Virginia Health Bulletin*, a pamphlet distributed free in the state. Devoted to a description of Virginia's midwifery education program, the article offered a quick synopsis of midwifery's history. It outlined the early practice of midwifery by white women in Jamestown Colony in the seventeenth century and implied that these women were superceded by slaves so that "in the eighteenth century midwives were in most cases Negro slaves trained on the plantations. Every plantation had its Negro Midwife" (*Virginia Health Bulletin* 1951, n.p.). The linkage of African American women with childbirth may have had its negative consequences to the extent that midwifery was perceived as being polluting as well as being a plantation craft and therefore reserved for black women.

Seen from another perspective, however, midwifery in Green River worked much like a guild. Informants suggested that only African American women possessed the appropriate combinations of practical skills and spiritual gifts necessary to attend childbirth. Dougherty (1978) writes of the midwife's role in an African American community in Florida as "supernaturally validated." According to Holmes (1986), retired Alabama midwives also referred to their spiritual connection to God. In Green River, such validation was also thought to be important.

Only those who knew how to connect with and read the supernatural world were reliable during childbirth. Perhaps there was the shared cultural assumption between blacks and whites that African American women were spiritually more powerful than white women, at least in the domain of reproductive care. In a study of eighteenth-century Virginia, Mechal Sobel (1987) writes of the mutual areas of overlapping cultural values and traditions between whites and free and enslaved African Americans. In an earlier work, Sidney Mintz and Richard Price (1976) suggest the complex interweaving of African and European cultural forms in the Caribbean and mainland North America. This possibility is important to consider because despite their struggles with physicians, midwives had considerable authority by virtue of their knowledge of the body. In her study of midwives in Texas, Ruth Schaffer (1991) writes that midwives acted as power brokers because of their connections to influential whites and their recognized expertise in health care.

Usually the midwife was related by blood or marriage to the women she attended, and when no such links existed she became a fictive member of the extended family by virtue of her involvement in the intimacies of birth and of her role as an experienced advisor to mothers. Mr. Jackman marveled that people still approached him more than four decades after his grandmother's death: "Both colored and white, they will come up to me and say 'She was my mammy. She helped to birth me.'" In some fashion, these individuals felt a certain connectedness to Mr. Jackman through his grandmother.

In the far past, informants remember that everyone valued older folks' experience and knowledge of roots and herbs that could, for example, cure illness, fortify the body, treat snakebites, hasten childbirth, and rid children of worms. At least one member of the immediate family knew how to prepare, where to find, and when to reap the most commonly used medicinal plants. For rarer remedies and more recalcitrant illnesses, a few elderly women could be consulted. One woman, for example, was particularly adept at setting broken bones by applying appropriate medicinals, although no one with whom I spoke remembered the names or types of remedies that she used. Another made powerful poultices for upper respiratory diseases. These poultices were said to draw the phlegm from the body. Other individuals knew all about female complaints. Yet although there were always individuals who could be referred to as healers or medical specialists, their knowledge was not perceived as esoteric. Any ordinary person came to know the greater repertoire of remedies. Perhaps in a limited sense, the midwife was the only specialist whose knowledge of birth rituals greatly superseded that of others. Yet even in this instance, it was believed that a woman became a good midwife not merely from long experience but because she was called by God, who had given her this gift. Only then could she put the training she received as an apprentice to a more experienced midwife to use.

Anecdotes about midwives' medical and social power cropped up in conversations on many occasions. The grandmother of Mrs. Mann (early seventies) practiced into the late 1930s. Mrs. Mann also remembered "poor" whites coming "into the yard" to solicit medical advice from her grandmother, as well as middle-class women who hired this well-respected midwife to attend them during birth and for the postpartum period. Another woman speaking of her aunt remembered that "she had just as many white people that she delivered for as she had black and she took care of them. And she had some of the richest people here in Green River County." Thus African American midwives provided a point of intimate contact between the races and across social class even as they also carved out an occupational niche for themselves.

Given the emergent structural division of reproductive labor along gender and racial lines—white male science/African American midwifery—and efforts to discredit and eliminate midwives, Mrs. Harris's narrative is one of triumph for her mother and for midwifery in general. Her recollection of these events provided proof that the traditional midwife was capable and did offer birthing services comparable to that of physicians. The mythic quality of her narrative relates to its reversal of the expected interaction between the races. A white couple become the supplicants in a black household.

The importance of this narrative in Mrs. Harris's life history stemmed in part from the subsequent problems she faced during her tenure as a midwife. Her great-grandmother, her grandmother, and to some extent her mother experienced few if any substantive challenges to their personal, social, and professional identities as midwives. By contrast, Mrs. Harris began her career during the period when public health officials increasingly encouraged women to rely on physicians and to deliver their babies in the hospital. She spoke with pride of her training under the auspices of the local public health clinic but expressed much anger about nurses' and physicians' derogatory attitudes toward midwives and their approach to birthing. As a fourth-generation midwife and the last in her family, she witnessed and experienced the demise of midwifery as a spiritually sanctioned and essential craft. Ostensibly about her mother's heroism, the events remembered in this narrative nourished Mrs. Harris's sense that she had taken the right path despite the obstacles placed in her way. She recalled that ever since she was a child she had wanted to "wait on sick people." Her mother's role in this birth may have served to validify Mrs. Harris's emerging belief that she was called to be a midwife.

Although a midwife performed some housekeeping functions, especially when attending middle-class and wealthy whites, they were not servants. For midwives, this was a crucial difference. Again, Mrs. Harris's story partially reveals the dynamics at work. She referred to the woman in labor as sick. On other occasions she described herself as someone who "waited on sick people." At first I misunderstood the use of the word. Because some midwives had reputations as healers who were especially knowledgeable about medicinal roots and herbs, I assumed that her reference was to this aspect of her practice. Once it became clear that the term applied specifically to her work as a midwife, I then inferred that she had adopted the terminology and perhaps the worldview of public health personnel and local physicians who considered birth to be a pathological event. This may be partially correct. But it is not the entire picture. The use of the term "sick" in Mrs. Harris's narrative provided a euphemism for speaking about pregnancy and childbirth, and I suspect that it customarily served that purpose. But more to the point, it also created an important social distinction between midwives and other women who worked in homes as domestics under the complete authority of the white household. Midwives were there to take care of "sick" women, and as such their craft was a specialized and skilled one.

The importance of this distinction to Mrs. Harris and historically to all midwives should not be underestimated. In this rigidly structured and racially discriminatory county, midwifery offered African American women an alternative to other kinds of employment. Mrs. Chandler, a woman in her sixties who migrated north in search of work during the 1940s, noted that many women of her generation left as teenagers. "For a young woman, there wasn't much of a choice as far as jobs were concerned—either work in domestic service, maybe a factory-type job would come along, or do some kind of farm-type work. So far as I can see, it was better to leave."

Given this limited field of opportunity for African American women, midwifery may have been perceived by some individuals as a means of gaining a measure of autonomy and respectability. A few women who received schooling became teachers. But midwifery did not require one to be literate. Being capable of signing one's name and filling out a birth certificate took on increasing importance by the early 1930s, but most women were probably able to find someone to do the required writing if they were unable to or unsure of their skills in this regard. For African American women in Virginia and in Green River County, midwifery was one of the few vocations open to them. This alternative was characterized by Mrs. Rawling in terms of complexion and respectability: "Only midwife around was colored, most of the time they were part-white. They wanted to do something different from the regular black people. They didn't mind you coming to their house because they kept it nice . . . but of course there were some jet-black ones too."

Though intriguing, I am unable to draw any firm conclusions as to the "complexion" of midwives and the symbolic role that this attribute played in the imaging of these women by whites and blacks. My point, here, is to show that for African American midwives, theirs was both a "calling" and a profession: it was a means of distinguishing themselves as ritual and reproductive specialists within the African American as well as the white community.

Mrs. Harris remarked, for example, that she had learned the "trade" from her mother and grandmother—a passing hint of the parallel drawn between midwifery and exclusively male "trades" such as carpentry,

blacksmithing, and so on. This perspective is remarkable for its divergence from the portrait of midwives in medical journals during the period under consideration. It also contrasts with the contemporary ambivalent perceptions of the traditional midwife by some African
Americans in the county. The sense of mission and faith in their skills
apparently expressed by midwives in Green River does fit, however, with
the occasional frustration expressed by physicians who complained of
"midwives's self-complacency" and independence.

Modes of Knowledge Transmission: Signs and Revelations

Midwives received their knowledge about birth, healing, and the body
and its treatment through different modes of transmission. In general,
older informants agreed that women were called to be midwives. But the
expression of that calling varied. Some women received signs in dreams;
others were imbued with a childhood interest in caring for the sick.
Others were picked by older midwives who themselves had been given
revelations about the suitability of a particular woman for the midwifery
calling. Some women started by helping in the delivery of family members and then gradually extended their practice outside of the immediate
family. Descriptions of these avenues to midwifery practice resemble
those of African American midwives in other southern communities
(Logan 1989; Dougherty 1978; Holmes 1986; Mongeau 1973; Reeb
1992; Susie 1988; Smith 1994).

The common thread linking these rural women is the emphasis on the
extrapersonal nature of the midwifery craft. Whether they inherited their
skills in a direct line of descent from female kin or were the first in their
families to practice, African American midwives from the rural South all
seem to have envisioned themselves as simply the vessels that God had
deigned worthy to fill with the practical and spiritual knowledge about
women's bodies and childbirth. According to residents in Green River,
the midwife's power came from a "higher authority." Yet as in other
aspects of life, it was up to the individual to read and interpret the signs
in her life. This reading could also involve the rest of the community
because they were expected to acknowledge and reaffirm, encourage or
discourage, the readings that persons placed on the signs they had been
given. The extent to which older residents were able to narrate the cir-

cumstances of an individual midwife's calling suggest that signs were shared information. It is easy to imagine familial or neighborhood discussions about the meanings of dreams and incidents in a person's life.

A legendary midwife who died in her nineties, the year before I arrived in the county, was remembered as having the most dramatic revelation. Aunt Annie Mae, as she was called, was the mother of nine children all delivered by a midwife. The children's father never actually lived with the family but visited regularly. I was told by informants that when Annie Mae began to feel "the pains of labor" with the birth of her tenth child, she delivered the baby, a breach birth, without the aid of a midwife or any other adult. Only after cleaning the child and herself and "straightening" the birthing room did she call her neighbors for belated assistance. Aunt Annie Mae's solitary endurance during childbirth was taken as a marker of her strong character and was interpreted by others as a sign that she had received the call to wait on women.

Annie Mae began her practice sometime in the mid-1930s, soon after she had recuperated. Informants noted as a further indication of her powers that unlike other midwives, she did not undergo any period of apprenticeship with a more experienced woman. Linda Holmes offers a narrative from Alabama that closely parallels that of Annie Mae. A woman who subsequently became a midwife tells of her decision to deliver her own child without informing members of her family who were, it appears, in an adjoining room. Holmes does not, however, interpret this remarkable story as part of the woman's initiation, so to speak, into midwifery. Rather, she simply presents it as an example of the way in which African American women "viewed birth as a natural phenomenon," "a spontaneous event" (Holmes 1986, 284–85). But was such an event as common as Holmes would have it? Under what circumstances would a woman decide to birth her own child without the support of others?

My data suggests that this occurrence was neither ordinary nor as unmarked as Holmes describes it. Her informant's extraordinary action occurred before she was a midwife and in a situation where help was close at hand. Perhaps, as in the case of Annie Mae, she wished to test herself as well as to indicate to others that she was indeed suited and called to be a midwife. In any case, we must be cautious not to impose our own desire to cast African American women as somehow more natural or closer to nature onto the stories that these women tell us. Actions taken in the past hold their own interpretations for the audiences for which they were intended.

In Green River, the force of Annie Mae's calling may have been necessary given the unusual situation of her personal life. The father of her children was white and married. Annie Mae was not, therefore, a Christian woman because she was "living in sin." She overcame these barriers and was accepted as a powerful and trustworthy midwife in large part because she delivered her own child. I heard many versions of this birthing story, from women who were themselves children when Annie Mae practiced her craft. Such narrative interest suggests that this was indeed seen as an unusual act by an unusual woman.

Mrs. Harris's life history is illustrative of another path to midwifery. In her household, her maternal grandmother and her mother were midwives, as was her great-grandmother, deceased by the time she was born. Her mother, she recalled, learned alongside her mother, and then she learned by listening to and watching the two women. She came to the craft at a relatively young age. Seemingly, the responsibilities entailed in being a midwife did not appeal to her sisters. Mrs. Harris was the daughter identified as having the gift to "take up the trade." The emphasis on divine sanction overlapped in this family with the long history of mother passing on the craft to daughter. In her account, Mrs. Harris emphasized that she took the initiative in expressing a desire to be a midwife: "I am the fourth generation. And growing up my mother used to go and wait on sick people, and I always wanted to wait on sick people. My mother encouraged me after I was old enough to go around with her. I think it must have been I always liked to do that work ever since I was a child, so it must have been a gift handed down and my mother encouraged me so it would always stay in the family."

From conversations with older women and men, it appeared that the usual pattern was for a woman to wait until she had herself given birth and raised her children before beginning to practice. In Mrs. Harris's case, however, she began to accompany her mother during her adolescence. It is likely that she did not actively participate during this apprenticeship period, but watched and helped as she was instructed. Yet even this level of participation was a bit unusual. After marrying in her early twenties, she stopped "going around" for a while but then began to attend women as an independent midwife sometime after the birth of her first child.

Mrs. Harris also was required beginning in the early 1950s to accompany a physician on his cases as a prerequisite to getting her yearly license. She recalled the evolution of midwifery from a calling to a licensed, secularized craft. She characterized the physician's primary role not as a teacher but as a monitor, some form of quality control expert:

> Well, mother I don't think they had to go around with the doctor but they asked us to go around with the doctor and the doctor will have to sign for you to get your license, you know. You can't just go on and get 'em like you used to. He got to see that you know something about that work. I went around with my mother, but still I had to go around with the doctor too. So that he could check what I know. Cause so many times, he would just sit back and he wouldn't tell me a thing. I would have to do the job. That's the way you would learn . . . I mean, that's the way I got my license.

Theoretically, licensure may have enhanced rather than diminished a midwife's authority. On the one hand it connected her to the county bureaucratic structure and thus connected her patients as well. Midwives were required to accompany pregnant clients to the clinic, and thus they may have enabled such women to more readily gain access to health and social welfare services. On the other hand, the license by its very official nature created an analogy between midwifery and nursing—a profession that had been a traditional avenue of opportunity for a few educated black women. In fact, as early as the 1920s, the public health clinic had encouraged midwives to replace their dark clothing and head wraps with white uniforms and caps (Bennett 1925). But what Mrs. Harris and her colleagues began to realize at least by the late 1940s was that they were losing a good measure of their autonomy. Furthermore, the emphasis on the spiritual calling of their craft was being displaced. Oftentimes, the local public health nurse picked young women who they thought would make likely candidates for lay midwives.

When researchers from the U.S. States Public Health Service, on a visit to Virginia, advised their local counterparts to train a younger woman in the neighborhood of each older one in order to meet that social "need" of midwifery and thus gradually eliminate the "unfit" midwife, they also offered a selection criteria. Among other qualities, they listed "an appreciation for cleanliness," which could be measured by judging the cleanliness of the candidate's home and children; education at no less than an eighth-grade level so that the candidate would understand "selected literature pertaining to general health as well as to maternity and infancy" (Daniel and Gafafer 1935, 1813). Based on these criteria, a good proportion of the women who would normally receive and take up the call to practice would have been eliminated. To the extent that public health personnel followed through on these and similar recommendations, they completely bypassed earlier norms of knowledge transmission and apprenticeship.

In her study, Mongeau (1973) reports that much to the frustration of clinic nurses, pregnant women ignored the "secularly" chosen and trained midwife. They preferred to engage the "old-style" midwife. Fragmentary evidence suggests that younger women in Green River may have preferred to use a licensed midwife who had trained with the public health department or with a physician. Some distinction seems to have been made between a "regular" midwife and one who had "been under training." Mrs. Stewart recalled that "younger mothers were more accepting [of her instructions] than the older ones." Yet I am unable to say if these younger mothers continued to perceive the spiritual validation of midwifery as a prerequisite to practice. Certainly in our conversation, older women, who would have been in this group of "younger mothers" in the 1940s, spoke of the "power" of midwives and the importance of being "called."

Lois Paul (1978) notes that spiritual sanction as a midwife was one, if not the only, way for Mayan women to achieve culturally approved authority and independence. As opposed to the socialized submissiveness expected of women, "the role of midwife," she writes, "demands that a woman be aggressive and authoritative in unfamiliar situations, that she observe none of the usual space and time boundaries applicable to other women, that she display unusual fortitude. She must withstand the terrors of night and of contact with the super-natural. She must overcome feelings of disgust and fear at the sight and handling of blood, of the newborn fetus, of potentially polluting birth substances" (Paul 1978, 130).

Although the same rules did not apply to the strict dichotomization of social roles between men and women in the African American community, women were generally expected to stay within the domestic sphere, caring for children and their households. Mrs. Murphy, for example, observed that "when I was coming along [in the 1920s] the women hadn't started out too much. Most of them were home." In this sense the midwife by virtue of her vocation was more likely to bend the normative pattern, staying away from home for extended periods of time when necessary, traveling at night, leaving the care of the household to other family members, and working with the county health care bureaucracy and with local physicians.

The inversion of authority relevant to the Green River data, however, relates more to race than to gender. African Americans, whether male or female, were perceived as standing in structurally and socially subordinate positions to the county's whites. African Americans neither enjoyed the same legal and political rights as whites nor the access to economic power. Social class, to be sure, overlayered racial stratification and the expected norms of racial interaction. Older residents took some interest in recalling white neighbors who were unable to provide for their families. They reminded me that neighboring whites were always "borrowing" food, tools, and even clothing. Mrs. Redding recalled that "mother lent my best Sunday dress and coat to a [white] neighbor girl when they had a death in the family." Stories also emerged about white men who fathered children with black women.

No matter what the private intimacies or the impoverishment of some whites, however, African Americans were generally expected to defer to whites, never overstepping the established public boundaries. The midwife, however, particularly in the first decades of the twentieth century, provided an essential service to the white household, whether rich or poor. From this perspective, midwives held a certain authority allowing for a greater latitude in negotiating the boundary between the races. She, for example, entered into the most private places of the white household and the white body at moments of intense vulnerability.

When whites referred to the midwife as "my mammy" or "aunt," we first hear the pejorative associations and the benovolent racism. Yet these apellations also indicate the acknowledgment of some kinship relationship with its related obligations. By virtue of her healing powers and importance in the birthing room, the midwife drew whites, rich and poor, into an implied reciprocal contract with her and by extension with her real kin. The working through of these connections is not immediately discernible in the present. Yet they can be glimpsed in statements from older residents such as Mr. Bowen, for example, who believed that because his grandmother had attended the wives of certain powerful men in the county, it had made it easier for him to obtain a loan to buy land and build his house during the 1940s. The local banker who also owned a lumberyard had been delivered by his grandmother. Thus, in this situation, the midwife's role led to the creation of patron-client ties between the local white gentry and her family—ties extending over two generations.

Midwifery Knowledge and Power

Heroism—or perhaps more accurately the dedication to service—appeared repeatedly in stories about midwives and midwife knowledge. Given my interests, informants, particularly relatives, who discussed these women may have considered it appropriate to highlight "achievements" and to downplay the ordinary or what they considered to be the negative. Yet having taken this likelihood into account, the common thread linking these kinds of stories appeared in conversations on other topics. The meaningful connection and the focus of much attention by older residents concerned the ability of people in the past to cope in the midst of crisis, to innovate, to make do, to use their common sense, to rely on and make use of their "God-given" talents or "gifts." These attributes fell under a category of knowledge and practice commonly referred to as "mother wit."

Mother wit was variously described as an intuitive capacity to adjust to unexpected circumstances, as knowledge of nature and how to use it, and as an ability to read signs or people's motivations and personality. Midwives were said to have mother wit. This kind of knowledge was discussed as both a spiritual and material substance. Thus, Mr. Marks (age eighty) told me that the acquisition of mother wit was a "mystery," a "gift from God." Similarly, commenting on his grandmother's use of herbal remedies and her knowledge about childbirth, Mr. Jackman expressed his puzzlement: "I mean, she . . . nobody didn't taught her. I mean, whar she get it from? She didn't go to school for it, so it had to be through God and her mother wit. That's the only thing that it could be. It was just a mystery, I mean, all that she could do."

Others provided a physiological explanation. Mother wit was transmitted from mother to child through breast milk. As proof of this matrilineal line of transmission, I was told that the younger generation had lost its "mother wit" because mothers had started using formula and stopped breast-feeding. According to Mr. Williams (age seventy), "they started using that old formula and the infant just couldn't get that mother wit, see. Cause you get it in that nursing." Whatever its manifestations—the ability to fix machinery, to play musical instruments without any formal training, to attend childbirth—mother wit enabled the individual to gain needed skills without "book knowledge." According to some informants, the loss of mother wit in the community and the increasing reliance on book knowledge was responsible for the eclipse of traditional medicine and the increasing dependence on doctors and hospitals.

I have previously commented on "giftedness" as central to the transmission of midwifery knowledge. In some manner, it is a concept analogous to right-handedness or left-handedness. This ability, according to informants, was something bestowed on particular individuals without their volition or direct intervention. Against the descriptions of the "natural" quality of this gift, however, it is important to recall Mrs. Rawling's comments that, at least in her neighborhood, midwives tended to be of lighter complexion and Mrs. Harris's reference to her "trade." This latter term brings to mind images of long-term apprenticeships, the acquisition of specific skills, and a conscious effort to transform oneself from a nonspecialist to a specialist.

References to individuals who "looked" like a midwife also suggest that there were some culturally recognized criteria for midwives. Furthermore, conversations with older residents suggest that women tended to become midwives on a full-time basis only after they were past active childbearing and their children were grown or able to take care of themselves. Thus the gift of midwifery was dissimilar to right- or left-handedness in that some women rather than others actively chose to learn midwifery and to take on the responsibilities inherent in such a vocation. It was important that women possessed the temperament and developed the appropriate skills and knowledge necessary to aid women in childbirth. Yet without the gift proffered by God, women would not be "good" midwives.

How might we interpret older informants' focus on midwifery as a supernaturally mediated "calling"? The concept of the midwife's "gift" or "calling" is discussed in the literature on southern African American midwives (Dougherty 1978; Mongeau 1973; Holmes 1986, 1996; Susie 1988). Dougherty (1978) writes of the tradition of "supernatural validation" of midwives in the community she studied during the early 1970s. Women dreamed that they were to become midwives. Furthermore, older midwives believed that God directed the selection of the younger women who would become their apprentices. The spiritual power and responsibilities held by the midwife was mediated through her close relationship with God. In some respects, a woman chosen to become a midwife was transformed from an ordinary to an extraordinary individual. Women in Dougherty's study emphasized that this transformation was beyond their control; it had been taken out of their hands. One woman asserted, for example, that becoming a midwife "was all in the plans of God, it was nothing on my part. No it was something I didn't have no control over . . . After I done got the call, I couldn't stay home; if I knowed a woman was in labor, I was gone. I just had to be there, just had to help" (Dougherty 1978, 153).

These utterances revealed the significance of supernatural validation and divine revelation to the midwifery vocation in this community. My work suggests a similar emphasis. Yet from a slightly different vantage point, I want to argue that in many arenas, older African Americans in Green River shifted the locus of knowledge acquisition away from individual will and toward the uncontrolled and uncontrollable nonmaterial world. Thus I was surprised to find Mr. Jackman, who was normally loquacious, grow silent and a bit shy in admitting that, like his grandmother, he also had gifts. Without formal training and without reference to written plans, he knew how to build houses. In the county he held a reputation as a master carpenter. It was important in Green River not to call attention to one's capabilities. Older informants received praises by deflecting them, pointing to God's role in their achievements and successes.

When the clerk in a local Baptist church read the minutes, she preceded her recitation with a prayer, ritually acknowledging that she stood without "form or fashion," humbled in front of the congregation and the Lord. Similarly, on other occasions, I noted that the pastor of this congregation would sometimes interrupt his sermon to tell those gathered that the Lord was "leading" him in what he said. On the one hand, the reference to divine inspiration emphasized his spiritual closeness to God; on the other, it was a means of telling the church that he was just a mere vessel. He at once remained ultimately human even as he took on the mantle of spiritual and moral leader.

The concept of the midwifery gift in Green River may be understood in these terms. It would have been inappropriate and unwise for women in this community to claim that their knowledge came from within the individual rather than from some external spiritual force. As in the Mayan community described by Lois Paul (1978), African Americans in Green River County expressed "marked ambivalence toward hierarchy and any demonstration of assertiveness or ascendancy that accrue[d] to the individual office holder rather than the office" (1978, 131).

As a midwife, a woman stood apart. She claimed special knowledge and was given authority by community members. People believed in her. Yet a good midwife was an individual who served everyone, who was willing to defer payments, who did not abuse her spiritual gifts or flaunt her powers. She remained humbled in front of the women she attended even as they gave themselves up to her authority. Midwives were gifted with the ability to attend births and safely bring women and children through this physically dangerous life event. Yet older informants seemed to regard this gift as eventually a communal one, shared by all the women and families who trusted midwives and to whom she was obligated to offer her services, day or night, on muddy roads or in well-appointed bedrooms.

The high value placed on mother wit in older residents' narratives contradicted to some extent their conviction that modernity is desirable. Yet from another perspective, these are different but not necessarily contradictory points of view. Because the younger generation had lost its capacity to draw on this source of practical and spiritual knowledge, it was necessary to rely on "book knowledge" and the resources it made available. Younger people, I was told, had grown "wiser" in some things and "more foolish" in others.

Narratives about midwives returned to this basic theme. They provided commentary not only on the skill of individual women but on the former independence and self-reliance of the African American community. The midwife, in this respect, took on heroic proportions. "I never seen her tired," Mrs. Mann recalled of her aunt. "She always had a hand for somebody. Don't make no difference who. Everybody was the same." The midwife was "backward" and "superstitious" in some people's eyes, but for others she represented the capacity of African Americans to transform the objective conditions of deprivation and to sustain self, family, and community. She also represented a worldview that older informants now characterize as "disappeared."

I should caution that informants rarely used such phrasings either to describe the history of midwifery or of the community. Rather, it is through the details of stories that they spoke most fervently on these matters. For Mrs. Harris, the story of her mother's rescue of the "white lady" provided the ground on which she then proceeded to build her case in defense of traditional midwifery and midwives in general. Submerged in these and other memories of midwives is the creation of an oppositional transcript. The weak and subordinate assert their sense of power when they recall the past. Older residents commented on the mutability of seemingly inflexible racial and socioeconomic boundaries: whites, too, depended on the midwives' skills and knowledge. The lines of authority, at least in the treatment of the body, hadn't always been from the top down. In the past, "book knowledge" had its limits, and those individuals who possessed mother wit and special gifts from God often succeeded where science failed.

The distinctions made between "book knowledge" and "mother wit" in Green River County resembles Carlo Ginzburg's (1980) discussion of "high" and "low" knowledge. Low or common knowledge he finds to be that normally held by the powerless in a society, although in whole or in part it is often used and exploited by the elite. Low knowledge, according to Ginzburg, consists of skills, insights, mode of inquiry, and problem-solving techniques grounded in the details of ordinary, everyday experience.

Yet such knowledge is neither reinvented by each new perceiver nor idiosyncratic. Rather, both innovations and accumulated traditions are verbally transmitted between generations and among the community of users. Common knowledge does not depend on the rigid application of a set of fixed rules but on the flexible use of what Ginzburg calls the "conjectural paradigm" (Ginzburg 1980, 12).

By contrast, high knowledge, normally kept out of reach of the powerless or nonspecialist, is codified through the written word. Characteristically, such knowledge involves the strict application of preestablished procedures and rules to obtain replicable results. This is the basis of the natural sciences, Ginzburg writes. In a hierarchy of values, high knowledge is considered to be of greater value because of its supposed removal from the realm of direct experience and its association with state power. Ginzburg also shows that despite its frequent cooptation by the elite, low knowledge is historically devalued by them (Ginzburg 1980, passim).

Distinctions between these two means of gaining knowledge of the world clearly emerged in conversations with older residents of Green River County, particularly in narratives about the midwives' ability to rise to unexpected events or circumstances. While certainly not denying the importance of "book learning," which residents believed to be essential for the younger generation to "get ahead," they described it as standing in some antagonistic relationship to mother wit. From this perspective, older African Americans used the midwife's acumen to say something about the distinguishing features of their community and their minds in the past. That is, "book learning" had its constraints: it could only "take you so far" before it would be necessary to call on deeper sources of skill and expertise. These could not usually be provided by white physicians. Obliquely, older informants referred to the fact that, for the most part, whites were not endowed with any large measures of mother wit.

In this construction of the "other," African Americans did not offer explanations as to why whites continued to hold economic and political power. I was also frustrated in my attempt to link these affirmations of African American medical and spiritual versatility to any structural critiques of the cooptation and eventual elimination of midwives. Nonetheless, discussions of midwives' power was often balanced against commentary on the relative inefficacy of medical science in the first half of the century.

Some informants did speak with great respect for individual physicians. A seventy-five-year-old woman, for example, remembered the occasional visits of one of the county's few doctors in the 1920s: "As soon as Doctor Mueller—he was an old German man—came into that room it was like we just knew everything was going to be all right. You just started feeling better." Respect for the individual physician, however, did not entail complete or exclusive confidence in scientific medicine or its approach to treatment of the body. In their discussions of white doctors, informants largely focused on their relative willingness to treat black patients, to accept barter rather than cash, on whether they inspired trust. They focused, in other words, on the personal characteristics of the physician.

Informants were less likely to comment on the efficacy of the physicians' pharmaceuticals and often expressed doubt about whether doctors could have significantly altered the course of an illness. Descriptions of a "good" doctor fit closely with what Paul Starr (1982) has categorized as "personal" as opposed to "collective" authority: "Before the professionalization of medicine was institutionalized in the late nineteenth and early twentieth centuries, physicians might win personal authority by dint of their character and personal knowledge. But once [authority] was institutionalized . . . it no longer depended on individual character and lay attitudes; instead it was increasingly built into the structure of institutions" (Starr 1982, 19–20).

In their recollections about the past, informants suggested that rather than the inherent power of scientific medicine, the most important factor in judging a biomedical practitioner was the strength of his character. An assessment of a physician's character involved, of course, his relative willingness to offer his services to African Americans. Recollections that focused on the goodwill of some physicians existed alongside bitter memories of segregated and inferior hospitals, of the exclusion of the county's African American population from the local doctor's office except for a weekly "coloreds' day," of being unable to afford medical care when it was available. On the one hand, informants remembered some caring, relatively unbiased physicians; on the other, they recalled a system of health care delivery that consistently discriminated according to race and economic status. They expressed pervasive ambiguities about this situation.

Mrs. Lawton lived through a major flu epidemic in the early 1900s. Her sister, then in her twenties, died after contracting pneumonia. Now in her nineties, Mrs. Lawton recalled the extraordinary generosity of the local physician. When her sister developed a "high fever," he had "allowed" the family to have a daily block of ice from his icehouse, though it was the height of summer when ice was a valued and scarce commodity. She also remembered the same physician's attendance when another sister fell ill soon after childbirth. Nonetheless, in both cases, Mrs. Lawton believed that "there was nothing that he could really do for them."

Given the unreliability of the medical care system, when the physician was called, he was considered to be one element—and not necessarily the most important—in a range of therapeutic approaches used to cure an illness or treat a medical emergency. Informants attributed such multifaceted health care strategies both to the value of traditional medicines and healers and to the impoverished economic situation of families who had to be self-reliant and use their mother wit. Typically, as expressed in the proud recollection of a man in his late sixties, the physician was rarely needed: "Mama didn't go to the doctor for every little thing. She did all the doctoring for us eight children and raised us all up to be grown [everyone reached adulthood]."

Because of her special gifts, the midwife played a central role in the life of the community. Some variation of the phrase "she was just like a doctor" occurred frequently in conversations. People referred to the community's "faith" in midwives. Mrs. Bowling recalled that her mother "doctored" and delivered the children of the town clerk, a white man. She was consulted whenever anyone in the clerk's household became sick. "They'll tell you that today. They won't deny it. He [the clerk], he says, 'Doctor what,' That [Mrs. Bowling's mother] was my doctor, and so that's the way it was. Any of his little children get sick or get a cold or something, he'll send after her. I don't know what she do . . . Just what I said, like a doctor, she could fix up . . . I don't know how she do it. But I don't care how ill you be, she could get and break your fever or whatever."

Here the doctor's skills become the abstract standard against which the midwife's expertise is judged. Yet her skills are discussed as essentially different from the physician's because she had to "learn them natural." The healing and midwifery skills of the midwife did not "come from man but from God." It is apparent from older residents' testimony, however, that acknowledgment of difference did not, as it now does, lead to the view that the two medical systems were mutually exclusive.

Mr. Jackman recalled an instance when his grandmother's knowledge of home remedies restored a diabetic patient to health after a regular physician had "given up the case." This account resembles Mrs. Harris's narrative: the doctor is replaced by the midwife who then proceeds to effect a cure. But it also shows that individuals, when they could, moved between scientific and traditional medical systems in their search for resolution of the body's dysfunction. Mr. Jackman orates the interaction between the midwife, her patient, and the doctor, shifting between telling the story and reproducing the dialogue between participants:

There was this fellow, his sister had sugar diabetes. The doctor had given her up completely you know. Her toes was coming off. He [the doctor] said, "No need you coming to see me no more, nothing I can do for you." And I don't know what my grandmother did, but I do know she went and got some huckleberry leaves, I'll never forget, and goose-berry leaves.

She boiled them, made a tea . . . and six months' time . . . [*interrupts himself*] well, just like she [the woman patient] would say, "Well, since I ain't got no change, no how, I'll try it." And six months' time the lady went back to her doctor and the doctor couldn't find no sign of sugar [diabetes]. No sign. She [the patient] said he [the doctor] asked her what she was doing. She said she told him, I'll never forget, she said [addressing the midwife], "I told him that you [the midwife] was the doctor. That's one thing I ain't gon tell how, but that you was the doctor." See, my grandmother just boil those leaves and made a tea. And six months' time she [the patient] didn't have no sugar and that woman lived . . . I know she lived 'bout twenty-five years after that. Evidently the leaves take the sugar out the body.

Mr. Jackman's and other narrations suggests that the midwife's calling was not restricted to parturition and childbirth. In the sequence of events recounted here, the confrontation between midwife/healer and medical doctor occurred over the body of a diabetic woman who moved between the two practitioners. It is likely that the physician had the appropriate technology to manage the diabetes, as these events occurred sometime in the 1930s when insulin treatments were available and used by at least one other person in the county. (I was told by an informant in her sixties that her diabetic mother gave herself daily injections of insulin.)

The physician's reported comment that he could do nothing for the patient is difficult to interpret. Perhaps from the patient's point of view, the physician's techniques were not having the desired effects. They did not bring about any noticeable changes. She then turned to the midwife, who shared her perspective on the nature of blood and its role in causing illness. Yet she reserved a certain skepticism. She drank the tea as a last bid: it could help and certainly wouldn't harm her. Mr. Jackman's narration is in part about this woman's conversion to the midwife's healing approach, coming after a loss of faith in the medical doctor.

Blood as the loci for illness diagnosis and treatment is a core motif in the medical belief systems of African Americans in the United States and the Caribbean (Hill and Mathews 1981; Moerman 1975; Laguerre 1987; de Albuquerque 1979; Dressler 1982; Snow 1978). It is not surprising, therefore, that the dissatisfaction in the preceding narration occurred around the issue of the appropriate treatment of the sick woman's blood. Mr. Jackman's reference to "sugar diabetes" conforms to the idea held by other informants that it was caused by having blood that is too sweet or thick. The sugar, therefore, has to be "drawn" out of the blood in order to restore it to the right consistency or "flavor," to use Moerman's (1975) descriptive category. In this illness narrative, the patient is first abandoned by the physician and then resurrected by the midwife, who knows just what herbal medicines to use in order to "take the sugar out of the body."

In her role as a healer, Mr. Jackman's grandmother understood the language of blood spoken by the woman. According to her grandson, she gathered the huckleberry and gooseberry leaves and boiled a tea, without hesitation. She knew just what was needed. His memory of her quick action and knowledge of bodily disease is a commentary on this woman's skills as a healer. It is also reflective of the oft-repeated opinion that such skills and abilities had disappeared. In other conversations, Mr. Jackman told me, for example, that most people no longer knew how to gather the roots and herbs for illnesses. But they need not have tried. As an example, he commented that, "You hardly see gooseberry around." Thus the connection between the physical landscape and the landscape of the body that undergird his grandmother's healing gifts no longer existed. Yet this link had been central to the midwife's craft. Not only did she make teas for "sugar diabetes" but other remedies intended to ease childbirth pain or protect against colds.

The pursuit of treatment by the woman in Mr. Jackman's story involved her in the medical belief system of the midwife—one that she, to some extent, shared. But this did not situate either woman in a strictly closed domain. In this telling, after six months, the woman returned to the physician both to confront him with her healed body and to use his methods of diagnosis to confirm that the sugar had disappeared. Mr. Jackman reconstructs their interaction. The physician detects no signs of diabetes with his instruments of measurement. He asks for an explanation: the expected hierarchy of the "medical interview" is temporarily suspended. Having been subject to the authority of the white physician, the African American woman now gets to say her piece. Her victory rests in silence and veiled speech. She names the midwife as her "doctor." But she leaves the rest in mystery: neither the method nor the form of her successful treatment is revealed.

Having proved the doctor wrong, the woman returns to re-create the encounter for the midwife. She may have expressed her gratitude. It is equally likely that by telling of her cryptic handling of the physician's questions, she wanted to reassure the midwife that no secrets had been betrayed. It is easy to imagine the repetition of similar scenes during the period we have been considering.

In Mr. Jackman's story, the "high knowledge" of scientific medicine interacted with the "common knowledge" of midwifery—a head-on collision worked through in an illness episode. Given the emphasis on flexibility in the medical worldview of midwives and Green River's residents, however, there was the potential for other kinds of interactions. Midwives frequently shared techniques and concepts of the body with scientific medical practice and seemed not to have placed them in a separate category of knowledge. In fact, the common-sense techniques developed by midwives were likely as reflective of their lives as wives of farmers or farmers themselves—working with animals, observing nature, and "making do" with the tools and resources available. We are reminded of Mrs. Stewart's (the white public health nurse) memory of a midwife being called straight from the field to attend a neighbor in labor. Whatever the exact provenance of the midwife's practice, it is the syncretic nature of her craft that most concerns us here.

The handling of a premature infant illustrates the ingenuity of a midwife who practiced into the 1940s. It also introduces the web of social relations surrounding childbirth. The midwife derived her authority as divinely sanctioned birth specialist not because of her isolation from others but as a result of her close connection to and involvement in a set of familial and communal relationships. In Mr. Jackman's story, the diabetic woman was unrelated to the midwife/healer, although he did specify that the woman's brother brought her to the midwife's attention, thus he acknowledges that the woman was not a stranger to his grandmother. Typically, midwives rarely attended women who were unfamiliar. They delivered the children of women related by blood or marriage, and when those connections did not exist, the fictive title of "aunt," "mom," or "mammy" established the midwife–patient relationship as a kin-based one.

Mrs. Bynum, who recalled her grandmother's treatment of the premature infant, was raised in an extended family. Her grandmother, grandfather, mother, siblings, and cousins lived in the same household, and aunts, uncles, cousins, and in-laws resided close to or within a few miles of the "homeplace." The homeplace was a central reference point in this and other narratives. It usually referred to the original site or house on land owned by the grandparents or parents of informants.

Now in her late sixties, Mrs. Bynum was a young mother when these events occurred. She returned to the family home with her first child while her husband served in the army during World War II. Despite the presence of their grown children and grandchildren, the grandparents were still considered household heads. They were shown respect. The idea of respect and its links to the transmission of mother wit and everyday knowledge informed Mrs. Bynum's conversations about her grandmother. One gained knowledge about the world by watching and by "showing respect to those above you."

Although hospitals may have been available with the facilities to accommodate a premature birth, it was likely that the family did not have the funds for such extended treatment or was unaware of them. Instead, the grandmother devised her own program of care.

> *Mrs. Bynum:* I had a cousin . . . and her first baby was Jasmine, and she was, ah, what would you say? a small, a very small baby, what you call a premature baby . . . and, ah, that child didn't weigh no more but a coupla pounds. And now you got incubators and things in hospitals. But at that time my grandmother made hers, you know what I mean?
>
> *Gertrude:* No, how did she do that?
>
> *Mrs. Bynum:* She always kept hot water in a bottle and she kept the temperature for that baby. She kept hot water in the crib under the blanket. And she raised that baby, she raised it up until it was about six months. Jasmine got about six months old and was just a fine a baby as you ever want to see.
>
> *Gertrude:* Where did she learn what to do?
>
> *Mrs. Bynum:* You know, I don't know. I don't think she took any training. I think it just came natural. But now if a baby get like that you have to have them in the hospital.

The infant's mother was "not allowed" to breast-feed. Instead, the midwife took complete charge of the infant's care, feeding her cow's milk through the first six months, first with an eyedropper and then with a bottle. When the baby developed "loose bowels," a new regimen was introduced. As Mrs. Bynum remembers, her grandmother "boil[ed] rice and give the baby rice water, water from the rice, took it off the milk for a day or so." In our conversations, Mrs. Bynum focused on the ability of her grandmother to act decisively and to draw on diverse domains of expertise in her ordinary life and at moments of crisis. She inspired confidence: "Anybody in the neighborhood got sick. They sent for Aunt Lucie you know. Aunt Lucie, that's what they used to call her, or Mom Lucie, and everybody believed in her. Didn't matter who they were."

Family and community deferred to "Aunt Lucie" in matters related to health care. Treatment of her great-granddaughter exemplified the emphasis placed on innovating with what one had available. Underlying this concept of innovation was a dual concern with empirical knowledge gained from watching and doing and with conviction or faith in one's spiritual (natural) powers (mother wit). Older informants, even those ambivalent about remembering midwives, returned again and again to these issues. Management of the premature infant, in the preceding story, is remarkable for its affinity to medical practice. Indeed, Mrs. Bynum made these connections explicit. "Aunt Lucie" adopted a flexible strategy. The hot water bottle replaced the "incubator," a piece of modern technology unavailable to the family. Keeping the baby's temperature was a principle based on a physiological understanding of the body that was shared, in its basic form, with scientific medicine. Similarly, the use of an eyedropper for an infant without a developed suckling response fit within the range of medico-scientific techniques. Beyond the specifics of treatment, however, the most compelling part of this and other stories about midwives for my informants was that knowledge of the body came "natural" to these women. They needed no "book learning."

This attribute was described as positive rather than negative. The emphasis on literacy and on "book knowledge" emerged in the public health campaigns launched in the 1920s and consolidated in the 1930s. Here we begin to make out the tensions that would erode the "respect" given to elderly midwives. In the system of evaluation developed by public health personnel, older, illiterate women were the first to be asked or encouraged to retire, to "give up the work" (Bennett 1925, 526; *Virginia Health Bulletin* 1951, 10). These women were judged according to some experts as "mentally unfit" to practice (Daniel and Gafafer 1935). As in other southern areas, emphasis was placed not on the experience of the elderly but on the educational malleability of younger women. But this process was not a unilinear one.

Information from older informants suggests that African Americans as well as whites in Green River utilized both African American and scientific birthing practices well into the 1950s. In a similar vein, Moerman (1981) reports that folk medicine on St. Helena island was complementary rather than antagonistic to biomedicine. For Moerman, however, treatment, diagnosis, and physiology in the medical belief system of St. Helena islanders were based on a totally different series of principles (Moerman 1981, 286) from those of scientific medicine. Hill and Mathews (1981) make a different argument. They agree that biomedicine and African American folk medicine do not necessarily compete. Scientific medicine is integrated into, although not coterminous with, African American medical practice. Thus some concepts of the body, illness, diagnosis, and treatment are shared, but not all. Shared concepts, in turn, do not necessarily result in similar approaches to diagnosis or treatment. Mongeau (1961, 1973) and Dougherty (1978) also write that midwives incorporated biomedicine into their practice. In their view, however, such a process was often involuntary. Medical personnel pressed midwives to secularize their practice and to abandon techniques and rituals now labeled superstitions. This pattern clearly occurred in Green River County.

The balance between traditional and scientific birthing shifted permanently toward biomedicine sometime in the late 1950s. Dr. Gilman—the first African American physician to practice in the county—recalled that by the time he arrived in 1953, the youngest midwife in the area of the county he served was in her late sixties. No younger woman took her place when she died. Thus with a few exceptions, midwives were not training apprentices to follow in their footsteps. According to Mrs. Stewart, the public health nurse, there were only fifteen midwives, some not active, in the county in the early 1950s. Mrs. Harris must have been one of the youngest members of this final group. Ironically, and I am reluctant to pursue this line of reasoning as I did not fully explore these issues with informants while I was in the field, some women may have been relatively more willing to acknowledge the secular authority of physicians in hospitals because these individuals were not considered a part of the community. Their skills had a different source.

As Moerman (1981, 297) argues for St. Helena islanders, the commodified arena of the body's treatment was perceived as occurring outside of the community's boundaries. Their bodies were not subject to the same rules. In the end, the embeddedness of the midwife in a specific set of social relationships may have worked against her as women increasingly opted to use physicians and hospitals, even though costs were often higher. Mrs. Harris made poignant comments about the marginalization of her craft. People, she told me, stopped thinking the midwife's services were worth any payment. Thus even those individuals who could afford her fees (considerably lower than the hospital's) sometimes neglected to pay her: "It's not worth that, they'll say." The sources of her spiritual authority as a midwife became perceived as without value by childbearing women. She recalled that by the late 1940s, physicians began to vigorously challenge those lessons she had learned under her mother's tutelage. They literally and figuratively attempted to empty the contents of the midwife's bag. Noting her mother's injunction against women eating certain foods immediately after childbirth, for example, she told me that "in my time the doctor say, 'Well, weren't nothing to it.' That's what the doctors used to say and a lot of things that the doctors don't believe in is still true today. But they say is nothing to it."

As the new secular medical authority debunked the midwife's methods and rituals and with fewer women receiving the call, the midwife's gift lost its value to pregnant women. There was indeed "nothing" to it. The "value-added" childbirth experience now occurred in the hospital under the physician's authority. Even when a few women continued to use the midwife, they viewed this option as "second best," a decision made out of necessity rather than choice.

10

Pregnancy and Birthing

In this chapter, I turn more directly to women's remembered experience of birth and of the midwives who attended them. By beginning an inquiry on the collective memory, we may fruitfully direct attention away from forgetting or silence and instead ask, What do older women remember about their experiences?

In Green River as well as in other African American communities, there is a recognized genre of "lying" tales—events in which speaker and audience share a transcript in which deception is both expected and the point of the communicative interaction (Abrahams 1964; Levine 1978). The communicative events that are the subject of this chapter do not fall into this category. Nonetheless, the boundaries between "personal experience" and "collective imagination," between what "happens inside" and what "happens outside," are no less fixed.

As one way out, I want to walk the tightrope between the personal and communal truths that older African American women told about their bodies and the experience of childbirth. What were the expected social rhythms associated with pregnancy, labor, and the postpartum period? Focusing on the midwife's role as ritual specialist, I shift between individual women's stories of their own bodies—"that's how it happened to me"—and of the socially determined expectations of women based on their shared biology—"that's the rule the old midwives went by." My intent is to offer a glimpse into the ways in which African American women experienced childbirth in the first half of the century. These women are not historical figures, yet they often spoke about their experiences of body and self as historical artifacts, something no longer valid in the modern world. At best, I think my work explores the meanings given to these historicized experiences. It does not and cannot make any claims to reconstructing an ethnography.

Older women's reluctance to speak about their experience of pregnancy means that my understanding of this aspect of birth is most fragmentary. It also means that I have few details to balance the rather programmatic descriptions offered in the context of conversations on other topics. These descriptions should be seen as idealized statements. Women who contributed to the household economy by working outside the home would not have been able to observe the same behavioral norms. A more experienced and older mother might have felt less subject to the advice and monitoring of older women than would a young woman going through her first pregnancy.

Midwives and Conception

Although accounts of the midwife's involvement in the early stages of pregnancy rarely appeared in my informants' it is likely that she was nonetheless involved. Typically, midwives attended women who were related to them through marriage or by blood or familiar to them because they lived within a few miles of her residence. Unlike the situation described by Susie (1988) for urban African American lay midwives in Florida, midwives in Green River rarely traveled great distances outside their immediate neighborhood. Midwives were closely associated with specific residential clusters. Informants were able to generate lists of midwives who practiced "around in the different neighborhoods." A midwife was in close contact with her potential clients, as members of the same church congregation, as neighbors, and as kin. At the time that a woman became pregnant, she already had extensive interaction with her midwife in situations not directly connected to childbirth. An impending birth, therefore, may have intensified the relationship between these women, but it did not in most circumstances initiate it.

Midwives were often among the first to know that a woman had conceived. Mrs. Wells (age eighty-two) recalled that for each of her clients, the midwife would "try to remember from the time of the pregnancy" in order to "keep account as best as she could." According to other informants, the midwife marked the progress of pregnancies in the neighborhood by reference to the moon's phases. His mother knew "by the moon," according to Mr. Leawright, when it was a woman's "time" to deliver:

> It worked perfect. How I do not know. Only she would say, if the moon change. If there would be a full moon, she know that this person is close to the time, and she would get her things ready 'cause she say, ah, tomorrow, and she would get her bag and everything ready, her apron, because they used to wear those aprons, everything so that in case they do come she would be ready. And there used to be a dirt road along here and when they cross the bridge in the horse and buggy coming to get her she would hear it, cause she be looking for it anyway and by the time they get to the house, she would be just about ready to leave. When the time come, oh, she never miss it. It was like a gift to her.

Knowledge of the land yielded remedies while the ability to read the firmament offered essential clues about women's bodies. Much as farmers planted crops according to the moon's phases, midwives tracked the course of pregnancies by watching and interpreting the moon's cycles. Mrs. Judkins, now in her sixties, remembered commenting in the presence of a midwife that a pregnant woman looked "about ready to take in," to which the midwife replied, "No, the moon ain't right." As part of their ritual duties, midwives kept close account of the pregnancies in their area of residence.

Mrs. Judkin also recalled that "it wasn't nothing for a woman, her mother and sister to have their monthlies at the same time." I regret not being able to gain more information on the cosmological mapping of pregnancy and menstruation against the moon's cycles. Knowledge about this aspect of birthing and women's bodies is now fragmentary, and no one could (or would) give me any details. Perhaps the remnants of such knowledge reflect a more coherent set of beliefs and practices that guided midwives and their clients in the past.

Commenting on the midwife's intimate knowledge of the body, Susie (1988) also suggests such a possibility based on her interviews in Florida and contiguous states, where she found that "many women believed the midwife 'knew' when the baby would come: 'she know the hour.'" Interpreting these assertions, Susie suggests that "intuition born of charisma" must have played a part in midwives' reported capabilities in this regard. Such "charisma," however, may well have been based on these women's informed readings not only of the cycles of women's bodies but of the relationship of those cycles to lunar movements. The evidence from recent experiments strongly suggests that midwives' observations may have been based on the direct relationship between the lunar cycles and the patterning of menstrual rhythms. Summarizing recent findings, Thomas Buckley writes that "the timing of ovulation in certain nonhuman mammalian females and in female humans can be manipulated by exposure to light relatively stronger than that to which subjects are accustomed at a given time of day or night. There is evidence that light of the intensity of the full moon can affect the timing of ovulation and hence of menstruation in human females" (Buckley and Gottlieb 1988, 274 n. 9).

I am drawn to the possibility that the connection between the moon, pregnancy, and the menstrual cycle remembered by people in Green River expressed what Lamp (1988) describes as "an ecology of the body in a cosmological context" (Lamp 1988, 231). The scrap of knowledge retained by Mr. Jackman may have its roots in West African lunar calendars as described by Lamp as well as in the empirically observed menstrual cycles of women living in the same household or neighborhood.

In his study of the ritual links between menstrual and moon cycles among the Temne of Sierra Leone, Lamp posits that there may well have been a physiological synchrony of women's menstrual cycles with the moon's phases. Such a possibility should not be ruled out, given the ritual emphasis placed on the connections between the moon and women's bodies, on the coming together of women to perform collective rituals and the acknowledgment of ritual connections through a shared biology. In support of his call for further work, Lamp writes that "some Africans have a great deal more knowledge about human anatomy than we have credited them with. Observers have argued that traditional Sierra Leone women are ignorant of the uterus and of the processes of conception and and parturition. I suspect, however, that ritual practitioners possess a considerable science of the body, perhaps obscured to us through the abundance of linguistic metaphor and through ritual secrecy" (Lamp 1988, 230).

As a rule, Virginia's public health officials believed that midwives and the women they served were ignorant of the physiology of parturition. Researchers attempting to conduct a survey of midwifery complained, for example, that "few midwives made any reference to the month of the pregnancy, and many of the mothers were confused when they were asked the date of the last menstruation" (Daniel and Gafafer 1935, 1,809). There is a strong likelihood that, despite their insistence on scientific objectivity, these early scientists, much like their anthropologist counterparts in Africa, asked the wrong questions. Perceiving only haphazard ignorance, they missed the method—one based not on the solar but the lunar calendar.

Referring to the diminished interest in the women's ritual association, Lamp's informant told him that for young women, biology textbooks were now the source of information about the body (Lamp 1988, 230). Soo, too, did older residents in Green River refer to the increased importance of "book knowledge." They spoke about the midwives' ritual and empirical skills only as examples of the praxis of "mother wit," not as a viable alternative to the scientific knowledge of the body held by medical practitioners. The instrinsic appeal of literacy and science served to erode the knowledge of the body that was the midwife's specialty but that also seemed to have been to some extent shared by other women.

Fragmentary though they are, the remembered memories of the cosmology of the body in Green River reminds us that we should not assume a perfect correspondence between past and present physiologies. Lamp's analysis of menstruation symbolism suggests the various ways in which physiology and culture are interrelated. In their introduction to the work in which Lamp's essay appears, Buckley and Gottlieb write that "we presume . . . to 'know' what menstruation really is and turn our attention to nonscientific 'belief' systems armed with this knowledge. In studying menstrual cycles we have tended to take the bodies of women as empirical givens, quite separate from the multiple cultural variables that are the subjects of our inquiries" (Buckley and Gottlieb 1988, 43).

In Green River, midwives delivered their close female kin and neighbors, both black and white. They possessed ritual and physiological knowledge about women's bodies—knowledge that may well have reflected a "uniformity of physiological function" based on the proximity and close interaction of these women to one another and to the midwife. Lamp as well as others (Martin 1987; Rothman 1982; Scheper-Hughes and Lock 1987) remind us that "the body is more than a machine that functions independently according to invariable scientific principles" (Lamp 1988, 231).

Part of what is lost with the throttling of African American midwifery rituals in Green River is the opportunity to explore the ways in which physiology, culture, and cosmology might have operated in the bodies of African American and white women living and interacting in close proximity and sharing the mediation of midwives as ritual specialists.

Cosmologies of the Body: Pregnancy and Risk

Whatever the means used to pinpoint the time of conception, especially in the early part of the century, the social recognition of pregnancy occurred at the time that a woman began to "show." "Showing" referred to the beginning of the period when the physical changes in a woman's body could be seen by her neighbors and kin. According to older women, until such external bodily signs could be read, a woman rarely informed any but her closest kin—perhaps her mother, a close friend, or her husband—when she first discovered that she was pregnant. One informant told me that invariably if a woman dreamt about fish, particularly jumping fish, this was a sure indication that either the dreamer was "in the family way" or that some close female kin had conceived. (Interestingly, Kitzinger [1982, 195] reports that "teeming fish" is among the dream imagery connected to pregnancy in Jamaica.) It is likely, therefore, that dreams were discussed among women to establish who among them had conceived. But in general, the signs of the body were considered sufficient information for most other kin and non-kin in the neighborhood.

Speaking directly about one's pregnancy or the pregnancy of others could bring unwanted attention from malevolent spirits or individuals who wanted to cause harm to the mother or infant. It is unclear if women spoke more openly about their pregnancies with their close female friends. At least in public, however—in mixed company or in the presence of children—the tongue was averted from the vulnerable mother and fetus, and indirect speech was used to refer to the woman's condition. The vulnerability of the pregnant woman meant that not only could other people, whether inadvertently or purposely, bring harm, but a woman herself could damage or negatively influence the child's development.

Words and thoughts had their own power. Thus if a woman had "evil" in her mind, her child could be adversely affected. These effects could be physically manifested, as in a birth defect, or manifested in the personality of the child. It is difficult to know if many young women today share any of these concerns. One woman in her late twenties pointed out an eight-year-old-boy who had developmental problems. She confided that, while pregnant, his mother, a close friend, had seriously considered an abortion because she was having marital difficulties. Both women believed that the boy's subsequent mental and physical difficulties were a direct consequence of his mother's desire to abort.

Attempts to protect mother and child as well as to observe rules of etiquette concerning pregnancy meant that a woman stayed increasingly closer to home as her pregnancy progressed. The focus on the liminal status of the pregnant woman and her child echoed the concern in other societies, past and present, with closely managing the transitional passages connected to birthing (Kitzinger 1982; Spring 1978; Scholten 1977; Wertz and Wertz 1977). Although there seemed to have been no restrictions on receiving visitors, a pregnant women ideally kept her visiting, such a vital part of everyday life, to friends or kin who lived nearby.

In the final months of her pregnancy, the woman might have stopped going to the store or working in the fields if the family farmed. When there were older children in the household, they performed many of these chores. When I asked Mrs. Sewell (age seventy-five), the eldest daughter of thirteen children, if her mother helped with the farming, she recalled that "she would go out there when she could, but I would take the children out most of the time. Every year she was in the family way." According to informants, when the mother of a household was pregnant or undergoing a period of rest after childbirth, children, especially teenage daughters, often took on primary responsibility for sustaining normal domestic routines.

A number of explanations were given for the narrowing of social contacts during pregnancy and the increasing need for women to stay close to home. Just as in the curbs placed on speech, a woman ideally limited her mobility in order to reduce the risks to herself or her unborn child. Water, for example, presented an immediate danger if a woman crossed over it. Mrs. Wayne recalled that the "old folks used to say a woman weren't to cross a creek, or such." Because creeks and branches (small run-offs from creeks) are common features of the landscape in Green River County and walking was the most common means of transportation, women simply cut back on their visiting. Another informant laughingly remembered that "some men would carry their wife across the water if they went visiting somewhere. They would take her and carry her across." Stepping over watermelon vines carried a dual danger. On the one hand, the fetus could be affected because of the watery nature of the gourd; on the other, the vines themselves could "bind up the pregnancy" and make labor difficult.

Besides the naturally occurring dangers, women had to be concerned with those initiated or caused by humans. Chief among these were the conjure rituals and powdered roots that jealous individuals, especially barren women, were thought to use in order to cause a woman to lose her baby or to mark the child in some way. Pregnant women and members of the household were always on the lookout for powders sprinkled across the door sill or in the well, or on the places a woman would likely touch. These were signs that someone meant harm and that remedies needed to be taken.

A woman who could not have children was frequently the source of suspicion in such affairs. If a woman grew concerned that someone wanted to harm her, she could consult a midwife versed in such matters, or she could go directly to a conjurer, usually male, who determined which member of the household was being targeted. He could also tell exactly who had tried to cause harm and offer protective remedies or counter spells. Mrs. Boatwright remembered a pregnant woman who went to the nearby city to consult with a conjurer. He gave the supplicant "certain roots" in order to ward off the malevolence of a sister-in-law, a longtime enemy, with whom she shared a communal yard and well.

Efforts to control and define risk during pregnancy resembled in form a similar emphasis in biomedicine. Where obstetricians focused on a woman's inherent physiological state, whether she was high or low risk, for example, African American medical belief emphasized the external environment, disturbed social relations, and malevolent spirits, all of which could negatively effect the health of a woman and her unborn child. Given the danger of the world outside, a woman greatly reduced the risks to herself and child by limiting her exposure, moving progressively inward until she reached relative safety in the darkened seclusion of the birthing room during and after childbirth.

Informants rarely mentioned a specific role for midwives during this phase of parturition. They spoke instead of the normative standards that women were supposed to follow because of their "condition." Yet despite this emphasis on the woman's responsibility for protecting herself and the fetus against harm, older informants did not necessarily attribute blame to the mother or the midwife in the event of a miscarriage or some problem with labor, or on the death of a newborn. Rather, they argued instead that God had ultimate control over events. Humans could try to assert control, but in the end "you can't do no more than what he let you do."

The distinction between scientific medical and the African American view of pregnancy does not split along a boundary marked by "natural" on the one side and "pathology" on the other. By this I mean that older women spoke of pregnancy as a normal part of a woman's life, but in their descriptions of the potential dangers, they seemed to be saying that the female body was not in a "natural" but rather in an extraordinary, dangerous state during pregnancy, childbirth, and the postpartum period. In fact, as I have suggested in the previous chapter, these women describe younger women's bodies as having changed in an essential manner. Over time, informants suggest, the gap between the pregnant and nonpregnant, normal state of the body has diminished. Thus younger women are less vulnerable, less needful of the protective behavior that had been so necessary during the older women's childbearing years.

Using cross-cultural materials, anthropologists have discussed attitudes toward pregnancy that seem similar in essential ways to those expressed by older women in Green River (Kitzinger 1982; Cosminsky 1977, 1982; Spring 1978; Jordan 1983; Delaney 1988). Kitzinger refers to the symbolic change of status marked by pregnancy in a rural Jamaican community. Pregnant women are believed to be in ritual danger, and as a result they are subject to dietary and social interactional restrictions. As in Green River, for example, pregnant women were considered especially vulnerable to bad spirits, in this case the ghosts of ancestors, that could "lay hands on the baby in utero and make it sicken and die" (Kitzinger 1982, 191).

As in other rites of passage, the changes inherent in pregnancy place the individual in a liminal and dangerous state of being. Among the Luvale of Zambia, to take another example, beliefs focus on creating barriers between the outside and the inside in a literal and figurative sense. According to Spring (1978), a woman with a history of uncompleted pregnancies, or whose babies die soon after birth, is placed within a fenced space during the full term of her subsequent pregnancy. Experienced women perform rites to appease ancestral spirits and to discourage them from harming the unborn child. This seclusion, according to Spring, provided medical as well as social relational benefits (Spring 1978, 174).

Commenting on protective rituals in her work with Jamaican women, Kitzinger writes that the "concept of 'at risk' is basic to such rites, for the transition between different social identities is believed to be fraught with peril, not only for the individual on the journey but also for the social group in which the upheaval is taking place. An essential element in the drama is that all those participating believe in the danger" (Kitzinger 1982, 182). Although African Americans and medical personnel shared ideas about the risks involved in pregnancy and the necessity of prenatal care, the particulars of the "concept of risk" differed. During her tenure, Mrs. Stewart, the public health nurse, focused her energies on convincing women to come to the clinic in order to receive monthly health checkups and lessons on proper nutrition, infant care, and general hygiene.

Following in a public health tradition long-established in the state, her lessons integrated middle-class white norms of personal and familial conduct into more specific instructions on health care. Mrs. Stewart told me, for example, that she tried (unsuccessfully) to convince women to abandon the practice of sleeping with their newborns. What were the inherent risks in this practice? Except for a concern with smothering the baby, I was unable to get a clear sense of this public health policy. In any event, along with other health lessons, Mrs. Stewart struggled, in her words, "to get them [African American women] to improvise beds [for the newborn], cardboard boxes, bureau drawers or whatever was available."

Besides what might be termed behavioral lessons, the clinic visit registered the number of previous births, the age of the mother, and her blood pressure—medical indices of the relative risk of a pregnancy. Few women took advantage of these free services. By the 1950s, a clinic visit was a prerequisite for women who wanted to use a midwife. Only after pregnant women were certified as low risk by the clinic could midwives legally attend them in birth. This restriction was ostensibly intended to monitor midwives and to provide health services to indigent African American women. Nonetheless, women delayed their appearance at the clinic. "Sometimes patients didn't show up until the seventh or eighth month," Mrs. Stewart complained.

Mrs. Stewart reasoned that the lack of transportation may have hindered some who wanted to use the clinic. But she also interpreted women's avoidance of the clinic in other terms. In her view, most women just didn't "think prenatal care was important." Women, she told me, associated the clinic with being sick. Thus unless there was specific illness, it wasn't necessary to see the nurse or physician. They held a "pathology view" of pregnancy. By this she meant that women only considered treatment if they believed that something was wrong. They were "ignorant," more willing to rely on the knowledge of the older women in the community than on the public health nurse. Her sense of the problem mirrored that expressed by earlier public health nurses at the beginning of Virginia's involvement in infant and maternal health in the 1920s and 1930s.

The language of the body spoken by Mrs. Stewart differed from that spoken and understood by the pregnant women she served. From her view, the containment of risk required a focus on health maintenance through eating the proper foods, measuring the body's pressure, and learning about parturition and the appropriate response to the body's signals. Contrary to the public health nurse's assessment, African American woman were indeed concerned with the dangers inherent in being pregnant. They took myriad precautions to protect themselves and their babies. They sacrificed their mobility and gave up the much-treasured Sunday visits to relatives in other parts of the county, for example. But risk, as they defined it, was not an inherent physiological condition that could be measured from the inside. During pregnancy, the body lost its normal impermeability. Thus it had to be protected from material as well as nonmaterial, spiritual "stuff" that could work its way inside, thereby causing damage. According to informants, at the time of childbirth and immediately after, when all the woman's pores and veins were open, the body was most permeable, so that even exposure to air could be dangerous.

It was during this period that the midwife's role became important, for she guided the woman through childbirth and monitored her activity during the postpartum period. "Monitoring" is purposely used here to point to the nature of the midwife's role. Women with whom I spoke acknowledged the midwife's authority. She was not a peer usually but a senior and respected woman in the community. Her former clients commented, sometimes negatively, on her imperiousness. She offered support but was unyielding when it came to having things done the right way. In accepting the responsibility for bringing women and children through childbirth, the midwife expected a certain measure of obedience. Mrs. Eggleston recalled with some amusement that midwives were known to reprimand mothers who failed to follow their directions. She remembered being in the front yard a few days before "taking to bed" with her first child when she "spied the midwife turning the corner of the road" on a final prenatal visit. She quickly ran back inside before the old woman could see her "running around." By the time the midwife reached the house, Mrs. Eggleston was calmly seated, waiting to receive her.

Cosmologies of the Body: Labor and Birth

Memories offer only partial glimpses of childbirth. Far more so than with pregnancy, this area of experience was closed to me. Besides the issue of propriety, I wonder if the silence about the actual events of labor in women's narratives is connected to a ritual muting of this particular aspect of childbirth. That is, rather than the peak experience, labor was in some respects an anticlimactic end point, a mark of a passage safely undertaken over the past nine months. Sandwiched between pregnancy and the postpartum seclusion, labor, therefore, takes a minor role in the stories of these women. Kitzinger notes in the Jamaican case that "when talking of the total experience women often complain far more of the discomforts and trials of pregnancy than of any pain and distress in labor" (Kitzinger 1982, 190).

Bridgette Jordan (1985) writes of the marked cross-cultural variation in the behaviors associated with labor. She reports that among Mayan women, only subtle body movements ("micro-behaviors") indicate that contractions are under way or the baby is about to be born (Jordan 1985, 4). In Green River, loud vocalizations, walking around, and stooping seemed to have accompanied contractions and been accepted as normal behavior. Yet Mrs. Wood, we may recall, was praised by her grandmother and mother for being an "easy" mother. Thus some criteria existed for judging whether a woman had stayed within the boundaries regarding the length of labor, the ease of childbirth, her relative calm, and her degree of response to the instructions of the midwife or older women. In the Green River narratives, however, this experience is rarely mentioned. Or if it is talked about, there is little or no elaboration.

Mrs. Harris, who was relatively willing to discuss her work as a midwife, did not give details on labor or on the birth of the child, except to mention that some women liked to be "petted" during contractions, especially on the birth of their first child. "Petting" as far I can ascertain referred to her sense that some women needed extra gentle coaching and encouragement. She commented that it was often difficult to provide this attention in situations in which no other women were available to "help out." The presence of a close female friend or relative may indeed have lessened the anxiety for a first-time mother while freeing the midwife to attend to other important duties. But I can only guess at the dynamics that occurred. Even with pressing on my part, older women seemed uninterested in telling narratives about this aspect of their experience.

Intriguingly, while the birthing behavior of African American women did not replicate that of the Mayan women observed by Jordan, it is difficult to hear the differences in cultural perspective because, in their recollections, women downplayed the physical experience of labor and childbirth. Older women did speak of their apprehensiveness or fear of labor, especially on the birth of their first child. Women who died in childbirth or soon thereafter were remembered in conversations. Mrs. Rawling pointed out the graves of two young woman, close to her in age (early twenties in 1940), who had lived only a few days after the home birth of their children.

Yet memories of these women occurred not in the context of labor but when we spoke about the informal adoptions of the newborns by members of the extended family. Mrs. Beaumont, who delivered eleven children at home during the 1930s and 1940s, came closest to describing the experience of labor. She answered in response to a direct question about the midwife's role during the birth of her children: "When I started showing the signs of pain my husband he would go and fetch Selma Lucas [her midwife]. She was real nice. He went in a horse and buggy. And she would come and sit with me. They [midwives/her midwife] would just come and sit with you until the pains come. T'ain't nothing they could do but help you bear against them pains. They would sit with you and hold your legs and tell you what to do."

Other women gave similar answers. What did the midwife instruct? I longed for details, but few were forthcoming. None of the older women mentioned her feelings or response to the actual birth of the baby. The dissimilarity in our ages, the question of etiquette, the propensity not to focus attention on oneself, and the dimming of memory may all have contributed to the silence on this issue. Yet women remembered and spoke about other events that had occurred well in the past and that seemed to be as intensely personal. The seeming gaps in narratives are not fully explained either by reference to individual forgetfullness or to the conscious intent of women not to bring personal experience into the public sphere.

Going over my field notes and interviews, I noticed that, in their narratives, women gave far more details about the expulsion of the placenta or afterbirth than about the actual emergence of the newborn. To give a rough analogy, rather than describing the arduous climb up the mountain and the ensuing exhilaration at reaching the top, older informants focused more intently on the hazards of making the return descent to safety. Thus the birth itself did not appear to be the event that leads to the creation of complex and emotionally engaged texts.

I remained puzzled by what seemed an unexplainable and somewhat inappropriate response until Bridgette Jordan's work on the "universals" of childbirth was brought to my attention. She writes, "I now think that an immediate reaction to the the baby is not 'natural.' There is, right after the woman has finally pushed the baby out, a breathing spell, a rest period, a transition from the exertion of the pushing to the new reality . . . The immediate joyful reaction which is typical for the U.S. appears to be something women have to be trained for. I didn't see it, in this extreme form, in France, nor Germany, nor Holland, not to speak of Yucatán" (Jordan 1978, 5).

Because it is extremely difficult to determine what is "learned" or "natural" behavior, it is problematic to cast the dilemma in these terms. How, for example, would we determine if French or German or Mayan women have simply been culturally trained not to respond immediately to the newborn? Part of the answer may rest in the fact that until the placenta is expulsed, women continue to feel pain and experience strong contractions. More important, however, Jordan's data points to the necessity of understanding the specific historical and cultural contexts that shape experiences of the body. Among Yucatán women, she finds that while response to the arrival of the baby is muted, there is emotional intensity directed toward the expulsion of the placenta.

In the United States, by contrast, the emotional peak occurs at the actual emergence of the child. The goal has been attained. This focus on the fetus's arrival as the end point in the birthing process is also con-nected to what Emily Martin and Robbie Davis-Floyd have described as the predominant emphasis in scientific childbirth on the baby as the "product of the labor" (Martin 1987; Davis-Floyd 1992). All other con-cerns are secondary to this primary achievement. Jordan's research cor-roborates the view that the rhythm and pacing of responses to the stages of birthing are culturally and socially embedded. Regarding the variation in the nature of responses to the birth of the infant, she reports that "for Mayan indians this is merely a stage in a process, and if there is a high point, it is the birth of the placenta. I believe the same may be true for other societies where the period between the birth of the baby and the expulsion of the placenta is the most dangerous time. So we have to conclude that the reaction of birth participants, including the mother, also varies cross-culturally" (Jordan 1985, 6).

These findings provide clues to the stress placed in birth narratives from Green River on the period after the baby's safe arrival. Certainly, the birth of the child was important. But for both midwife and mother, events following close on the birth of the baby were most fraught with danger, on the one hand, and most likely to bring the midwife in direct confrontation with medical science and the law, on the other. Regardless of the birthing position taken by the mother, most midwives encouraged their clients to sit on a chamber pot if there was any delay during the delivery of the placenta.

Both the seated position and the pot itself were believed to contribute to quick expulsion of the whole placenta with a minimum of hemorrhag-ing. Public health officials actively discouraged this practice. They con-sidered it unnecessary and, at worst, superstitious, unseemly, and unhy-gienic. For example, researchers from the U.S. Public Health Service, in a study to rate a group of midwives from Brunswick County, Virginia, described three births. In two of these, midwives followed unapproved methods for delivering the infant and the placenta, and in the other, the midwife obeyed accepted protocol. The report is worth citing at length. Note the emphasis placed on the "dirty" conditions associated with un-approved birthing methods.

Two mothers had not been bathed; the third was bathed before the investigator's arrival. One bed had only a dirty mattress which was protected with dirty brown wrapping paper and a dirty cotton blanket;

the mother was delivered on her hands and knees; the placenta was delivered after the mother had gotten up on a slop jar.

The second mother was delivered on her hands and knees on the floor besides the bed; a folded quilt covered with newspapers protected a bare floor; the placenta was delivered spontaneously after the mother had gotten up on a slop jar; after the delivery of the child and the placenta, the mother was washed and helped into a clean bed. The third mother delivered both child and placenta in a clean, well-protected bed. (Daniel and Gafafer 1935, 1,811).

For midwives and mothers in Green River, conflicting models about how and where to deliver the placenta created tension and excitement. Such conflict accompanied the opposition between midwives' and bio-medicine's approach to labor and the birth of the baby. Conflicts might have been intensified, however, over the correct method of delivering the placenta. The danger of hemorrhaging and concerns about extracting placenta that was impacted or only partially expulsed brought midwives perilously close to the boundaries of what they were legally allowed to do. Mrs. Harris alluded to the nature of the dilemma in her discussion of situations in which her grandmother was compelled to enter the birth canal to extract the afterbirth.

A delayed afterbirth was considered an "emergency" situation by public health personnel and cause for summoning the physician. In practical terms, however, physicians were not immediately available or could not be easily contacted owing to distance and the lack of transportation. Thus a midwife sometimes had to decide between obeying the rules or possibly endangering a woman's life or taking the blame for a maternal death.

One Alabama midwife described to Linda Holmes (1986) her decision to break the rules when she found herself in such a moral quandary. She first established that she understood the law: "If they got where they couldn't deliver the afterbirth, then we just had to have a doctor to get it cause we wasn't allowed" (Holmes 1986, 276). But she then explained the extenuating circumstances and justified her actions, referring to a higher moral order:

Now I did it one time, but I knew it was against the law . . . We were a long way. It was on a Saturday. All the men were out of place. We didn't have a doctor nearer than Benton. We didn't have nobody to go get the doctor. So the girl laid there but t'wasn't nothing we could do. We put her over the slop jar and it wouldn't come. So finally I just decided. I said, now I know this is against the law. I hope this don't come against me now. I said, I know this is against the law, but it is against the law for you to lay there in this condition too long . . . I had to put my hand inside. I greased my hand and put it inside and lifted it up. When I did that, it come right on . . . The Lord must have put it into me . . . you know what to do for a lady when she was sick. (Holmes 1986, 277)

In Alabama, Mississippi (Logan 1989; Smith 1994), North Carolina (Mongeau 1973), Florida (Susie 1988), and Virginia, the issues were the same. The high drama for rural African American midwives and their clients participating in home births and under the regulatory and policing arm of the public health department may have in large part centered on the delivery of the placenta.

The fact that older women's narratives did not focus on the actual birth is also connected, I believe, to the view of newborns as belonging to some liminal state, not yet fully human. To anticipate the next chapter, part of what occurred during the postpartum period is that the child gradually became properly and safely human. Women believed that evil would be attracted to the child if too great attention was given to its presence. Thus, for example, the public health department's insistence on naming in order to properly fill out the birth certificate ran counter to the system of beliefs shared by midwives and their patients. The views of birthing and of the fetus and newborn that emerge from older African American women's narratives place them in a specific historical framework.

Only with the rise of scientific obstetrics in the late nineteenth and early twentieth centuries has the idea of the fetus as a separate entity with separate morality and personhood taken such firm hold (Petchesky 1984; Wertz and Wertz 1977; Martin 1987; Rapp 1988). These scholars have convincingly shown that the increasing sophistication of technological instruments and procedures to see "inside" the woman's body and to consequently "personalize" the fetus has further sharpened the cultural focus on the arrival of the child as the end point—indeed, the only point—of the birthing process. Taken together, these historical, physiological, and cultural factors explain the content and pacing of older women's narratives.

Only when the potentially dangerous process of the delivery of the placenta had taken place could the midwife relax and attend to the needs of the infant as well as to the comfort of the mother. Mrs. Cunningham, a woman in her late seventies, recalled the birth of her second child:

> He was a nine and three-quarter pound baby. The midwife said "I'll call it a ten pound baby." Then the afterbirth wouldn't come. I had to sit on a pot for some hours. The midwife, she was afraid to pull. She said she would call the doctor, and he came after a long while and when he got there, the afterbirth hadn't come so he pulled it and it finally fell on out. I guess it took so long cause I wasn't eating like I wanted to. I had an upset stomach for all the time [during her pregnancy]. It felt like phlegm filled up my insides.

Just as the phlegm had entered her body cavity during pregnancy, so, too, had the placenta filled her up and refused to descend spontaneously. Her body's unease prefigured the difficulty she would have with the afterbirth.

Once the placenta had been safely delivered, the social and physiological crisis had been surmounted. Yet to understand such emphasis on this aspect of the birthing experience, we have had to examine not only physiology but the specific historical development of African American midwifery and its relationship to biomedicine. Only then are we able to place Mrs. Cunningham's narrative and those of other African American women in their full context as individual and collective memories of the "lived experience of the body" (Scheper-Hughes and Locke 1987)—experiences shaped by history as well as by culture.

The Placenta, the Navel, and Resistance

As in other African American communities (Holmes 1986; Mongeau 1973; Susie 1988; Schaffer 1991; Reeb 1992), in Green River, the delivery and disposal of the afterbirth marked the end of one phase and the beginning of another. In the winter months, the midwife burnt the placenta as well as any newspapers or rags that had been used for the birth in the main fireplace or stove. If the birth occurred in the summer, she was responsible for burying the afterbirth in the client's yard, in a hole deep enough so that "the dogs wouldn't get it." One women recalled that the midwife burnt the placenta in the woodstove and then buried the ashes. Informants did not attach any particular significance to the disposal of the afterbirth. Yet it may well have been that its cremation or burial denoted that the placenta was perceived as having some qualities that marked it as more than simply the effluvia of birth. This certainly was the case for African American midwives in Alabama, who "performed with care and sometimes with ceremony . . . the burying of the after-birth" (Holmes 1986, 282). According to Holmes, "Although the disposal of the afterbirth was an obvious public health concern, the meticulous care provided . . . also reflected the pervasive view that the afterbirth was an extension of the human body, a part of life. The specific procedure for its burial . . . included making certain that it was buried deeply in the ground, at lest three to four feet under the earth, selecting a spot that was near the house and highly visible" (Holmes 1986, 282).

If there had been no delay in the period between birth and the final expulsion of the placenta, midwives' attention turned to the newborn and in particular to the umbilical cord. According to the testimony of informants, some midwives were more skilled in cutting and dressing the cord so as to produce a small, inwardly turned navel as opposed to a large, distended one. Mrs. Harris revealed her technique and contrasted it with that of modern-day physicians who were probably unaware of the aesthetics of the body that underlay the midwives' methods: "And you know what will make a big navel? Some don't know. After the babe is born you let the pulse stop beating, you let that die. My mother taught me that. And they'll have a nice navel. Some cut it . . . at least the doctor do. They cut it as soon as the baby is born. But if you [*addressing me*] ever deliver a baby, you feel that cord and the pulse is in there a few minutes and then you cut it. They won't have that big navel."

Sheila Cosminsky (1977, 1994) reports a similar emphasis among Guatemalan midwives, who prefer to wait for the expulsion of the afterbirth and for the pulse to die before cutting the cord. Apparently, these midwives do not voice a concern about the size of the navel but believe that "if the cord is cut before, . . . the child might die [or] the placenta might rise up in the woman's body and cause her to choke" (Cosminsky 1978, 215). Cosminsky does suggest a physiological correlate to the cultural practice. If the umbilical cord is severed too quickly, she reasons, "crucial blood is cut off from the baby" (Cosminsky 1994, 205). As in Virginia, she reports that Guatemalan physicians complained that traditional midwives "wait too long to cut the cord."

The umbilical cord—that final link between mother and child—was the focus of considerable attention in Green River and not surprisingly provided another area for the playing out of conflicts between midwives, medical personnel and mothers. Treatment of the umbilical cord proved to be a source of resistance long after women routinely delivered their babies in the hospital. Public health protocol required midwives to quickly cut the cord with a scissor sterilized over a flame or in alcohol. The scissor was in fact one of the only instruments that midwives were "allowed" to carry in their bags. They were then to tie the cord. No bindings, no form of medicinal salve, no other treatments were to be applied. Undoudtedly, from a public health standpoint, physicians and nurses wanted to reduce the risk of tetanus neonatorum infection of the umbilical cord, which is a source of infant mortality in societies that have or continue to rely on traditional midwives (Kitzinger 1982; Spring 1978; Gray 1982; Cosminsky 1982).

In Virginia's medical journals, however, I came across no specific references to tetanus as contributing to infant death or as connected to midwifery practice. Thus the injunctions against midwives' methods of treating the umbilical cord may have been conceptualized as a preventative rather than as a public health response to a particular problem. Medical opinions on the proper treatment of the cord underwent some changes over the first half of the century. Early on, "bindings" were considered appropriate treatment. Women who could afford it recalled sending away to Sears and Roebuck to buy "belly bands" for infants, suggesting that this item was a consumer good. By the 1940s, however, public health personnel seemed to have reconsidered their policies and determined that uncovered umbilical cords were more healthy. Midwives and mothers, however, did not immediately adapt to this change.

How did midwives' treatment of the cord diverge from public health policy? Midwives and the women they attended believed that the treatment of the cord during the early weeks could determine not only the neatness of the infant's navel but also whether or not the child thrived and grew up with a strong, straight backbone. There was considerable room for individual preferences in the treatment of the cord. Once the cord had been tied, some midwives burnt a small square of linen or flax which was then placed over the navel, after it had been amply greased with a lubricant.

Mrs. Cunningham's grandmother, who practiced well into her eighties, applied the scorched linen directly to the umbilical cord and then tightly wrapped the baby's midsection with a clean white bandage that the mother had normally washed and prepared in advance. According to Mrs. Cunningham, her grandmother "used to put this belly band after taking a piece of linen cloth, they used to have this cloth around that time. She would call it 'purify' by putting it over the stove. Then she would put the belly band to keep this linen just for protection. She said that if children would cry a lot then they'd have a big navel on account of them pushing it out, so the belly band serve to keep it [the navel] from bulging out."

Cross-culturally, the practice of scorching or burning dressings is a relatively effective and common means of sterilizing (Cosminsky 1977, 1982; Kitzinger 1982). Besides purification through scorching the dressing, other midwives used additional methods to achieve the proper navel shape. Mrs. Wainwright's midwife put a fifty-cent piece on top of the cord to "prevent the navel from poking out," before tightly wrapping and pinning the belly band around the baby's waist. Others used "greased gauze," which prevented the cord "from sticking, and it would heal that much nicer" (Mrs. Powell). Some midwives combined this practice with the use of gentian violet, which was recommended as a germicide by the clinic. Still others applied grated nutmeg to the navel, a practice that Kitzinger (1982) reports in Jamaica. She suggests that "nutmeg has antiseptic qualities and is slightly irritant," which may cause the cord to "slough off early" (Kitzinger 1982, 193). In Green River, the belly band was said to keep the navel from pushing out during the baby's everyday exertions.

Ever cautious, Mrs. Harris described her mother's technique and only implied that she had used a similar method. The past provided a important safety cushion for her critique of biomedicine: "My mother taught me to put Vaseline around the cord and she said it would rot quickly and it will [*raises her voice*], it will do it today but they don't allow us to put Vaseline or nothing on, just tie it and don't even dress it. Way back now, they'd burn this material and put it there on the navel and then pin that belly band around the baby. It would keep it warm or something. Anyway, the cord would drop off quick."

The quick healing of the cord lessened the risks of infection. It also reduced the possibility that air would get into the newborn. Midwives' visits in the postpartum period were in part to check on the navel's healing, to change dressings, and to rebandage the infant.

In general, the midwife stopped her daily postpartum visits after the baby's cord was judged to be sufficiently healed. If there were other women in the household, they took primary responsibility for supervising and caring for the newborn so that the mother could rest and recuperate. Thus Dee, for example, recalled that her midwife did not have to make the usual number of postdelivery visits because her husband's sister and mother changed the umbilical dressing and bathed the baby. Just as a pregnant woman and a newly delivered mother were at risk, so, too, was the infant. The navel was one point of entry for germs, spirits, and noxious powders placed by ill-intentioned persons.

One woman who had used a physician and did not have the support of female kin at home experienced great anxiety about the antenatal care of her last child, born in the early 1950s. Mrs. Tilden recalled that "when my mother had her children, her mother would help her, and when I had mine, my mother-in-law would always come." By the birth of her son, her mother-in-law was ill. On her release from the hospital, the doctor recommended that she have someone to "tend" to the baby because of her high blood pressure. But no one was immediately available. We begin to glimpse, in her narrative, the coming apart of expected helping traditions among neighbors and kin:

> I got here [to the house]. My mother-in-law was sick; she couldn't come. My husband would bring the basin to the bed and I would wash the baby. When it came to washing the diapers, he didn't do it. [*laughter*] He just throw them away. The rest of the ones [urine-soaked] he would just put them in the washing machine. I got tickled about changing the dressing [on the umbilical cord]. I don't want you [*directing her comments to me*] to get scared. But when I changed the belly band, the cord it look almost like a worm. I told him [her husband] he better find somebody to help me. The cord wasn't healed up. I was really frightened.

Even though she had already mothered four children, this woman was encountering, for the first time, a feeling of isolation and helplessness. The condition of the newborn's navel may have not been any worse than those of her other children at that age. But she had never before had to take care of the dressing and the belly band without the aid of other women and during the period when she normally had a period of rest and seclusion. Unaccustomed to being involved in care of the newborn, her husband did the best he could, perhaps, but given his inexperience he could not allay her fears or offer any substantive help. That these fears coalesced around the baby's umbilical cord is to be expected, given the usual attention devoted to this part of the child's anatomy by midwives and older women. Mrs. Tilden desperately needed some nurturing for her body and mind, but instead she voiced concern about the proper care and treatment of the newborn's navel—a call for help that could more easily be expressed and heard.

Besides preventing air from entering the baby and keeping the navel tucked in, the belly band supported the baby's back. Informants often told me that people today have weak backs and stooped postures because they were not "banded" properly when they were young. Children sometimes wore these waist bands long after the umbilical cord had healed. Depending on family tradition, babies wore bands until they emerged from seclusion with their mothers in their first month or until they reached three or four years old. Mrs. Stewart recalls seeing nearly school-age children with protective "belly bands." Children thought to be "weakly" or susceptible to drafts and colds were probably made to wear these "girdles" for longer periods of time. Mr. Jackman told me that his grandmother "believed in" the belly band for infants as well as just-delivered mothers. He thought that the weaker constitution of the young was connected to the disappearance of this once-essential piece of infant clothing: "Now that belly band support the back. They say that's why people today have a lot of trouble with the back, because they don't have nothing to strengthen the back. That's what the old people used to say. And then, a child you see with a belly band they stands up straight, you notice that."

Perhaps the community's farming past accounts for this emphasis on a strong and straight back. Additionally, because it both supported the back and covered the navel, the band prevented the entry of air into the child's body at a point considered to be particularly vulnerable.

As reported by informants, incidents of resistance to the educational agenda of medical personnel often occurred over these explicitly noninvasive methods of treating the body or maintaining its health. Public health personnel took as great, if not greater, umbrage at what they labeled "superstition" as they did at lapses in hygienic methods or at the use of herbal or other unsanctioned remedies or foods.

To use Jordan's (1985) phraseology, the "micro-behavior" of resistance may have clustered around seemingly small acts and small regions of the body. Martin (1987) suggests that we more finely differentiate among the forms and possibilities for women's resistance to dominant constructions and management of the body. In this respect, the kinds of opportunities open to African American women (midwives and their clients) probably fell into the category of "sabotage." As she defines it, "sabotage" involves "actions or words meant to foil some process or behavior perceived to be detrimental but intended not to be detected" (Martin 1987, 186).

In Green River, a midwife might have been hesitant to reach into the birth canal but might have quite readily burnt feathers in order to speed labor, or cut the umbilical cord according to her sense of timing and dressed it as she had been taught by her elders. A mother may have used a physician, as did Mrs. Wood, for example, but then followed the direction of her older female relatives in caring for the infant or her own body while at home. Mrs. Bynum told me that she conscientiously took her newborn son to the clinic for postnatal checkups but that before she made the trip, she took off the dressing and unwound the bandage placed on the baby's navel by her grandmother. As soon as she returned home, Mrs. Bynum replaced the dressing and repinned the bandage. Her public health nurse had instructed her to leave the navel open to the air. Both she and her grandmother thought that such treatment would not only hamper healing and weaken her son but also could endanger his life. She "got around" the doctors and nurses, doing what she considered best for her child. In a similar story, a woman who also gave birth in the 1940 recalled that the doctor told her that the belly band "was more harm than it was good." She continued to use it, however, because she found that her infants "were real skeptic" about sitting up without the added support. She noticed that babies today were bolder in this regard. She reasoned, therefore, that this is why they were able to sit up without the aid of the belly band.

As with the emphasis on the physiological differences in the development of babies' eyes between the "olden days" and the present, older women legitimized their experiences by reference to the biological necessity of past cultural practices. Only now, they seemed to be saying, when the bodies of infants and women are changed, has it been possible to abandon the techniques used by midwives. The use of belly bands is illustrative of this area of contestation. Informants reasoned that the differential physiology of the generations was responsible for the changes in the experience of pregnancy. At the same time, however, they used a similar explanatory model to talk about the reasons they resisted the efforts of public health nurses to abandon long-held patterns of treatment and managment of pregnancy, the newborn, and the mother. Thus it appears that initially women and midwives were not completely convinced that these nurses always knew what was best for their bodies and the bodies of their children.

As they do in other spheres of their knowledge about home remedies and the midwife's work, older women "explain" these transformations in experiences of pregnancy and the postpartum period by reference to biology. In Brazil, mothers explained to Nancy Scheper-Hughes that they were unable to breast-feed their infants because their milk was "sour, curdled, bitter, and diseased, a metaphorical projection of their inability to pass on anything untainted to their children" (Scheper-Hughes and Lock 1987, 17). In a similar fashion, the older women in Green River County discussed the displacement and dissolution of midwifery knowledge in terms of the changed physiology of the younger generation. Women's memories of their postpartum seclusion carry similar themes. On the one hand, this period of rest immediately after birth was seen as absolutely necessary. On the other, older women believe that these practices are not necessary in the present time and for the "new bodies" of their daughters and granddaughters.

11

The Postpartum

The experience of pregnancy for women and their offspring lasted well beyond the nine months of the fetus's gestation. During the culturally mediated postpartum period, women were returned to a state of physiological and social "normalcy" in the months after childbirth. For the child, the extended time spent in full or partial seclusion served a complementary purpose. According to descriptions offered by my informants, it was during this period that the newborn became fully enculturated as a social person and completed its physiological development. For mothers and infants, therefore, the period after childbirth was the last and crucial stage of birthing. What were the "rules" that supported and provided the context for women's behavior during the postpartum period?

Bodily Cosmology: Seclusion and Recovery

Mrs. Bynum had a resident midwife—her grandmother—a strong influence in the household, but this did not preclude the use of the clinic for antenatal care. Nonetheless, away from the clinic, other influences determined the postpartum management of the body. Besides the midwife, a woman's mother, mother-in-law, sisters, and other close kin offered their opinions and participated in the care of the infant as well as the recuperating mother. Mrs. Culler, in her late sixties, migrated to Baltimore, but she returned to her mother's home for each of her two deliveries. She recalled once rushing out to grab clothes off the line during a rainstorm only to be reprimanded by a neighbor: "Your baby only six weeks old and you in this rain, you gonna bring on a fever." Older women remembered that their opinions regarding their bodies and those of their infants were not necessarily given more or even equal weight compared with those of the senior women in the household or of the midwife. They used words and phrases such as "obey," "following or going by the rules," the "strictness of the older folk," and "not being allowed to" when they describe their postpartum experiences.

Just at the moment when they had affirmed their adulthood by undergoing childbirth and becoming mothers, they also reverted in some respects to a childlike relationship with senior women. I often asked whether women resented the imposition of these strictures. The muting of antagonisms or resentments over time may explain some responses, but invariably, as in the case of Mrs. Bynum, informants told me that "you come to rely on them telling you what to do. They was going to make sure that you did the right thing to protect you, and all."

The relationships between a woman, her family, and the midwife after childbirth were outside the direct control of public health officials. These relationships, as well as the postpartum experience, remain vivid in the memories of older women in Green River. Moreso than any other aspect of childbearing, the management of the postpartum period, then and now, signify for them the radical differences in the experience of birth between the generations.

By way of entry into a fuller discussion of the way in which older women remembered and talked about their postpartum experiences, I want to discuss some recent work on the cultural meanings of menstruation and blood symbolism in Western and non-Western societies (Martin 1987; Buckley and Gottlieb 1988; Gottlieb, 1988). The relevance of this work to our examination of African America postpartum practices will, I hope, become clear. I follow closely Buckley and Gottlieb's introduction to a collection of essays that offer new analyses of menstruation as a cultural and physiological construct.

The ethnographic description and symbolic analyses of menstruation in the anthropological literature roughly fall into two categories—the classic treatment and the (new) critical approach. Buckley and Gottlieb characterize the classic treatment of menstrual symbolism as ethnographically and theoretically narrow in scope. Regardless of the specific cultural context or the form of menstrual rituals, two themes have traditionally preoccupied anthropologists: "the concepts of taboo (supernaturally sanctioned law) and pollution (symbolic contamination)" (Buckley and Gottlieb 1988, 4). Classic approaches either describe menstrual blood as "symbolically dangerous or otherwise defiling," or they discuss the practices that are supposedly intended to restrict and constrain both the "negative potency of the substance" (Buckley and Gottlieb 1988, 5) and the women who produce the blood.

Why do the authors find these approaches problematic? First, they are suspicious of general theories that would squeeze the complexity and variation of individual and communal response to menstruation into such a tight box. They argue for greater ethnographic attention to women's view, for example, and for the "multivalent," sometimes contradictory meanings given to menstrous women and menstruation within the same society. Not only might similar, even identical, rituals have widely divergent meanings and functions cross- and intraculturally, but it is important to distinguish the specific content of ritual acts. Thus Buckley and Gottlieb correctly point out that rules prohibiting menstruating women from engaging in sexual intercourse have dramatically different implications from those that prohibit them from preparing food or cultivating the land (Buckley and Gottlieb 1988, 11).

Second, they reject the a priori assumption that in cultures where menstruation is culturally marked, women are necessarily subordinated. Rather than coding for woman's oppression, Buckley and Gottlieb wonder if seclusion of menstruating women, for example, might not indicate in some situations an effort to "restrict the behavior of others more than that of the menstruating woman herself" (Buckley and Gottlieb 1988, 9). In this case, menstrual seclusion may be seen as protective, affirmative of women's spirituality, shielding them from the unmenstruating, rather than as a means to prevent others from being polluted. Furthermore, women are well able to use seemingly oppressive social customs to their advantage and may in fact have a different set of meanings from men to explain the necessity and value of menstrual seclusion. Where Western eyes see isolation and degradation, women of a particular society might envision gender solidarity, release from ordinary routines, or a bothersome inconvenience. It should not be assumed that in all instances men have been responsible for constituting and then "imposing" menstrual restrictions on women.

The evidence from Green River County supports Buckley and Gottlieb's view that menstrual (and postpartum) behavioral norms cannot simply be understood as an instance of society's restrictive curtailing of women's activities because of their polluted state. Even with recollections of the constraints and proscriptions for between two weeks to a month after childbirth, women in Green River County described this experience as one of "taking care," "protecting" health, and avoiding things that could "work against" a good recovery. The narratives of women who gave birth during this period evoke a sense of protective care. The negative aspects of behavioral restrictions were balanced against the protective attention of the midwife, members of the household, and neighbors. Mrs. Billson described the lying-in period in this manner: "Mothers couldn't go outside. They would stay inside a dark room for about three weeks, no light except a little lamp light. The room had to be dark. No air, you know. They had to be careful that you didn't have any setbacks or anything like that. The midwife wouldn't let you even put your foot on the floor for about ten days to two weeks. Oh, yes, they took very good care of themselves in those days. Nowadays, I think the doctor send you home in about three or four days."

Pregnancy placed a woman in a spiritually and physically dangerous state—a state of intense susceptibility to the outside as her body opened to accommodate the fetus. The period of seclusion and rest afterwards gave the body time to heal, to close, and to regain its strength. For the woman, it established once again the boundaries between the inside and the outside, while for the infant it offered a period of acclimatization after having been enclosed in the womb.

The postpartum period lasted from between two to six weeks. Older women described two distinct periods of the postpartum: the initial seclusion of mother and child within the darkened birthing room and a longer period of staying indoors and restricting activity. Informants' descriptions suggest that over the decades there was a shortening of the total number of weeks that women were expected to stay in the birthing room and then within the space of the home. Women who gave birth in the 1920s and 1930s describe a period of at least nine days and as long as three weeks when they stayed in bed in a darkened room with the newborn and then longer periods of restricted movement within the home and the immediate vicinity of the porch and yard.

By the 1940s and 1950s, restrictions on the period of time in the shaded and dimly lit birthing room were lifted. Women in their sixties remembered that midwives encouraged them to stay put for about two to three days. Food was brought to the room, as were the necessary items for baths for the newborn and damp baths for mothers, who were not supposed to immerse themselves in water. It appears, however, that there was considerable variation in the later period concerning the amount of time that a woman should stay within the home and restrict her outdoor activities. Some women reported that even as late as the 1950s, midwives and mothers preferred that they not go outside or take the baby out before the end of six weeks.

Normally, the midwife visited the just-delivered woman daily for the first three days to check and redress the umbilical cord, to ensure that the baby's eyes were healthy, to give instructions on how to wash and take care of the newborn, and to help with household chores if there were no other adults in the household. As a means of marking the progression from her grandmother's practice in the first three decades of the century to her aunt's in the latter two decades, Mrs. Avery recalled that her grandmother made daily visits to help mothers but that her aunt did not provide this service because "the women were more wise and alert" about their bodies and those of their children.

The kinds of support offered by midwives of Mrs. Avery's grandmother's generation extended beyond the actual birth, while in her aunt's generation less time was spent with the mother either before or after birth. Mrs. Avery remembered that at times her grandmother would stay for up to two weeks if women were having difficulties after childbirth: "and some of the homes she [her grandmother] would probably stay a coupla days or more, especially if that patient wasn't feeling good. 'Cause I know we [herself and cousins] used to go back and forth on a horse and buggy and take food to her where she was staying—food for her and the patient—the mother of the baby—and she done that for colored and for whites."

Mrs. Avery's memory of taking food to the home of her grandmother's clients points to the involvement not only of the midwife but of the entire household both in supporting the midwife in her responsibilities and in enabling neighborhood women to recuperate from childbirth in situations where there were no immediate kin to help out. In a sense, therefore, the period of rest after childbirth was seen as necessary but not always an easy thing for some women to do.

Certainly for women with young children, with no supportive kin or mate, or for those whose labor was needed to sustain the household, the

postpartum period had to be shortened. One woman recalled the difficulty faced by a neighbor who was forced to curtail the time spent at
home after childbirth in order not to lose her position as a domestic to a
local white family. Yet even in this oppressive situation, she recalled that
the woman insisted on staying in for the first two weeks of intensive
seclusion in the darkened birthing room. My sense from narratives is
that this two week phase in which mother and child stayed in bed, away
from any light, was considered the least subject to compromise. Historically, the intensive seclusionary stage appeared also to have continued as
a fixed part of childbirth practice well into the mid-1950s, at a time when
increasing numbers of women delivered in the hospital. Women who
delivered in the hospital during this period, nonetheless, followed the
normative rules about restricting activity after childbirth.

Reporting on the positive attitudes of her Chinese informants toward
postpartum restrictions, Martin (1987) notes that, for these women,
such a period offered respite from work and from the demands of family
and household. She writes that "although women chafe at the confinement, they regard this period positively specifically because it is free of
work. I was told many sad tales of desperately poor families who were
unable to free a new mother from work for this long, and the dire consequences to her health that followed from her inability to regain her
strength" (Martin 1987, 99).

During the immediate postpartum period for my Green River informants, the special status of a woman, in a physiological and ritual sense,
was marked by the darkened room as well as by the close monitoring of
her activities—bowel movements, diet, mobility—by midwife and family
members alike. Just as her newborn did, a woman wore a form of a
binder or belly band that had been prepared in advance of her lying-in.
With the help of the midwife or a female member of the family, she
wrapped and pinned the binder made of white cotton firmly around
her midsection. Over the woman's period of confinement, the binder
was gradually tightened so as to lend support, according to informants,
as well as to aid in the reshaping of the woman's waist. Here, too, informants emphasized that women who wore binders regained their original waistline and musculature in a shorter period of time than women
"today."

Older women also explained to me that the period of time that they
spent in bed allowed their wombs "to set back into place." The physiological merits of the communally expected postpartum rest period were

pointed out by many informants. Mrs. Overton (seventy years old) expressed her view on this subject. She reasoned that "in the olden days, by the people being more careful, you didn't suffer with female problems and stuff like the peoples do now. To me, I believe that's why the old folk were so particular about such things."

In this regard, women who lived in two-story homes told stories about the special restrictions on their movements. I think they felt especially isolated upstairs because they were well removed from the hustle and bustle of the household below—isolation was complete. Mrs. Bynum, who lived with her grandmother, recalled that "if you were upstairs, you would have to stay upstairs for two weeks and no coming up and down the steps. They take you water, whatever you have to use. They didn't believe in you climbing those steps." The movement downstairs to the rest of the family during the day hours meant, however, that one had to stay down for the entire day until it was time to retire for the evening. Mrs. Garvey, for example, reenacted with mock-seriousness the way that she was required, by her mother, to descend the stairs every morning after the initial two weeks upstairs. First, a younger sister or her husband carried the baby with its clothing and other accoutrements. Then, after dressing and binding herself, she descended the stairs slowly on her rearend, so as to prevent any possibility of jerking her womb out of place. In the evening the procedures were reversed.

As Mrs. Garvey acted out the slow descent and ascent, the ritual aspects of this activity emerged. While explicitly directed to protecting the womb, the restrictions on stair-climbing marked the woman's special status as a mother and recently delivered woman. It brought her to the center of familial attention by her very dependence on others, on the one hand, and on the other, by her release from normal household and social duties. Informants argued that such social and familial support was only possible in the past when extended households were the norm and reciprocity a condition of family and communal life. According to Mrs. Wayne, "most in general at that time—most of the people lived at home. There was always somebody there to help, and you wouldn't have to do this, you wouldn't have to do that, 'cause somebody else would do it." Thus the proscriptions that seem so oppressive in our eyes were viewed in a generally positive sense by older women. Modern women, according to some informants, have been deprived of similar opportunities to recuperate and relax after childbirth, secure in the knowledge that others will "take care." At the heart of women's memories of these experiences is their recollection of the interdependence of family and community during major life-cycle events. Just as people expected to "help out" during birth, so, too, during illness or death.

What of the father's role during the postpartum period? Women rarely spoke of any specific part played by their husbands. He usually was the one who fetched the midwife at the onset of labor. Then the women took control of the birthing process and space. Mrs. Tilden recalled that her husband helped out when her mother-in-law fell ill. Other women remembered laughingly that the men "went as far out in the fields as they could get" when their wives were giving birth. Men were not expected to be able to sustain the noise and sight of childbirth. Furthermore, women suggested that they did not want men around at a time when they were so emotionally naked. They preferred to undergo childbirth only in the presence of other women—persons who had or would eventually undergo similar experiences and who would therefore not misinterpret their fear, their crying, their anger.

No one spoke directly about the norms of sexual interaction between husbands and wives immediately after childbirth. But it does appear that couples slept apart at least in the first phase of seclusion. The period during childbirth was one of intensified femininity, where the differences between the genders were accentuated. Paradoxically, however, it could also be a time when the sexual division of labor was inverted: if no female kin was immediately available to help during a woman's confinement, then it was expected that her husband or mate would care for the other children and prepare meals for the family. When I asked directly, some women recalled that while they were recuperating, their husbands and older kids took charge of the household.

Both childbirth and menstruation involved the woman in a special relationship to the world and to those around her. Besides the risk to her person, she presented certain potential dangers, particularly to men. Invariably, when conversations touched on these issues, women spoke more warily. Some laughed a bit embarrassingly or deflected questions. Some men, it seems, avoided eating food cooked by midwives or by menstrous or postpartum women. Male avoidance of food may not have been universal; nonetheless, both men and women with whom I spoke had heard about this practice. Some older men alluded to a connection between diminished virility and food that had been prepared by women "at that certain time of the month."

When they talked about this subject, women gave differing emphasis to its importance. Pushing the proscription into the past, Mrs. Bynum said that this had been a practice "way back then." Mrs. Harris laughingly suggested that this attitude was not universal but that there were some men who "didn't want anything" that their wives cooked during menstruation or after childbirth. She also asserted that "right today some men don't like anything that a midwife fix. No, they don't want it." Yet her husband, father, and brothers ate the food cooked by the midwives in the household. On the other hand, Mrs. Powell, who was so reticent about revealing other dimensions of her experience, told me that her father absolutely refused to eat food cooked by her mother or herself if they were menstruating. He preferred to eat cold sandwiches or leftovers if nothing else was available. Such avoidances on the part of men did not prevent women from cooking for themselves or others in the household.

During the postpartum period as well as during menstruation, the woman's body was socially marked as in an extraordinary state. Those around her adapted their behavior in order to accommodate these changes—for short periods during menstruation and for significantly longer periods after childbirth. Certainly in Mrs. Bynum's case, her father's refusal to eat gave the menstruating woman a respite from the regular obligations of meal preparation. It also meant that he had to fend for himself, forgo a hot meal, or cook after returning from work in the fields.

Whatever their experience of the cultural norms governing postpartum seclusion or menstruation, older women in Green River never spoke of these customs in any direct relationship to supernatural or spiritual mandates. A woman who left the birthing room prematurely may have jeopardized her health or offended people's sense of propriety, but there was never any suggestion that the community or her family members suffered because of her ill-advised actions. "Rules" in the sense used here refers to those which are meant to guide behavior rather than the "supernaturally sanctioned laws" discussed by scholars of menstrual "taboos" in other societies.

Bodily Cosmology: Sacred and Profane

Buckley and Gottlieb create a distinction between "taboos" (spiritual sanction) and "rules" (common sense, "by local standards," praxis).

They give these two examples. Among the Beng of the Ivory Coast, restricting sexual intercourse during menstruation because it is "messy" is a menstrual rule. The "Levitican" threat of "spiritual retribution" for the same act is a menstrual taboo. They write that "menstrual taboos are quite different from menstrual rules. When stated as taboos they must have some kind of spiritual or mystical foundation that is apart from any practical effects that might be their by-product. In order to understand such taboos it would seem that systems for symbolically constructing reality, and their religious expressions, must be analyzed first and that the practical implications of these systems cannot be seen as generative of them" (Buckley and Gottlieb 1988, 24).

Here the authors wish to counter theorists who explain menstrual taboos by reference to their origins in biological or practical states of the body or in the relationship of the body to its environment. They do well to critique such theorists.

In creating the distinction between menstrual rules as "common sense" and taboos as "spiritual," however, Buckley and Gottlieb paint themselves into a corner. I would argue for a different, perhaps vaguer use of the term "menstrual rule." Older women in Green River County never connected menstruation or postpartum management of the body to any direct spiritual or religious domain, but at the same time their descriptions of and conversations about physiology contained a "spiritual" dimension quite apart from the explicit behavioral norms that they described. The "common sense" explanations offered to account for their and the midwives' treatment of the body are not explanations in of themselves but rather reiterations of communally shared concepts of the body and the self.

The body itself deserved a certain respect both in its corporeal form and in its connection to the spiritual (supernatural) and material world (see also Dougherty 1978; Hill and Mathews 1981; Holmes 1986; Laguerre 1987; Mongeau 1973; Susie 1988). Thus a promiscuous woman was said not to "respect" her body. In the same manner, one followed the "rules" regarding childbirth and menstruation because in "respecting" the body's limitations, a woman was both safeguarding her health and maintaining her body's sanctity and moral equilibrium.

The relationship between the embodied self and God was a direct and visible one in the view of older African Americans in the county. This relationship could be expressed in a number of ways. Thus, for example, the concept of mother wit expressed the manifestation of a specific kind of knowledge that was transmitted from God to man. For some informants, such a transmission was mediated through the woman's body in the form of breast milk. In any case, however, they believed that the acquisition of mother wit was an expression of the individual's special and ultimately physical connection to the spiritual realm. The same might be said for the idea of the "gift." For midwives in particular, their desire and ability to wait on women was discussed as a divinely inspired attribute. The midwife was, in fact, simply a "vessel": she depended on the Lord to guide her actions and decisions and to know what best to do for her patients.

Similarly, at the level of ideal behavior, African Americans in Green River County did not seem to dichotomize the sacred and the profane, the physical and nonphysical. Rules about menstruation or postpartum behavior were not taboos, in the strict sense, but they were about the appropriate decorum and treatment of the body as both a spiritual and physiological entity. When they remembered the behavior expected of women during menstruation or after childbirth, therefore, my informants described the close attention to the physiological changes in and rhythms of the body as morally mandated. In her role as a ritual specialist, the midwife helped to "bring" women "through" their experience of the spiritually and physically dangerous process of birthing. In the same manner, senior women in the household and neighborhood watched to ensure that younger women observed the appropriate rules regarding menstruation and postpartum behavior. In addition to watching, however, they actively helped to ensure that women were able to take appropriate care of their bodies during such periods. Thus women recalled that neighbors and kin helped with the cooking and with child care during the times that a woman had to "rest" after giving birth. One woman recalled that "they just expect to do it [offer help] for one another."

Furthermore, when they explained rules for particular behaviors during menstruation or the postpartum period, women expressed their answers or comments in terms of cause and effect: "we did this to prevent that" or "if you did that this negative or positive effect would occur." At the same time, however, they seemed not to have been concerned with explanation, with the "why" of many of the rules they had followed and now recited to me. These were the body's requirements. They were com-

munally constructed and supported. Yet as seems to have been characteristic of other African American communities, distinctions were rarely
made between secular and morally sanctioned rules about how the body
should be treated during the postpartum period.

Informants discussed measures taken to protect the body, on the one
hand, and to restrict it, on the other. Most women were able to produce
a list of foods that were allowed and those that were to be avoided.
Appropriate foods included oatmeal, eggs, bread and butter, sassafras tea
(to clean the blood), applesauce, smothered but not fried chicken, and
boiled white potatoes. Foods to be avoided included pork, beef, collard
greens, lima beans, tomatoes, and sweet potatoes. These could not be
eaten because they were said to cause fevers or to "make against the
mother."

Other protective measures were taken after childbirth as well as during menstruation to shield the body from drafts or "winds." Besides these
named dangers, older women also alluded to, but never named, general
risks, material and nonmaterial, to the woman. Women suggested that
they were more vulnerable during menstruation and after giving birth:
pores, veins, and other parts of the body were closed in the normal state
but opened up during the menstrual flow and in childbirth.

The body's need to expel impurities and to provide a path for the birth
of the next generation made it necessary to regularly lose its impermeability, to "open up." Good health entailed the crossing between boundaries. To reduce fevers or "draw phlegm" out of the body, home remedies
were sometimes used. But in the "opened" condition, special precautions
had to be taken to release what needed releasing from the body, without
taking in unwanted or harmful "elements" from the outside. Mrs. Fields,
a woman in her early sixties who delivered three children at home under
the care of a midwife, explained that "your veins is all open and you can
catch a cold by having the air get into you." She recalled a woman who
had "taken to bed and died" after having "exposed herself" too soon after
child birth. These kinds of deaths confirmed the wisdom of sheltering
the body and reducing the chance of exposure.

Bodily Cosmology: Staunching and Maintaining Flow

Postpartum seclusion and behavioral restrictions during menstruation
did not signal the imposition of rules marking women's inferior status.

Rather, they provided an important means of managing the body so as to maintain its equilibrium and health. The focus on impurities was not specific to women's bodies and childbirth, for men and children also received seasonal purges at the beginning of spring. In some senses, however, the woman's ability to both take purges and rid herself of impurities through menstruation and childbirth made her body more suited to maintaining balance and cleanliness. In this regard, Buckley and Gottlieb's assertion that the cultural construction of menstruation may have contradictory meanings is well taken. Women may pollute food and reduce male virility during menstruation, but they are nonetheless more able to expel contaminants and keep their blood clean and well-circulating.

In a survey of the literature on African American folk medicine, Laguerre (1987) finds a cluster of related concepts regarding the flow from outside to inside and across the boundaries of the body. He also suggests, but does not develop the hypothesis, that for African Americans in different regional and cultural contexts, the physiology of gender is implicated in concepts about maintaining a "pure" blood supply.

The purity of blood is a sign of well-being. Once the blood is contaminated, the body has a mechanism through which it expels the bad blood for the maintenance of health. According to Snow, "a majority of Bahamians, Cubans, Haitians, and Puerto-Ricans believed the function of menstruation to be that of ridding the body of unclean wastes or unnecessary blood" (Snow 1978, 82). If menstruation is the moment when the bad blood is expelled from the female body, then men expel their bad blood through sweating (Snow and Johnson 1978). If the blood does not get out through these normal processes, it is possible that it will come out through skin eruption (Laguerre 1987, 70). The problem women faced during menstruation and after childbirth was to control the channeling of impurities while avoiding situations that would allow for new impurities to enter the body.

As a primary precaution, women avoided washing their hair or taking full baths. The connection between bathing and the risk of "pathogens" entering the body, especially the womb, is immediately clear. By contrast, the avoidance of washing the hair or wetting the head does not refer to a direct physiological link. Yet older women stressed this behavioral injunction. I was told on many occasions that people "back then, were very particular about wetting the head" while they were menstruating as well as after childbirth. Why the concern with the hair and head? Few explanations were forthcoming, except for a general reference to the increased possibility of "catching cold." The apparent incongruity of linking these two parts of the body to gynecological processes suggests that older women were working with models that do not mirror scientific anatomical ones. If one washed, this would have an effect on the body and on its ability to maintain its equilibrium during menstruation or the postpartum period.

The seeming incongruity between the head and the womb as conceptualized in Green River is reduced, although not explained, by the appearance of similar beliefs in other societies. Skultans reports that her informants in South Wales avoided "washing, especially washing the head" during menstruation. During menopause, the ceased outflow of blood is thought to go to the head (Skultans 1988). There is for these women a physiologic and symbolic connection between the head/hair and the womb. In her analysis, Skultans argues that the concern with inflow and outflow, purging and retention involved the movement of blood and impurities through the system from head to womb. The details are not identical, but for older women in Green River, similar concepts of flow from inside to outside and from head to the rest of the body seemed to have been important. In an analogy that first struck me as inappropriate, Mrs. Bolen, a retired hairdresser in her early sixties, said that her clients often compared her to a doctor. She recalled one woman in particular who used her services: "she used to get those clogged sinuses and she'd come to me every time she got clogged up. I'd give her a shampoo and massage her head and that would drain all the stuff. She'd sit in the chair and every minute blow her nose. [*snorts to demonstrate*] She said my treatment was the only thing that cleared her congestion. You could say that I was almost like a doctor." In the context of menstruation or after childbirth, this was precisely what women seemed to want to avoid: opened pores, flow of fluids out of the system through the head, or the intake of dangerous substances or impurities.

A connected precaution taken during the first days after childbirth encouraged the flushing of impurities, especially any that remained as a consequence of the birthing process or pregnancy. This was again a controlled opening and cleaning of the system. During the nine months that she carried her child, a woman's body did not have the regular cleansing that accompanied menstruation. Informants recalled that the midwife administered castor oil mixed with lemon juice to facilitate the expulsion of impurities and to "clean out the insides." Should this step be circumvented, then the body might take longer to recover or else the woman might contract puerperal fever.

In what must have been a sobering occasion for family and friends, especially for the younger women of the household who had not yet had children, I was told of the near death of a woman whose system had not been "cleaned out" right after she gave birth. The events occurred sometime in the 1930s. At the time, Mrs. Evers, now in her mid-sixties, was unmarried, with no children, and still living at home. This story was narrated in the course of our conversations about the midwife's role in taking care of a woman's body after childbirth:

> Now say for instance that your baby was born yesterday. The next day they would give you castor oil. You had to have that big dose of castor oil after the baby was born cause I remember when my sister-in-law . . . with one of her children . . . I believe that it must have been her second or third child and I was younger than her. But I do remember that she had bed fever [puerperal fever], and she didn't take the castor oil. You know a lot of people don't like it 'cause it taste so bad and she got the bed fever . . . took her hair out and everything. She was real sick with it. I think she didn't take the oil or maybe she didn't take it in time. She had a high fever; she was real, real sick. That's why they had to be so particular about such things."

The release of impurities cleaned the body from the inside out and prepared it for its eventual return to normality. Given people's view that these procedures and precautions were so essential, they are oftentimes bewildered by the absolute disregard for this approach in biomedicine's management of the body.

The emphasis on the physiological cleaning and recuperation of the woman's body after childbirth also had its correlate in a symbolic sweeping of the house at the end of the postpartum period. The midwife also played a role in the normalization of the new mother's status. Holmes (1986) refers to similar "re-emergence" rituals that marked the end of the postpartum period in Alabama. In Green River, older women remembered that by the time they were free to move about the house or to sit on the porch if the weather was warm, the midwife returned in her final appearance as a mediator between the body and the spiritual and social

world. Dee recalled that the midwife escorted her slowly around the
house and then returned to take the newborn in the same cycle. Here the
symbolic excursion to the outside testified to the health of the woman
and child while introducing them as intimately connected to each other,
to the family and community.

Whether because these practices fell into general disuse or because
informants were unwilling to elaborate on their details, descriptions of
the specific nature of the midwives' ritual behavior are fragmentary. For
example, the allusion to "smoking" also surfaced in women's description
of the walk around the house. But no one wished to discuss the exact
nature or purpose of this practice. Holmes (1986) suggests that in Alabama, enveloping the mother in smoke symbolized purification. It is
also likely that the smoking may have offered some final protection for
mother and child, but I am unable to say more.

The child's introduction to the wider social network occurred when he
or she was taken to church for the first time. Informants recalled that
people gathered around to greet mother and child, to give compliments,
and to make formal acquaintance with a new member of the congregation. Only with these various indications that a woman was safe and
once again integrated into normal routines could it be said that the process of parturition was completed. From the time of conception through
childbirth and the postpartum period and to the final transition back to
"adulthood," a woman was involved in a process whose goal was not
simply the birth of a baby. Family members, the midwife, her husband,
and her neighbors were implicated in returning the woman's body to its
state of ordinariness and health.

As a specialist in the area of childbirth and woman's health, the midwife played a central role. Yet her role depended in great part on others'
acceptance of her authority and on their complementary involvement in
helping to support the postpartum woman and in taking on the extra
burdens necessitated by her release from the ordinary routines of living.
The dissolution of this social contract lie at the heart of older women's
conversations about their childbearing years and experiences of childbirth. The generational gap in their construction is not merely one of
viewpoint but of a physiological and essential break between the past
and present.

Conversations about their experiences of birth provided a context for
speaking and thinking about the past. The past as I use the term here
does not simply refer to elapsed time in a historical sense. Older resi-

dents often seemed to speak of the past in terms of the body/mind—how it changed and why, of the body's relationship to the unembodied world and to forces outside the direct control and comprehension of human beings. But an outsider has to listen closely and with patience to hear about this past. It is covered, as I have argued elsewhere, with a thick veneer of present time and social conditions. New visions of the body/mind take precedent. Only in talking about the past did older informants evoke models of the body and community that significantly diverged from dominant scientific and social constructions.

Contained within older women's memories of birthing is a powerful critique of scientific childbirth. But such a critique remains hidden and powerless. Although older African Americans, both men and women, implicitly question the models of scientific medicine, they rarely challenge the historical denigration of their own medical knowledge. Aspects of traditional midwifery that would speak to their concerns and beliefs about the unity of mind and body, the organic and the supernatural, and the religious and the secular are now fragmented. In the past few years, Mrs. Harris has rarely attended any births in her community, but she has experienced a brief resurgence in activity outside of the county. Now that there has been an increasing interest in "natural" childbirth among middle-class white women, she has on a few occasions been engaged to aid in a home birth. The "natural" childbirth requested by her new clients does not necessarily fit with Mrs. Harris's approach in all its particulars. Nonetheless, however, these families, she informed me, "appreciate" her presence, and they do not hesitate to remunerate her. In the course of our conversations, Mrs. Harris never elaborated on her sense of the irony in this situation. In one sense, she may indeed not have considered her involvement in such births as paradoxical. During her many years of practice she had attended both white and black women. But perhaps most important, in her view, she was a midwife. She offered her skills as a service to women and to God.

Maybe this is the final irony. Children, grandchildren, and great-grandchildren of the women I interviewed still struggle to gain access to health care resources. They do not under these circumstances untangle the web of history in order to take back what is good and whole and useful in their own medical traditions. Instead they turn to progress with the blessing of their elders, while other, more affluent women turn with nostalgia to the vestiges of a worldview taken completely out of its cultural context.

12

Conclusion

Most African American midwives and the women they served had no forum through which to voice their experiences of changes in childbirth. How they responded to the medicalization of the birthing arena remained largely invisible. In my long talks with older residents in Green River County, I have come to appreciate the difficult choices they faced: few options were presented to them where benefits were not accompanied by losses. This work, therefore, is a study of the ways which people tried to respond to reproductive transformation. It avoids simple oppositions—between resistance and accommodation, or rejection and acceptance, for example—and explores instead the realm of ambiguity, of contradiction.

The Question of Choice

Memories of medical transformation are influenced by the very success of the scientific project, so that only occasionally do the women and men with whom I spoke directly recall their own or their midwives' response to the more dominant voice of medical authority. What this means is that the received view from the medical texts—of an inevitable, rather smooth process of transition from midwifery to scientific obstetrics— predominates in their narratives. I have not written the "story" in this manner. I have tried to expose the uphill battles that science/public health faced in making its logic seem "natural" to midwives and their clients.

African Americans wanted to take advantage of the benefits offered by medical science, but they probably did not envision that these advantages would eventually lead to the elimination of the midwife. We should recall, for example, that at first Virginia's State Board of Health encouraged the use of prenatal clinics, together with home deliveries attended by midwives.

It is doubtful that physicians and nurses working in the first half of the century realized themselves the full dimensions of the problem they created when they promoted a reduction in the numbers, and finally the complete elimination, of midwives. In a sense, they, too, shared in a vision of progress as intrinsically good for the polity and for all its citizens. Thus despite the competitive dimension of their intolerance of the midwife, their initial intent in pushing for scientific childbirth may not have been to deprive poor and African American women of good birthing care but to create a more efficient science, available to all. The coercion was real and effective, but this should not prevent us from acknowledging that African American women and their birth attendants actively sought to participate in the movement to improve health conditions. They wanted to offer their children increased access to the medical care that had been so long denied their race. From this perspective, the narratives of Green River's African American residents offer not so much a refutation as a different reading of the same historical events.

It has been difficult to identify the connections between an explicitly African American approach to birthing and a biomedical one. It is equally problematic to uncover those adaptations brought about by coercive means and those voluntarily adapted by midwives and the women they served. We should not assume that these women reacted in any uniform way to the transformations in childbirth. For example, even when increasing numbers of women gave birth in the hospital or used physicians, they continued to draw on the midwife's expertise concerning postpartum care of mother and child. We have shown that ideas about birth and its intimacy still inform older women's views of pregnancy. Medical personnel portrayed the struggle against the "midwife problem" as inexorably leading to triumph over midwifery. But the recollections of residents do not lead to a similar view of events as they unfolded.

The multifaceted behavior on the part of individuals in search of treatment and explanation should caution us against proposing too rigid a separation between the belief systems of the midwife and that of medical personnel. It is also important to point out explicitly what should by now be obvious. "Traditional" midwifery was neither static nor homogeneous. "Mother wit" epitomizes the emphasis placed on creative improvisation, within a set of shared rules and motifs. The rigidity in approach to the conceptualization and treatment of the body (especially in childbirth) came for the most part from medical personnel, who, as they gained power against the backdrop of the developing administrative concerns of the state and national governments, insisted that people (especially parturient women) make a choice.

As a corollary, therefore, medical incursion into midwifery should be seen as remarkable only to the extent that it heralded a new use of power to administer to bodies and society, to the exclusion of other possibilities and systems of belief. The historical development of African American midwifery in Green River County and, I suspect, in the rest of Virginia does not lend itself to interpretations derived from a "before" and "after" model of change.

Jean Comaroff (1981) develops a case, based on African traditional medical belief systems, for dispensing with such analytic models, which she labels "synchronic" or "closed." "Synchronic models," she writes, "do not simply reduce complex data to manageable proportions, as is usually claimed in apology for them; rather they create a static and unchanging 'reality' in the eye of the beholder. As Feierman and Janzen have pointed out, the study of medical systems in Africa strongly belies the assumption that 'pluralism' and socio-cultural proliferation are purely modern phenomena, associated with social change and the 'opening' of 'closed' systems" (Comaroff 1981, 368).

Both at the level of folk practitioner and patient, individuals in Green River County testified that they combined different therapeutic and philosophical approaches. This was not a random process of undirected trial and error. Rather, individuals worked within a generally accepted set of ideas about illness, health, and the functioning of the body. Within these beliefs, there was room for individual flexibility and innovation.

In Green River County, acceptance of the differences in the provenance of the midwife's and the physician's expertise did not lead to outright rejection of one or the other practice by residents. I believe that this helps to explain why midwives did not at the beginning perceive public health policies regarding reproduction as a threat either to their livelihood or to birthing practices. Coexistence with scientific medicine was neither alien nor untenable.

The emphasis on a pluralistic approach to health care is a consequence of the history of syncretic medical and religious practice in African American communities. As Mintz and Price (1976) cogently argue, none of the sociocultural traditions of African slaves reached the New World completely intact. The basis for survival of individuals as well as of cultural forms depended in great part on the flexible and adaptive contouring of New and Old World traditions under the constraints of plantation slavery. The works of Comaroff (1981), Janzen (1978), and Mullings (1984), to cite a few examples, suggest that the emphasis on flexibility—though taking different forms under different social and economic conditions—is a widely shared feature of African traditional medicine. In the New World, with the fragmentation caused by slavery, African American medical practice probably drew on this underlying perspective.

An emphasis on innovation and creative adaptation challenged a main principle in medical personnel's debates about the "midwife problem." Those involved in regulating midwives had argued with frightening conviction that the African American midwife was "ignorant," a slave to superstition, and unable to generalize from particulars. In response, public health personnel insisted on the strict application of rules as a means of teaching midwives "proper" childbirth techniques. From the midwives' perspective, this approach was antithetical. Their philosophy of praxis required flexibility. Innovation based on empirical experience was valued. Just as important, midwives drew on their ability to act on inspiration. Yet this kind of innovation was precisely what most disturbed medical personnel. The contradictions in their construction of midwives and midwifery meant that they were blinded to the possibility that midwives' skills and approaches could contribute to scientific knowledge about childbirth or that these women were indeed using the principles of scientific inquiry—innovation, reasoning from the particular to the general—in their work with pregnant women.

We must qualify our use of the word "choice" to describe the movement of women away from home births and midwives. For most women, it may have become safer rather than riskier to have a child at home under the care of a midwife. Physicians could easily be called and transportation found to take the woman to the nearest hospital. But the structuring of the discourse over the earlier decades had all but closed off that possibility. Women chose "progress" when it became defined as the only, as well as the best, alternative. One informant voiced a generally held view when she told me that in the hospital "you feel kind of surrounded by good doctors."

By the 1960s, midwifery care was perceived by many as a form of deprivation. Segregated hospitals with inferior facilities were being integrated and upgraded. Women wanted to gain equal access to these institutions. Furthermore, the long postpartum seclusion and the other correlates of midwifery practice no longer fit the realities of most women's working lives in the factories and the homes of the nearby cities. Unlike the situation in which the older women of Green River had delivered their children, women in the 1950s had moved out of the agriculturally based household economy. Older residents remembered that starting sometime in the 1940s, women who had not migrated to the North would "go in carloads" to the nearest city in order to work as domestics in white homes or as workers in the tobacco factories. We cannot challenge the choices they eventually made nor question their motivations in accepting the elimination of the spiritually bound midwife tradition.

Writing of the historical specificity of women's decisions to undergo abortions, Rosalind Petchesky (1984) argues for a reconceptualization of our approach to understanding individual's decision-making. Abortion practiced in cultures where female children are devalued or "illegitimacy stigmatized," for example, encode a different set of constraints and possibilities than in societies where it is an act of individual self-determination (Petchesky 1984, 11). Similarly, we have tried to unravel some of the variables that led to the shift of women away from midwives in Green River County. As Petchesky writes,

> To paraphrase Marx, women make their own reproductive choices, but they do not make them just as they please; they do not make them under conditions they create but under conditions and constraints they, as mere individuals, are powerless to change. That individuals do not determine the social framework in which they act does not nullify their choices nor their moral capacity to make them. It only suggests that we have to focus less on "choice" and more on how to transform the social conditions of choosing, working, and reproducing. (Petchesky 1984, 11)

Observer and Observed

An important part of this agenda is to understand the ways in which narratives about the experiences of home births and of the value and power of midwifery knowledge provide a counterdiscourse. Because they do not directly challenge, and oftentimes seem to explicitly accept, the dominance of the scientific discourse, this does not mean that men and women in Green River reject their own visions of the body and its relationship to the land, to the history of the community, and to the systems of belief they share with their ancestors.

My own wish to hear strong praise for midwives and denunciation of the forces that pushed them to the margins sometimes threatened to get in the way of the stories that informants wanted to tell. Only by suspending this desire for clarity could I expect to hear about the shape and textures of my informants' sense of place, of history, and of the lived experience of the body.

As an African American woman, I have an intellectual and emotional investment in reclaiming/celebrating the history of African American midwives. In my work, I argue implicitly, if not explicitly, that the patterns of community life that disappeared along with midwifery were intrinsically valuable. But African Americans in Green River clearly stand in a much more complex relationship to their past. It is that complexity, I would argue, that is missing in the work of scholars who have examined African American midwifery in retrospect (given the few active practitioners). For one thing, they assume for the most part that there is a direct correspondence between memory and reality. The resulting descriptions provide too simple a perspective on the "ethnographic past." There is a tendency to ignore the role of power in the kinds of narrations people offer. Such power is inherent in the relationship between participants in the exchange of information. Distinctions in educational level, in cultural perspective, in the experience of being female, and in socioeconomic status and race no doubt influence both the nature and content of the data.

Furthermore, in the case of the work on African American midwives, one cannot ignore the parallels in the professional encounters between past and present. Outside researchers interview traditional midwives just as public health personnel and physicians probably interviewed and scrutinized these women or their earlier counterparts. To what extent did the replication of roles (inferior-superior/questioner-respondent) structure midwives' responses? This question has to be posed, despite the fact that these new "observers" are sympathetic and supportive of the midwifery tradition and perhaps overtly antagonistic toward medical science and its bureaucracy. An inversion of the historical stance is also problematic. In attempting to provide a corrective to past injustices, there is a danger of "exoticizing" informants, presenting them either as victims or as saints. This, too, involves the application of power.

In their uses of silence, informants spoke eloquently about power and the way in which it contoured their reality. My use of "power" in this context refers to administrative and legislative power, to the power of the dominant culture to offer and withhold resources, as well as to the power of communal rituals. From this perspective, the world created by the discourse of my informants stands in some subordinate relationship to the world created by the discourse of medical science or the legal and economic system. It is the nature of that subordination and the ways in which persons communally and individually understood, explained, and gave credence to or rejected the terms of that subordination that has concerned me in the work.

I doubt that older African American residents of Green River County would be unreservedly enthusiastic either about the manner in which I have brought their past into the public sphere or the readings that I have given it. My sense of what the "struggle" entails is not theirs. I hope to have suggested the dimensions of the ways in which they spoke of the eclipsed world of midwives and birthing and to have given coherence to their present situation.

Discussions of the "midwife problem" in medical journals allowed an examination of white medical personnel's constitution of reality, of their representations of self and other and their uses of power to shape the social order to their image. Similarly, I have presented the construction of the midwife and birthing in Green River County in order to bring new voices to the discourse—voices of persons who historically have had little power to impose their "realities" on others.

Notes

Prologue

1. My gratitude to David Sapir, a colleague in the Department of Anthropology, the University of Virginia, and an expert in photo-ethnography, who presented me with my very own original copy of *Life* for December 1951. Another documentation of the southern African American midwife in the 1950s was *All My Babies*, released in 1952. Written, directed, and produced by George Stoney, the film was commissioned by the Georgia Department of Public Health.
2. Although I have no specific documentation, it is possible that 1950s African American readers of *Life* would have had a rather different response to the images, even if they agreed with the political and ideological motivations of W. Eugene Smith. The level of exposure created by the photographs is disturbing. A project on such a topic would be well worth pursuing.
3. I am tempted to say that "I'm not a historian, but I play one in this book."
4. Usage patterns of midwives by class and ethnicity are undergoing fascinating changes. Declerq (1992, 1993), in an analysis of National Center for Health Statistics figures, reports a dramatic decline in the use of midwives outside hospitals by women of color and low-income women and an increase for white affluent mothers from 1975 to 1988. Four of the five states with a decrease in the use of out-of-hospital midwives were in the South (Declerq 1993 682–83). African American mothers accounted for most of these changes. The picture is quite different for in-hospital births. There has been an increase in the use of midwives for in-hospital births among low-income and of women of color. The established pattern is that nurse midwives in hospitals (4 percent of all hospital births) attend a majority of ethnic women. Declerq writes that nurse midwives "attended mothers who were distinctly younger, less educated and more likely to be non-white and unmarried" (Declerq 1992, 1,000). He suggests that nurse midwives are being used for this population because they are more cost-effective. See also Parker (1994), whose figures show that between 1982 and 1989, approximately 14 percent of African American mothers were delivered by nurse midwives in

hospitals as opposed to 3 percent of white mothers. In summary, out-of-hospital midwifery-attended births are a middle-class phenomena, supported by white families. In the hospital, poor women and women of color get nurse midwifery care, whereas white women get obstetricians. Ironically, as Declerq shows, this is good care, but it may well be perceived as second rate by women who cannot choose to have an obstetrician.

5. Many thanks to Eric Perkins for pointing me to Lyman's work and its resonance for the uses of silence and speech in narratives of the past in Green River County.

1. Introduction

1. Another North Carolina song was based on the hymn "I Have Made a Covenant with My Lord" (Hudson 1987, 69): "Done Made a covenant with my nurse *(repeat three times)* / I will keep in touch with the doctor and nurse *(repeat three times)* / Send my certificate in on time *(repeat three times)* / Done Made a Covenant with my Nurse *(chorus)*."

2. Shared cultural elements of southern midwives existed before the public health initiatives. I am arguing, however, that the production of training material, the presence of nurse supervisors, and the similar protocols of campaigns, even the details of how midwife lessons were to be taught, created a shared set of constructs oriented toward a medical, routinized model. The origins and composers of these midwife songs are not at all clear. A version of the song that Campbell attributes to the composing skills of Georgia midwives was sung by a group of Mississippi midwives at a club meeting during the late 1940s, according to James Ferguson's "eyewitness" account (1950, 90–91). Apparently midwives did have cross-state contacts during the time of the midwife institutes. Furthermore, an account from South Carolina noted the attendance of visiting public health nurses as observers who came to learn how to teach midwives.

3. Appropriations totaled $272 million, with all but three states participating across the United States. All three of those refusing funds were in the North (Ladd-Taylor 1988; Mulligan 1976). Beardsley (1990) questions the eventual generosity of a program that relied on matching local funds but notes that most southern states responded with some resources.

4. In 1930, fewer than 10 percent of public health nurses were African American (Hine 1989, 227). Even in southern states with a majority African American population, black nurses could rarely secure positions in county health departments. One set of calculations show a total of only twenty-nine African American public health nurses in the entire South in the 1920s (Beardsley 1990, 114–15). A few southern boards of health (Virginia, North Carolina,

Tennessee) hired a sole African American nurse to address African American health issues (McBride 1991, 79). Aware of the dire need, northern philanthropic organizations such as the Rosenwald Fund allocated resources to establish public health training for nurses in black hospitals (remember that southern health institutions were segregated, usually with separate, independent, and underfunded hospitals for African American patients). Some scholars regard the increase of such trained nurses to just under 150 by the 1930s in largely positive terms. But it is important to point out that, in this same period, the total population of southern African Americans was nearing 10 million.

5. For more on the intricate web of social security legislation, philanthropies, and African American activism in the public health arena, see Beardsley (1990), Hine (1989), Gordon (1994), McBride (1991), and Smith (1995).

6. See, for example, the 1943 letter of W. A. Plecker: "registrar, to local registrars, clerks, legislators, and others responsible for, and interested in, the prevention of racial intermixture." Thanks to Bob Vernon for making me aware of this letter.

References

Abrahams, Roger. 1964. *Deep Down in the Jungle: Negro Narrative Folklore from the Streets of Philadelphia*. Chicago: Aldine Press.

Albuquerque, Klaus de. 1979. "Folk Medicine in the South Carolina Sea Islands." In *Proceedings of a Symposium on Culture and Health: Implications for Health Policy in Rural South Carolina*, ed. Melba Varner, 33–79. South Carolina: College of Charleston, Center for Metropolitan Affairs and Public Policy.

Andrews, C. J. 1924. "How Can This Woman Best Be Delivered?" *Virginia Medical Monthly* 22:148–154.

———. 1944. "The Maternal Mortality Situation." *Virginia Medical Monthly* 71:366–370.

Armstrong, David. 1983. *Political Anatomy of the Body: Medical Knowledge in Britain in the 20th Century*. Cambridge: Cambridge University Press.

Arney, William. 1982. *Power and the Profession of Obstetrics*. Chicago: University of Chicago Press.

Axelsen, Diana. 1985. "Women as Victims of Medical Experiments: J. Marion Sims' Surgery on Slave Women, 1845–1850." *Sage* 2:10–12.

Baer, Hans. 1982. "Toward a Systematic Typology of Black Folk Healers." *Phylon* 43:327–343.

Barker-Benfield, G. J. 1976. *The Honors of the Half-Known Life: Male Attitudes toward Women and Sexuality in Nineteenth Century America*. New York: Harper & Row.

Baughman, Greer. 1928. "A Preliminary Report upon the Midwife Situation in Virginia." *Virginia Medical Monthly* 54:748–751.

———. 1929a. "How May We Improve Our Obstetrical Mortality." *Virginia Medical Monthly* 56:382–384.

———. 1929b. "The High Obstetrical Death Rate with Suggestions as to Its Cure." *Virginia Medical Monthly* 55:849–852.

Bear, Joseph. 1928. "A Brief Review of Some Old and New Obstetric Problems." *Virginia Medical Monthly* 55:524–529.

Beardsley, Edward H. 1990. *A History of Neglect: Health Care for Blacks and Mill*

Workers in the Twentieth Century South. Knoxville: University of Tennessee Press.

Behar, Ruth. 1991. "The Body in the Woman, the Story in the Woman: A Book Review and Personal Essay." In *The Female Body: Figures, Styles, Speculations,* ed. Lawrence Goldstein. Ann Arbor: University of Michigan Press.

Bell, Peggy. 1993. "'Making Do with the Midwife': Arkansas's Mamie O. Hale in the 1940s." *Nursing History Review* 1:155–169.

Bennett, Emily. 1925. "Midwife Work in Virginia." *Public Health Nurse* 17:523–526.

Blackburn, Laura. 1935. "A One-Day County Institute for Midwives." *Public Health Nurse* 27: 17–18.

———. 1937. "Searchin' the Midwife's Bag." *Public Health Nurse* 29: 119–121.

Blake, John. 1965. "Women and Medicine in Antebellum America." *Bulletin of the History of Medicine* 34(2):108–134.

Blum, John, and Kenneth Stampp et al. 1985. *The National Experience.* New York: Harcourt, Brace & Jovanovich.

Bolt, John. 1929. *Causes and Prevention of Neonatal Mortality.* Washington, D.C.: Children's Bureau Publication.

Bradbury, Dorothy. 1962. *Five Decades of Action for Children: A History of the Children's Bureau.* Washington, D.C.: Children's Bureau Publication #35.

Bradley, Frances. 1924. "'P'int de Toes o' Dem Shoes Out'ards.'" *Hygeia* 2(9):544–546.

Brown, E. Richard. 1980. *Rockefeller Medicine Men: Medicine and Capitalism in America.* Berkeley: University of California Press.

Buckley, Thomas, and Alma Gottlieb, eds. 1988. *Blood Magic: The Anthropology of Menstruation.* Berkeley: University of California Press.

Campbell, Marie. 1946. *Folks Do Get Born.* New York: Rinehart.

Cassedy, James. 1965. "The Registration Area and American Vital Statistics: Development of a Health Research Resource." *Bulletin of the History of Medicine* 22:221–235.

———. 1969. *Demography in Early America: Beginnings of the Statistical Mind, 1600–1800.* Cambridge, Mass.: Harvard University Press.

Chase, Allan. 1978. *The Legacy of Malthus: The Social Costs of the New Scientific Racism.* New York: Knopf.

Christian, Barbara. 1985. *Black Feminist Criticism: Perspectives on Black Women Writers.* New York: Pergamon.

Clark, Katherine. 1996. *Motherwit: An Alabama Midwife's Story.* New York: E. P. Dutton

Clayton, Elizabeth. 1948. *A Birth Registration Handbook for Colored Midwives.* Washington, D.C.: Federal Security Agency, National Office of Vital Statistics.

Clifford, James. 1983. "On Ethnographic Authority." *Representations* 1:118–46.

Comaroff, Jean. 1981. "Healing and Cultural Transformation: The Tswana of Southern Africa." *Social Science and Medicine* 153:367–376.

Commander, Lydia Kingsmill. 1972 [1907]. *The American Idea.* New York: Arno Press and the *New York Times.*

Cooper, George. 1953. "Virginia's Health Rating." *Virginia Medical Monthly* 81:76–79.

Cosminsky, Sheila. 1977. "Childbirth and Midwifery on a Guatemalan Finca." *Medical Anthropology* 1(3):69–104.

———. 1994. "Childbirth and Change: A Guatemalan Study." In *Ethnography of Fertility and Birth,* ed. Carol MacCormack. New York: Academic Press.

Crede, Karl. 1932. "The Prevention of Inflammation of the Eyes in the New-Born: The Commonest and Most Important Cause of Blindness." *Medical Life* 2:533–542.

Daniel, Josephine, and W. Gafafer. 1935. "The Rural Midwife: Her Social and Economic Background and Her Practices as Observed in Brunswick County, VA." *Public Health Reports* 50:1807–1815.

Davis-Floyd. 1992. *Birth as an American Rite of Passage.* Berkeley: University of California Press.

Declerq, Eugene. 1992. "The Transformation of American Midwifery." *American Journal of Public Health* 82:680–684.

———. 1993. "Where Babies Are Born and Who Attends Their Births: Findings from the Revised 1989 United States Standard Certificate of Live Birth." *Obstetrics and Gynecology* 81(6):997–1004.

Delaney, Carol. 1988. "Mortal Flow: Menstruation in Turkish Village Society." In *Blood Magic,* ed. Thomas Buckley and Alma Gottlieb, 75–93. Berkeley: University of California Press.

DeVries, Raymond. 1985. *Regulating Birth: Midwives, Medicine, and the Law.* Philadelphia: Temple University Press.

Dewberry, Mayhew, and Josephine Daniel. 1936. "The Development of a Technique for Measuring the Knowledge and Practice of Midwives." *Public Health Reports* 51:757–797.

Donegan, Jane. 1978. *Women and Men Midwives: Medicine, Mortality, and Misogyny in Early America.* Westport, Conn.: Greenwood Press.

Donzelot, Jacques. 1979. *The Policing of Families.* Translated from the French by Robert Hurley. New York: Pantheon Books.

Dougherty, Molly. 1978. "Southern Lay Midwives as Ritual Specialists." In *Women in Ritual and Symbolic Roles,* ed. Judith Hoch-Smith and Anita Spring. New York: Plenum Press.

———. 1982. "Southern Midwifery and Organized Health Care: Systems in Conflict." *Medical Anthropology* 6:114–126.

Dressler, William. 1982. *Hypertension and Culture Change: Acculturation and Disease in the West Indies.* South Salem, N.Y.: Redgrave Publishing.

Duden, Barbara. 1985. "Historical Concepts of the Body." Unpublished Manuscript. Presented to the American Academy for the Advancement of Science. May 28. Symposium on Medical Sciences: Alternative Insights and Approaches.

Eakins, Pamela, ed. 1987. *The American Way of Birth.* Philadelphia: Temple University Press.

Ehrenreich, Barbara, and Dierdre English. 1973. *Witches, Midwives, and Nurses: A History of Women Healers.* Old Westbury, N.Y.: Feminist Press.

———. 1978. *For Her Own Good: 150 Years of the Expert's Advice to Women.* Garden City, New York: Anchor Press.

Farley, Reynolds, and Walter Allen. 1989. *The Color Line and the Quality of Life in America.* New York: Oxford University Press.

Ferguson, James. 1950. "Mississippi Midwives." *Journal of the History of Medicine and Allied Sciences* 5: 85–95.

Flannagan, Roy. 1930. "Medical Jazz—a Plea for Harmony in Medicine." *Virginia Medical Monthly* 63:659–664.

Foote, J. A. 1919. "Legislative Measures against Maternal and Infant Mortality." *American Journal of Obstetrics and the Diseases of Women and Children* 80:534–551.

Foucault, Michel. 1980. *The History of Sexuality.* Vol. 1, *An Introduction.* Translated from the French by Robert Hurley. New York: Vintage Books.

Fraser, Gertrude. 1991. "Race, Class, and Difference in Hortense Powdermaker's *After Freedom: A Cultural Study in the Deep South.*" *Journal of Anthropological Research* 47(4):403–415.

———. 1995. "Modern Minds, Modern Bodies: Midwifery and Reproductive Change in an African American Community" In *Conceiving the New World Order: The Global Politics of Reproduction,* ed. Faye Ginsburg and Rayna Rapp. Berkeley: University of California Press.

Gebhard, Bruno. 1976. "The Interrelationship of Scientific and Folk Medicine in the United States of America since 1850." In *American Folk Medicine,* ed. Wayland Hand, 87–98. Berkeley: University of California Press.

Ginsburg, Faye, and Rayna Rapp, eds. 1995. *Conceiving the New World Order: The Global Politics of Reproduction.* Berkeley: University of California Press.

Ginzburg, Carlo. 1980. "Morelli, Freud, and Sherlock Holmes: Clues and Scientific Method." *History Workshop* 9:5–36.

Glassie, Henry. 1984. *Passing the Time in Ballymenone: Culture and History of an Ulster Community.* Philadelphia: University of Pennsylvania Press.

Gordon, Linda. 1994. *Pitied but Not Entitled: Single Mothers and the History of Welfare.* Cambridge, Mass.: Harvard University Press.

Gottlieb, Alma. 1988. "Menstrual Cosmology Among the Beng of Ivory Coast." In *Blood Magic: The Anthropology of Menstruation.* Berkeley: University of California Press.

Gouchenour, David. 1925. "Observations of a Medical Man Among the Malay Tribes of the Suler Archipelago." *Virginia Medical Monthly* 25:561–565.

Gray, B. M. 1982. "Enga Birth, Maturation, and Survival: Physiological Characteristics of the Life Cycle in the New Guinea Highlands." In *Ethnography of Fertility and Birth,* ed. Carol P. MacCormack, 75–114. New York: Academic Press.

Greene, Melissa Fay. 1991. *Praying for Sheetrock: A Work of Nonfiction.* Reading, Mass.: Addison-Wesley.

Greiner, Alfred. 1922. "The Trend of the Healing Art." *Virginia Medical Monthly* 68:141–145.

Hall, Arthur, and Peter Bourne. 1973. "Indigenous Therapists in a Southern Black Urban Community." *Archives of General Psychiatry* 28(1):137–142.

Haller, John, and Robin Haller. 1974. *The Physician and Sexuality in Victorian America.* Urbana: University of Illinois Press.

Haller, Mark. 1963. *Eugenics: Hereditarian Attitudes in American Thought.* New Brunswick, N.J.: Rutgers University Press.

———. 1972. "The Negro and the Southern Physician: A Study of Medical Attitudes, 1800–1890." *Medical History* 16:239–44.

Hammer, James. 1931. "Management of a Normal Labor in the Home." *Virginia Medical Monthly* 58:376–379.

Hangar, P. 1918. "Notice to Doctors and Midwives." *Virginia Medical Journal* 46:15–16.

Hardin, E. R. 1925. "The Midwife Problem." *Southern Medical Journal* 18:347–350.

Harris, Percy. 1924. "Reply to Greer Baughman." *Virginia Medical Monthly* 55:852.

Harris, Seale. 1950. *Woman's Surgeon: The Life Story of J. Marion Sims.* New York: Macmillan.

Haskell, Thomas. 1977. *The Emergence of Professional Social Science.* Urbana: University of Illinois Press.

Hill, Carole. 1992. "Reproduction and Transformation of Health Praxis and Knowledge among Southern Blacks." In *African Americans in the South: Issues of Race, Class, and Gender,* ed. Hans Baer and Yvonne Jones. Athens: University of Georgia Press.

Hill, Carole, and Holly Mathews. 1981. "Traditional Health Beliefs and Practices among Southern Rural Blacks: A Complement to Biomedicine." In *Social Science Perspectives on the South,* ed. Merle Black and John Shelton Reed, 307–322. New York: Gordon and Breach Science Publishers.

Hill-Collins, Patricia. 1990. *Black Feminist Thought: Knowledge, Conciousness, and the Politics of Empowerment.* New York: Routledge.

Hine, Darlene Clark. 1989. *Black Women in White: Racial Conflict and Cooperation in the Nursing Profession.* Bloomington: University of Indiana Press.

Hoch-Smith, Judith, and Anita Spring. 1978. *Women in Ritual and Symbolic Roles.* New York: Plenum Press.

Holmes, Linda. 1986. "African American Midwives in the South." In *The American Way of Birth,* ed. Pamela Eakins, 273–291. Philadelphia: Temple University Press.

———. 1993. "Midwives, Southern Black." Entry in *Encyclopedia of Childbearing.* Phoenix: Oryx Press.

Holmes, Linda, and Margaret Charles Smith. 1996. *Listen to Me Good: The Life Story of an Alabama Midwife.* Ohio State University Press.

Hudson, C. C. and M. P. Rucker. 1923. "Maternal Mortality in Richmond: A Preliminary Survey." *Virginia Medical Monthly* 50:300–304.

Hudson, Lynn Marie. 1987. "Twentieth Century Midwives in North Carolina." M.A. thesis, University of North Carolina at Chapel Hill.

Hymes, Dell. 1980. *Language in Education: Ethnolinguistic Essays.* Washington, D.C.: Center for Applied Linguistics.

Jackson, Bruce. 1976. "The Other Kind of Doctor: Conjure and Magic in Black American Folk Medicine." In *American Folk Medicine,* ed. Wayland Hand, 259–272. Berkeley: University of California Press.

Jackson, Edward. 1928. "Relation of Ophthalmology to Blindness." *American Journal of Ophthalmology* 11, ser. 3:147–149.

Jackson, Michael. 1983. "Knowledge of the Body." *Man* 18, n.s.: 327–45.

Jaffre, Yannick, and Alain Prual. 1994. "Midwives in Niger: An Uncomfortable Position between Social Behaviours and Health Care Constraints." *Social Science and Medicine* 38(8):1069–1073.

Janzen, John. 1978. *The Quest for Therapy in Lower Zaire.* Berkeley: University of California Press.

Johnson, Charles. 1941. *Shadow of the Plantation.* Chicago: University of Chicago Press.

Johnson, James. 1975. "The Role of Women in the Founding of the U.S. Children's Bureau." In *"Remember the Ladies": New Perspectives on Women in History,* ed. Carol George, 179–196. Syracuse, N.Y.: Syracuse University Press.

Jonas, Stephen. 1978. *The Training of Doctors in the United States.* New York: W. W. Norton.

Jones, Gordon. 1966. "Will There Be a Place for Nurse Midwives." *Virginia Medical Monthly* 43:173–175.

Jones, Jacqueline. 1985. *Labor of Love, Labor of Sorrow: Black Women, Work, and the Family.* New York: Basic Books.

Jones, James. 1981. *Bad Blood: The Tuskegee Syphilis Experiment.* New York: Free Press.

Jordan, Bridgette. 1983. *Birth in Four Cultures: A Cross-Cultural Investigation.* Montreal: Eden Press.

———. 1985. "Biology and Culture: Some Thoughts on Universals in Childbirth." Paper Presented at Symposium on Birth in Biocultural Perspective. American Anthropological Association, December.

———. 1989. "Cosmopolitical Obstetrics: Some Insights from the Training of Traditional Midwives." *Social Science and Medicine* 28(9):925–944.

———. 1991. "Technology and Social Interaction: Notes on the Achievement of Authoritative Knowledge in Complex Settings." Unpublished Manuscript for the Institute for Research on Learning and Work Practice and Technology System Sciences Laboratory. Xerox Palo Alto Research Center.

Kennedy, David. 1970. *Birth Control in America: The Career of Margaret Sanger.* New Haven, Conn.: Yale University Press.

Kerns, W. W. 1927. "Why Young Physicians Are Not Locating in the Country." *Virginia Medical Monthly* 54:369–370.

Kevles, Daniel J. 1985. *In the Name of Eugenics: Genetics and the Uses of Human Heredity.* New York: Knopf.

Kitzinger, Sheila. 1982. "The Social Context of Birth: Some Comparisons between Childbirth in Jamaica and Britain." In *Ethnography of Fertility and Birth,* ed. Carol MacCormack, 181–203. New York: Academic Press.

Kleinman, Arthur. 1995. *Writing at the Margin: Discourse between Anthropology and Medicine.* Berkeley: University of California Press.

Kobrin, Francis E. 1966. "The American Midwife Controversy: A Crisis in Professionalization." *Bulletin of the History of Medicine* 40:350–363.

Kraker, Florence. 1925. "Reply to E. R. Hardin." *Southern Medical Journal* 18(5):349.

Ladd-Taylor, Molly. 1988. "'Grannies' and 'Spinsters': Midwife Education under the Sheppard-Towner-Act." *Journal of Social History* 22:225–275.

———. 1992. "'Why Does Congress Wish Women and Children to Die?': The Rise and Fall of Public Maternal and Infant Health Care in the United States, 1921–1929." In *Women and Children First: International Maternal and Infant Welfare, 1870–1945,* ed. Valerie Fildes, Lara Marks, and Hilary Marland. New York: Routledge.

Laguerre, Michel. 1987. *Afro-Caribbean Folk Medicine.* South Hadley, Mass.: Bergin & Garvey.

Lamp, Frederick. 1988. "Heavenly Bodies: Menses, Moons, and Rituals of License among the Temne of Sierra Leone." In *Blood Magic,* ed. Thomas Buckley and Alma Gottlieb, 210–231. Berkeley: University of California Press.

Laneford, Burneley. 1924. "Better Obstetrics: How Such May Be Obtained." *Virginia Medical Monthly* 51:491–494.

Lange, Deola. 1949. "'Plantation Granny': A Necessity." *Public Health Nursing* 41(11):603–609.

Langston, A. 1929. "Diagnosis and Normal Delivery." *Virginia Medical Monthly* 56:379–382.

Laqueur, Thomas. 1986. "Female Orgasm, Generation, and the Politics of Reproductive Biology." *Representations* 14:1–82.

Lassiter, Irene. 1941. "Nurse Teaches Midwife." *Public Health Nurse* 33: 460–466.

Leavitt, Judith. 1986. *Brought to Bed: Childbearing in America, 1750–1950.* New York: Oxford University Press.

Lemons, J. Stanley. 1973. *The Woman Citizen: Social Feminism in the 1920s.* Urbana: University of Illinois Press.

Levine, Lawrence. 1978. *Black Culture and Black Consciousness: Afro-American Folk Thought from Slavery to Freedom.* New York: Oxford University Press.

Lewis, Michael. 1993. "Driving Miss Onnie." *New Republic,* 16 August, 11.

Litoff, Judy. 1978. *American Midwives: 1860 to the Present.* Westport, Conn.: Greenwood Press.

————. 1986. *The American Midwife Debate: A Sourcebook on its Modern Origins.* Westport, Conn.: Greenwood.

Logan, Onnie Lee. 1989. *Motherwit: An Alabama Midwife's Story as told to Katherine Clark.* New York: Dutton.

Lowenberg, Eugene. 1928. "Prenatal Care." *Virginia Medical Monthly* 54:267–272.

Lukes, Stephen. 1978. "Power and Authority." In *A History of Sociological Analysis,* ed. Robert Nisbet and Tom Bottomore. New York: Basic Books.

Lyman, Peter. 1981. "The Politics of Anger: On Silence, Ressentiment, and Political Speech." *Socialist Review* 11(3):55–76.

McBride, David. 1991. *From TB to AIDS: Epidemics among Urban Blacks since 1900.* Albany: State University of New York Press.

McCleod, W.W. 1927. "Why Doctors Should Locate in the Country." *Virginia Medical Monthly* 54:524.

McGregor, Deborah 1985. "Silver Sutures: The Medical Career of J. Marion Sims." Ph.D. dissertation. State University of New York, Binghamton.

Malinowski, Bronislaw. 1967. *A Diary in the Strict Sense of the Term.* Introduction by Raymond Firth. Translated by Norbert Guterman. New York: Harcourt, Brace & World.

Martin, Emily. 1987. *The Woman in the Body.* Boston: Beacon Press.

————. 1994. *Flexible Bodies: Tracking Immunity in American Culture from the Days of Polio to the Age of AIDS.* Boston: Beacon Press.

Maternal Health Committee. 1942. "Selected Case Report of Maternal Death." *Virginia Medical Monthly* 61:35–37.

Mathews, Holly 1992. "Killing the Medical Self-Help Tradition among African Americans: The Case of Lay Midwifery in North Carolina, 1912–1983." In *African Americans in the South: Issues of Race, Class, and Gender,* ed. Hans Baer and Yvonne Jones. Athens: University of Georgia Press.

Meigs, Grace. 1917. *Maternal Mortality from All Conditions Connected with Childbirth in the United States and Other Countries.* Bureau Publication 19, ser. 6, Washington, D.C.: Government Printing Office.

Michie Law Codes 1919. *Virginia Code of 1919.* Charlottesville, Va.: Michie Co.

————. 1924. *Virginia Code of 1924.* Charlottesville, Va.: Michie Co.

Mintz, Sidney, and Richard Price. 1976. *An Anthropological Approach to the Afro-American Past: A Caribbean Perspective.* Philadelphia: Institute for the Study of Human Issues.

Moerman, Daniel. 1975. "High-Low, Bitter-Sweet: An American Folk Medical System." In *Proceedings of the Central States Anthropological Society* 1:47–50.

————. 1981. "Masterful Marginals: Black Life on a Carolina Island." In *Social Perspectives on the American South,* ed. Merle Black and John Reed, 285–300. London: Gordon & Breach.

Mongeau, Beatrice. 1961. "The 'Granny' Midwife: Changing Roles and Functions of a Folk Practitioner." *American Journal of Sociology* 66:497–505.

————. 1973. "The 'Granny' Midwives: A Study of a Folk Institution in the Process of Social Disintegration." Ph.D. dissertation. University of North Carolina.

Morantz-Markell, Regina. 1982. "Feminism, Professionalism, and Germs: The Thought of Mary Putnam Jacobi and Elizabeth Blackwell." *American Quarterly* 34(5):359–468.

————. 1985. *Sympathy and Science: Women Physicians in American Medicine.* New York: Oxford University Press.

Mulligan, Joan. 1976. "Three Federal Interventions on Behalf of Childbearing Women: The Sheppard-Towner Act, Emergency Maternity and Infant Care, and the Maternal and Child Health and Mental Retardation Planning Amendments of 1963." Ph.D. University of Michigan.

Mullings, Leith. 1984. *Therapy, Ideology, and Social Change: Mental Healing in Urban Ghana.* Berkeley: University of California Press.

Navarro, Vicente. 1976. "The Fetishism of Industrialization: A Critique of Ivan Illich." *Monthly Review* 28(5):34–46.

Nelson, Margaret. 1986. "Birth and Social Class." In *The American Way of Birth,* ed. Pamela Eakins. Philadelphia: Temple University Press.

Oakley, Ann. 1980. *Women Confined: Towards a Sociology of Childbirth*. New York: Schocken.

———. 1984. *The Captured Womb: A History of Medical Care of Pregnant Women*. Oxford: Basil Blackwell.

O'Neill, John. 1985. *Five Bodies: The Human Shape of Modern Society*. Ithaca, N.Y.: Cornell University Press.

Parker, Jennifer. 1994. "Ethnic Differences in Midwife-Attended US Births." *American Journal of Public Health* 84:1134–1141.

Paul, Lois. 1978. "Careers of Midwives in a Mayan Community." In *Women in Ritual and Symbolic Roles*, ed. Judith Hoch-Smith and Anita Spring, 129–149. New York: Plenum Press.

Perkins, Frances. 1937. *The Children's Bureau: Yesterday, Today, and Tomorrow*. Washington, D.C.: U.S. Government Printing Bureau.

Petchesky, Rosalind Pollack. 1984. *Abortion and Woman's Choice: The State, Sexuality, and Reproductive Freedom*. New York: Longman.

Plecker, W. A. 1914. "The Midwife Problem in Virginia." *Virginia Medical Semi-Monthly* 19:456–458.

———. 1918. "The First Move toward Midwife Control in Virginia." *Virginia Medical Monthly* 12–13.

———. 1924. *Midwifery and Childcare Manual*. Richmond: Bureau of Vital Statistics.

———. 1925. "Virginia Makes Efforts to Solve Midwife Problem." *The Nation's Health* 8(12):809–811.

———. 1933. "Progress in Midwife Control." *Virginia Medical Monthly* 59: 84–87.

Poovey, Mary. 1986. "'Scenes of an Indelicate Character': The Medical 'Treatment' of Victorian Women." *Representations* 14:137–169.

Portelli, Alessandro. 1981. "The Peculiarities of Oral History." *History Workshop* 12:96–107.

Post, Lawrence. 1931. "Fifty Years of the Crede Procedure." *American Journal of Ophthalmalogy*. 14:1271.

Price, Laurie. 1987. "Ecuadorian Illness Stories: Cultural Knowledge in Natural Discourse." In *Cultural Models in Language and Thought*, ed. Dorothy Holland and Naomi Quinn, 343–368. Cambridge: Cambridge University Press.

Rabinow, Paul. 1977. *Reflections on Fieldwork in Morocco*. Berkeley: University of California Press.

Rapp, Rayna. 1979. "Anthropology (Review Essay)." *Signs* 4(3):497–513.

———. 1988. "Chromosomes and Communication." *Medical Anthropology Quarterly* 2(2):143–157.

Reeb, Rene. 1992. Granny Midwives in Mississippi: Career and Birthing Practices. *Journal of Transcultural Nursing* 4(2):18–27.

Reeb, Rene, and Joyce Booth. 1993. "Mississippi's Granny Midwives: Pre and Post Civil Wars." *The Mississippi RN*, Nov/Dec: 20–22.

Reed, Louis. 1932. *Midwives, Chiropodists, and Optometrists: Their Place in Medical Care.* Publication of the Committee on the Costs of Medical Care, #15. Chicago: University of Chicago Press.

Reverby, Susan. 1987. *Ordered to Care: The Dilemma of American Nursing, 1850–1945.* Cambridge: Cambridge University Press.

Riggin, I. C. 1935. "Public Health Statistics." *Virginia Medical Monthly* 61:607–608.

———. 1942. "Public Health Statistics." *Virginia Medical Monthly* 70:688–694.

———. 1945. "Public Health Statistics." *Virginia Medical Monthly* 72:204–210.

Roberts, Edna, and Rene Reeb. 1994. "Mississippi Public Health Nurses: A Partnership that Worked." *Public Health Nursing* 11(1):57–63.

Robinson, Sharon. 1984. "A Historical Development of Midwifery in a Black Community: 1600–1940." *Journal of Nurse-Midwifery* 29:247–250.

Rocereto, LaVerne. 1973. "Root Work and the Root Doctor." *Nursing Forum* 12(4):414–427.

Roper, M. D. 1948. "The Virginia Hospital Survey and Construction Program under the Hill-Burton Act." *Virginia Medical Monthly* 75:108–109.

Rosenberg, Carrol, and Charles Rosenberg. 1973. "The Female Animal: Medical and Biological Views of Woman and Her Role in Nineteenth-Century America." *Journal of American History* 1:332–356.

Rosenkrantz, Barbara, ed. 1977 [1917]. *The Health of Women and Children.* New York: Arno Press.

Rothert, Frances. 1933. "Maternal Mortality in Virginia in 1927 and 1928." *Virginia Medical Monthly* 60:237–251.

Rothman, Barbara Katz. 1982. *In Labor: Woman and Power in the Birthplace.* New York: W.W. Norton.

Rothman, Sheila. 1978. *Woman's Proper Place: A History of Changing Ideals and Practices.* New York: Basic Books.

Rothstein, William. 1970. *American Physicians in the 19th Century: From Sects to Science.* Baltimore: Johns Hopkins University Press.

Royster, Lawrence. 1942. "Do You Know Your Nurse Maid?" *Virginia Medical Monthly* 69:44–45.

Rucker, M. P. 1941. "Maternal Deaths in Virginia." *Virginia Medical Monthly* 68:138–147.

———. 1942. "Conservative Obstetrics." *Virginia Medical Monthly* 69:440–448.

Savitt, Todd. 1978. *Medicine and Slavery: The Diseases of Blacks in Antebellum Virginia.* Urbana: University of Illinois Press.

———. 1982. "The Use of Blacks for Medical Experimentation and Demonstration in the Old South." *Journal of Southern History* 68:330–340.

Savitt, Todd, and James Young, eds. 1988. *Disease and Distinctiveness in the American South.* Knoxville: University of Tennessee Press.

Schaffer, Ruth. 1991. "The Health and Social Functions of Black Midwives on the Texas Brazos Bottom, 1920–1985." *Rural Sociology* 56(1):1991.

Scheper-Hughes, Nancy. 1992. *Death without Weeping: The Violence of Everyday Life.* Berkeley: University of California Press.

Scheper-Hughes, Nancy, and Margaret Lock. 1987. "The Mindful Body: A Prolegomenon to Future Work in Medical Anthropology." *Medical Anthropology Quarterly* 1(1):7–41.

Scholten, Catherine. 1977. "On the Importance of the Obstetrick Art: Changing Customs of Childbirth in America, 1760–1825." *William and Mary Quarterly* 34:426–45.

Scully, Diana. 1986. "From Natural to Surgical Event." In *The American Way of Birth,* ed. Pamela Eakins, 47–59. Philadelphia: Temple University Press.

Showalter, A. N. 1922. "The Management of Normal Labor." *Virginia Medical Monthly* 49:136–140.

Shyrock, Richard. 1962. *Medicine and Society in America, 1660–1860.* Ithaca, N.Y.: Cornell University Press.

Sims, J. Marion. 1884. *The Story of My Life.* New York: Appleton.

Skultans, Vieda. 1988. "Menstrual Symbolism in South Wales." In *Blood Magic,* ed. Thomas Buckley and Alma Gottlieb, 137–160. Berkeley: University of California Press.

Smith, Susan. 1994. "White Nurses, Black Midwives, and Public Health in Mississippi." *Nursing History Review* 2:29–49.

———. 1995. *Sick and Tired of Being Sick and Tired: Black Women's Health Activism.* Philadelphia: University of Pennsylvania Press.

Smith, W. Eugene. 1951. "Nurse Midwife: Maude Callen Eases Pain of Birth, Life, and Death." *Life,* 3 July 135–145.

Smith-Rosenberg, Carrol. 1985. *Disorderly Conduct.* New York: Oxford University Press.

Snow, Loudell. 1978. "Sorcerers, Saints, and Charlatans: Black Folk Healers in Urban America." *Culture, Medicine, and Psychiatry* 2(1):69–106.

Snow, Loudell, and S. Johnson. 1978. "Folklore, Food, Female Reproductive Cycle." *Ecology of Food and Nutrition* 7: 41–49.

Sobel, Mechal. 1987. *The World They Made Together: Black and White Values in Eighteenth-Century Virginia.* Princeton, N.J.: Princeton University Press.

Spring, Anita. 1978. "Epidemiology of Spirit Possession among the Luvale of Zambia." In *Women in Ritual and Symbolic Roles,* ed. Judith Hoch-Smith and Anita Spring, 165–189. New York: Plenum Press.

Stevens, Rosemary. 1971. *American Medicine and the Public Interest.* New Haven, Conn.: Yale University Press.

Starr, Paul. 1982. *The Social Transformation of American Medicine.* New York: Basic Books.

Stern, Bernard. 1946. *Medical Services by Government.* New York: Commonwealth Fund.

Stevens, Rosemary. 1971. *American Medicine and the Public Interest.* New Haven, Conn.: Yale University Press.

Strathern, Marilyn. 1987. "An Awkward Relationship: The Case of Feminism and Anthropology." *Signs* 12(2):276–292.

Susie, Debra Anne. 1988. *In the Way of Our Grandmothers: A Cultural View of Twentieth-Century Midwifery in Florida.* Athens: University of Georgia Press.

Taussig, Michael. 1980. "Reification and the Consciousness of the Patient." *Social Science and Medicine* 14:3–13.

Taylor, Lloyd. 1974. *The Medical Profession and Social Reform, 1885–1945.* New York: St. Martin's Press.

Thompson, Sharon. 1984. "Search for Tomorrow: On Feminism and the Reconstruction of Teen Romance." In *Pleasure and Danger: Exploring Female Sexuality,* ed. Carole Vance, 351–384. Boston: Routledge & Kegan Paul.

Thoms, Herbert. 1933. *Chapters in American Obstetrics.* Springfield, Ill.: Charles C. Thomas.

Tyler, Stephen. 1986. "Post-Modern Anthropology." In *Discourse and the Social Life of Meaning,* ed. P. Chock and J. Wyman. Washington, D.C.: Smithsonian Press.

Van Blarcom, Carolyn Conant. 1914. "Midwives in America." *American Journal of Public Health* 9:197–207.

———. 1930. "Rat Pie: Among the Black Midwives of the South." *Harper's* 60:322–332.

Virginia Health Bulletin. 1949. "Midwifery Education," July, 7–9.

1951. "Midwifery in Virginia." January, 5–13.

Virginia State Board of Health. 1924. *Midwife Instruction: A Series of Lectures. Prepared for Nurses.* Richmond: Virginia Board of Health.

Wallerstein, Immanuel. 1983. *Historical Capitalism.* New York: Schocken.

Ware, Harry. 1931. "A Discussion of the Prevention of Foetal and Maternal Mortality." *Virginia Medical Monthly* 58:245–248.

———. 1936. "Cesarean Section in Richmond, Virginia." *Virginia Medical Monthly* 68:82–86.

Weiss, Nancy Pottisham. 1974. "Save the Children: A History of the Children's Bureau, 1903–1918." Ph.D. dissertation. University of California, Los Angeles.

Wertz, Dorothy, and Richard Wertz. 1977. *Lying-In: A History of Childbirth in America.* New York: Schocken Books.

White, Harrison. 1992. "Cases Are for Identity, for Explanation, or for Control."

In *What Is a Case?* ed. Charles C. Ragin and Howard Becker. Cambridge: Cambridge University Press.

White, J. A. 1918. "Ophthalmia Neonatorum." *Virginia Medical Monthly* 46:12–15.

Wiebe, Robert. 1977. *The Search for Order, 1877–1920.* New York: Hill and Wang.

Williams, T. J. 1936. "Factors in Maternal Mortality." *Virginia Medical Monthly* 63:68–74.

Willumson, Glenn. 1992. *W. Eugene Smith and the Photographic Essay.* Cambridge: Cambridge University Press.

Wilson, Elizabeth. 1977. *Women and the Welfare State.* London: Tavistock.

Zelizer, Viviana. 1985. *Pricing the Priceless Child: The Changing Value of Children.* New York: Basic Books.

Index